"THEREFORE REPENT!
IF YOU DO NOT, I WILL COME TO YOU
SOON AND FIGHT AGAINST THEM
WITH THE SWORD OF MY MOUTH."
REVELATION 2:16

Published by IDW (www.idwpublishing.com) in the United States.
Published by No Media Kings (www.nomediakings.org) in Canada.

Library and Archives Canada Cataloguing in Publication

Munroe, Jim, 1972-
      Sword of my mouth : a post-rapture graphic novel / Jim Munroe ; [illustrations by] Shannon Gerard.
ISBN 978-1-60010-604-0
      I. Gerard, Shannon, 1973- II. Title.
PN6733.M85S86 2010   741.5'971   C2010-901341-7

Digital Painting: Scott "Secret Weapon" Waters

Editor: Alison Kooistra

Valuable Feedback: Suzanne Andrew, Carol Borden, Susan Bustos, Jhon Clark, Nicholas Di Genova, Greg Dunford, Sarah Gwisdalla, Nalo Hopkinson, Josh Kostka, Guy Leshinski, Adam Morris, Liam O'Donnell, and Tate Young.

Character Models: Atique Azad, Willy Brown, Rick Conroy, Adrienne Costantino, Luke Dickerson, Emma Gerard, Robyn Gerard, Sue Gerard, James Greer, Doug Harvey, Dajuan Holbrook, Justin Labine, Eric Mathew, Gideon Naef, Erin Nims, Colin Rogers, Ayako Shimizu, Simone Sicard, Shaheer Szazai, Hayden Thomas, and L'il Gee as the baby. Many thanks, also, to countless O-kids for stepping in as background characters. Special thanks to those who were willing to stand in as characters with completely different personalities from their own.

We would also like to thank the people behind some of the Detroit projects that inspired this story, and hope they don't mind us referencing them: Catherine Ferguson Academy, detroityes.com, the Heidelberg Project, Hamtramck Disneyland, sweet-juniper.com, and Trumbullplex. Thanks also to Chris Butcher, Mike O'Connor, Max Douglas, Terry Lau, Carolyn Leadley, El-Farouk Khaki, Curtis McGuire, Gayla Trail, and the Ontario Arts Council.

IDW Publishing
5080 Santa Fe St., San Diego, CA 92109

ISBN 978-1-60010-604-0
13 12 11 10   1 2 3 4

ONE

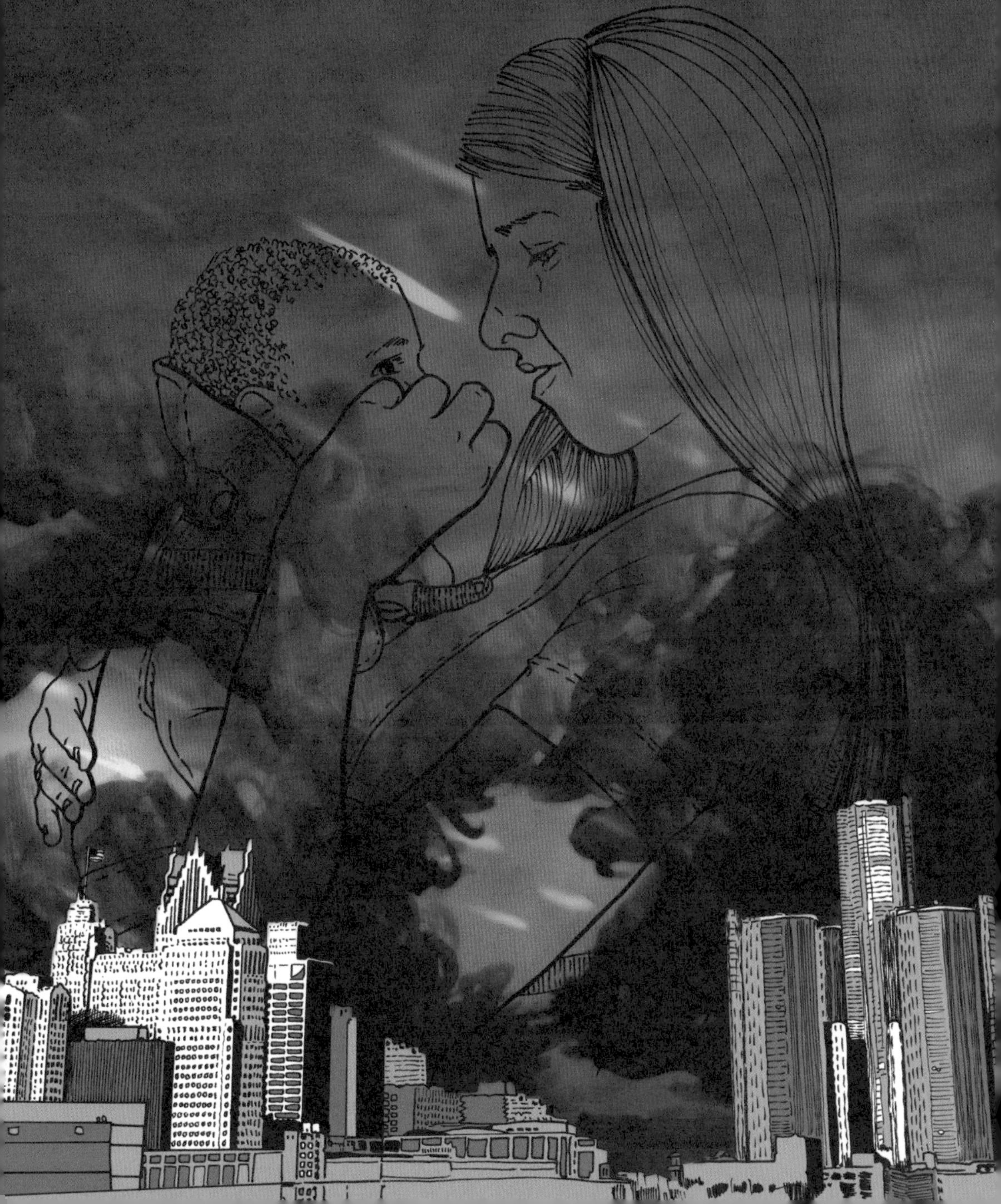

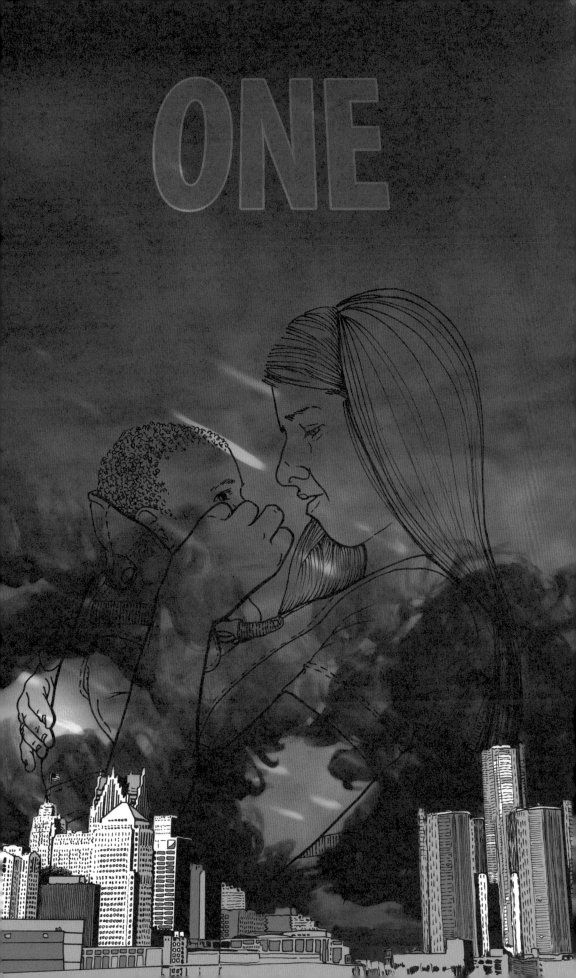

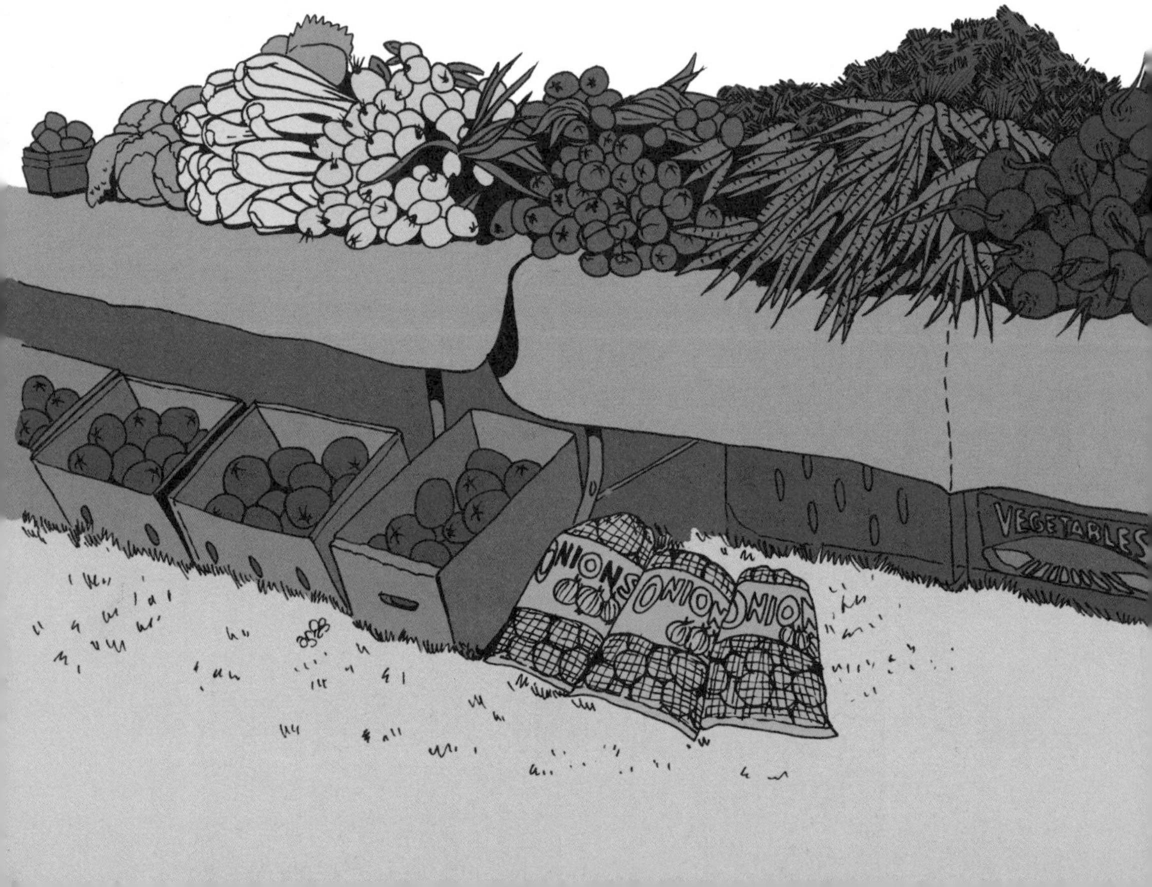
ONIONS
VEGETABLES

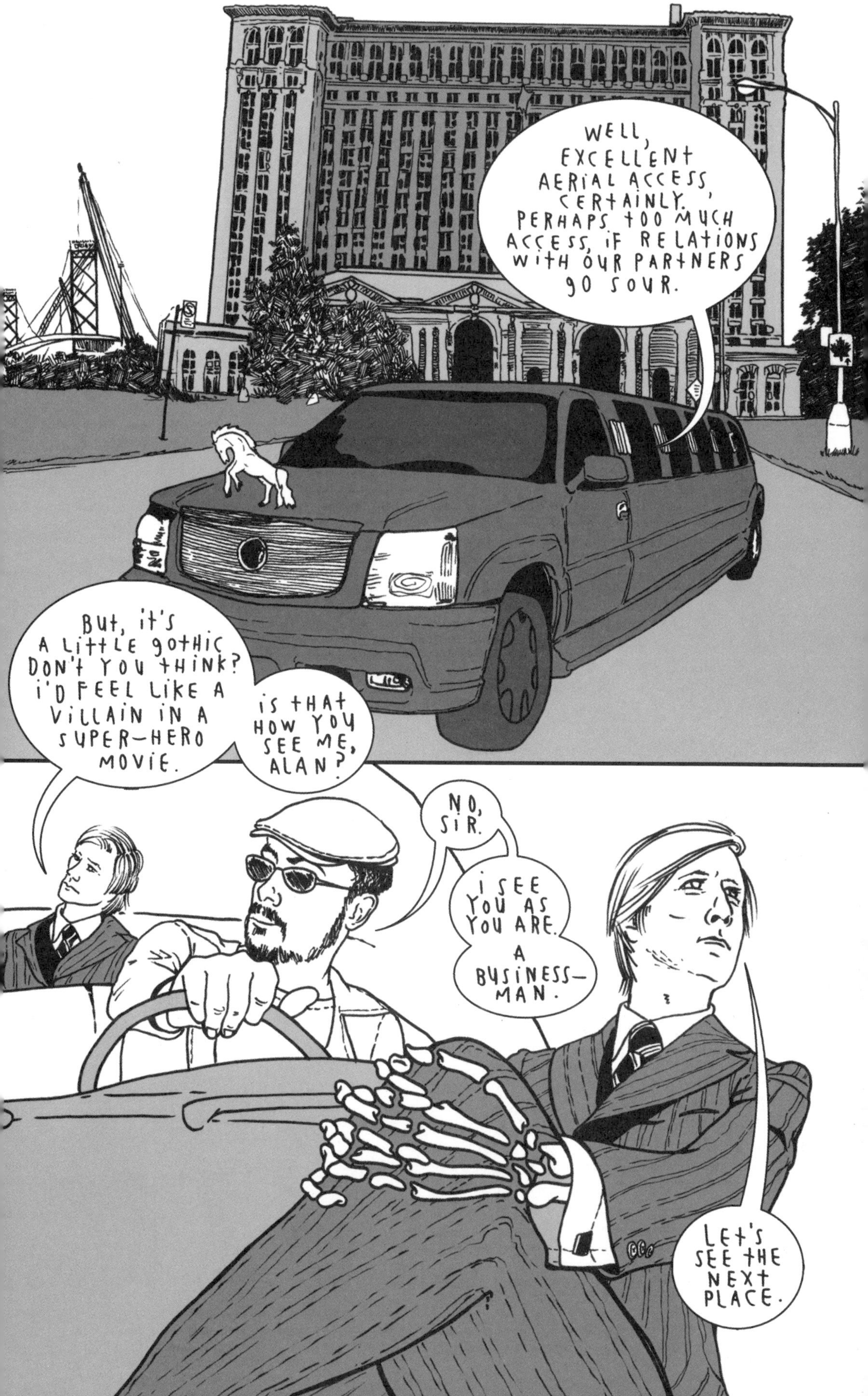
WELL, EXCELLENT AERIAL ACCESS, CERTAINLY. PERHAPS TOO MUCH ACCESS, IF RELATIONS WITH OUR PARTNERS GO SOUR.
BUT, IT'S A LITTLE GOTHIC DON'T YOU THINK? I'D FEEL LIKE A VILLAIN IN A SUPER-HERO MOVIE.
IS THAT HOW YOU SEE ME, ALAN?
NO, SIR.
I SEE YOU AS YOU ARE.
A BUSINESS-MAN.
LET'S SEE THE NEXT PLACE.

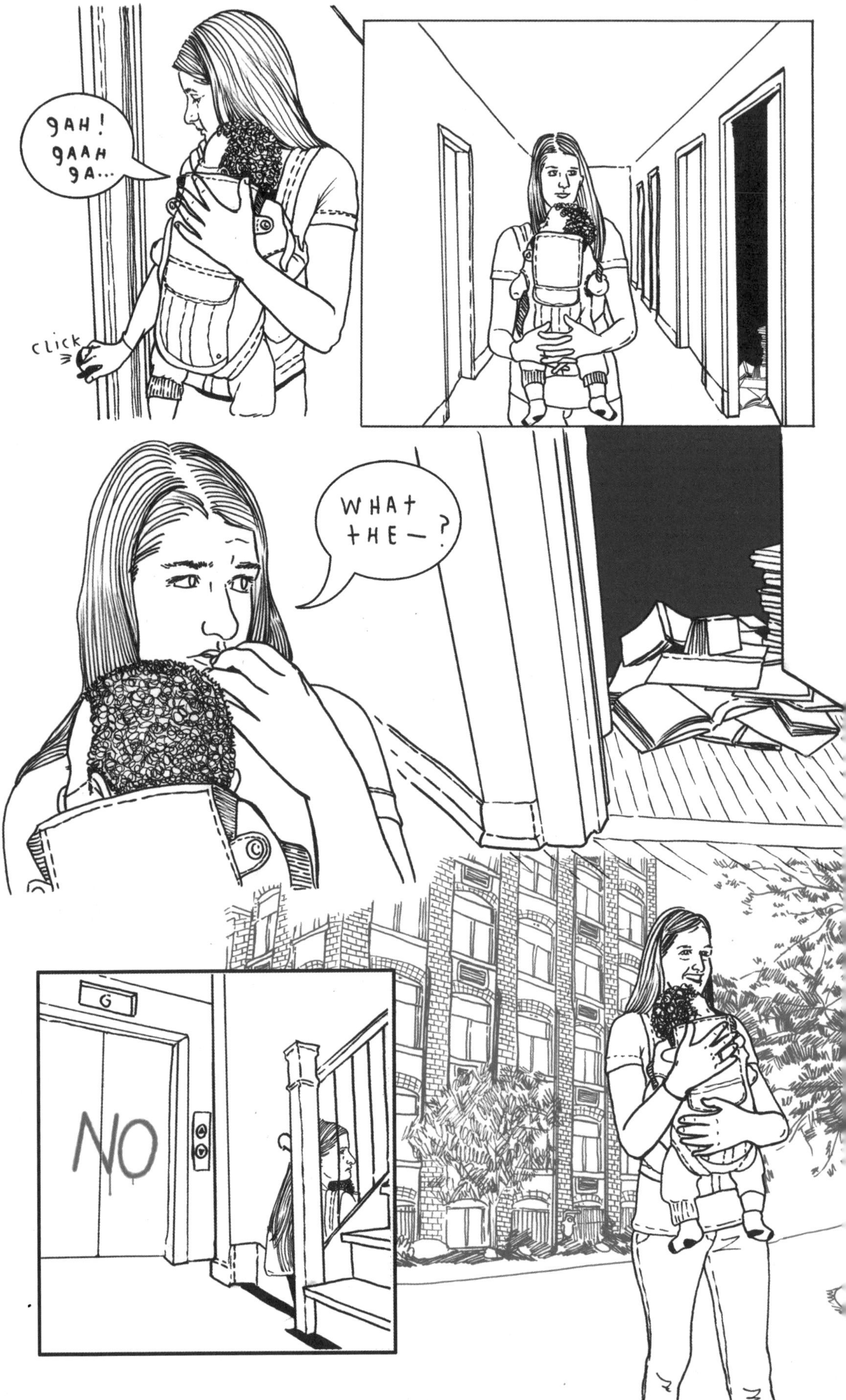
GAH! GAAH GA...
CLICK
WHAT THE—?
G
NO

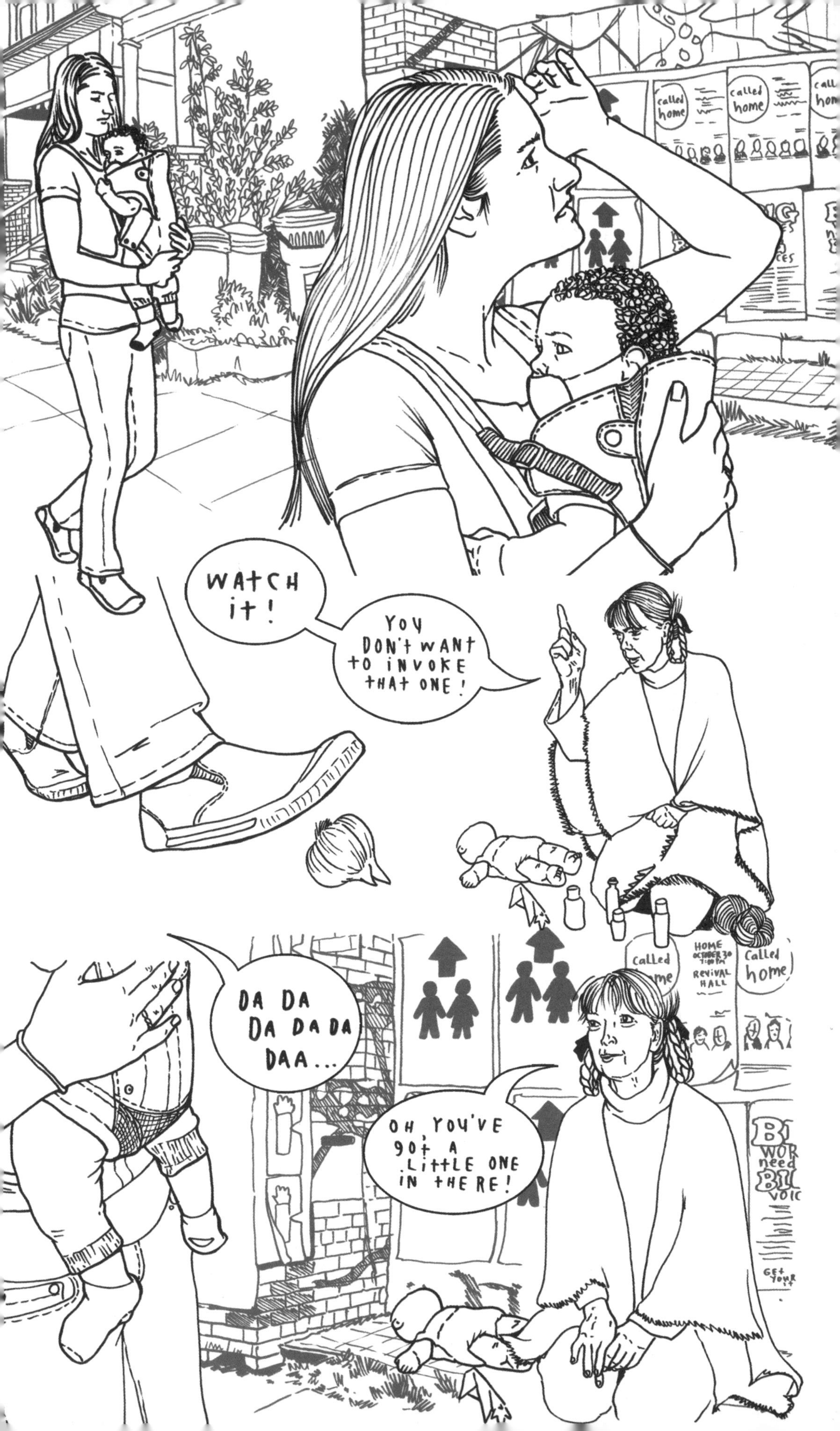
called home
called home
WATCH it!
YOU DON'T WANT TO INVOKE THAT ONE!
DA DA DA DA DA DAA...
Called home
HOME OCTOBER 30 7:00 PM REVIVAL HALL
OH, YOU'VE GOT A LITTLE ONE IN THERE!

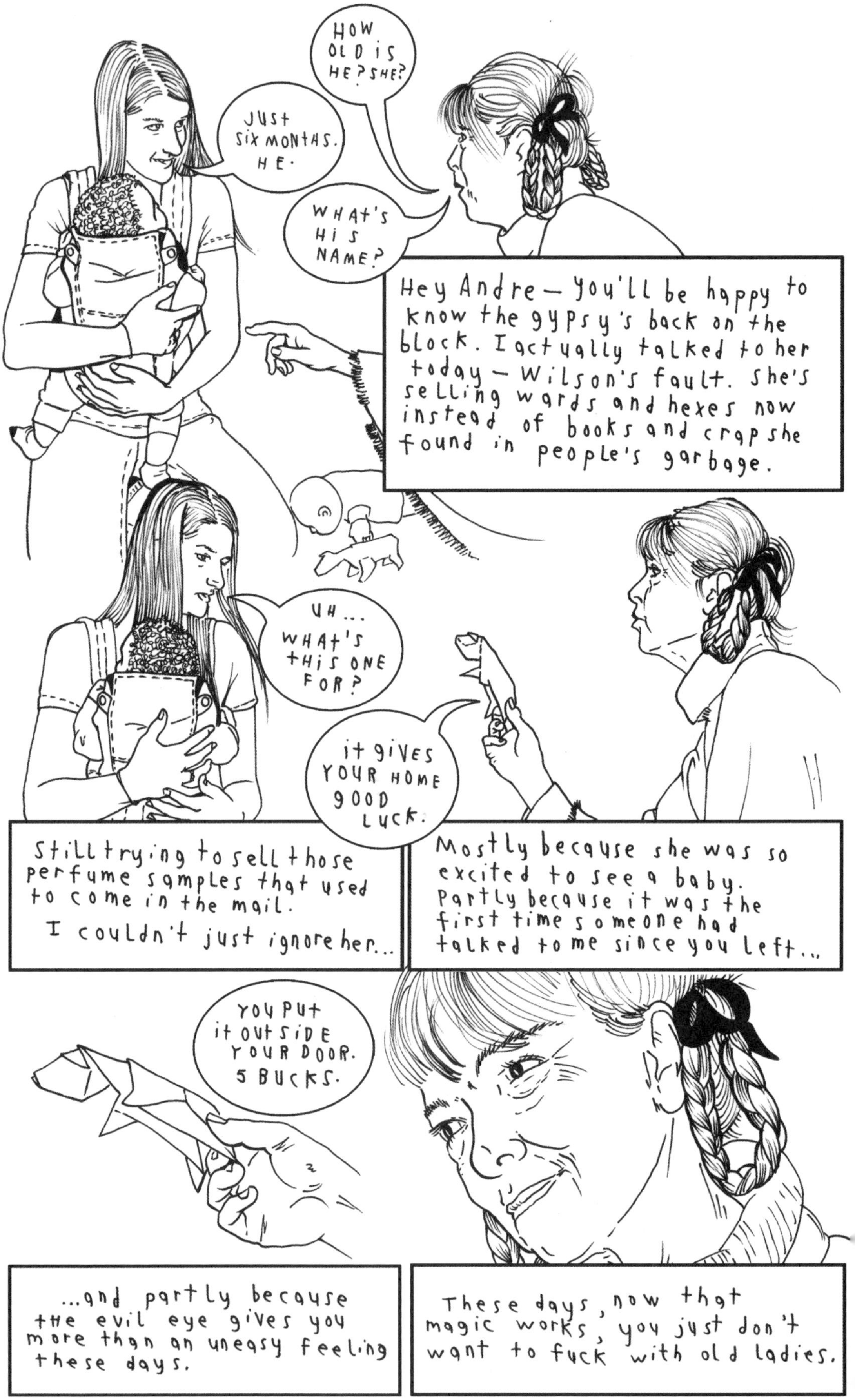
HOW OLD IS HE? SHE?
JUST SIX MONTHS. HE.
WHAT'S HIS NAME?
Hey Andre — You'll be happy to know the gypsy's back on the block. I actually talked to her today — Wilson's fault. She's selling wards and hexes now instead of books and crap she found in people's garbage.
UH... WHAT'S THIS ONE FOR?
it gives YOUR HOME good LUCK.
Still trying to sell those perfume samples that used to come in the mail.
I couldn't just ignore her...
Mostly because she was so excited to see a baby. Partly because it was the first time someone had talked to me since you left...
YOU PUT it OUTSIDE YOUR DOOR. 5 BUCKS.
...and partly because the evil eye gives you more than an uneasy feeling these days.
These days, now that magic works, you just don't want to fuck with old ladies.

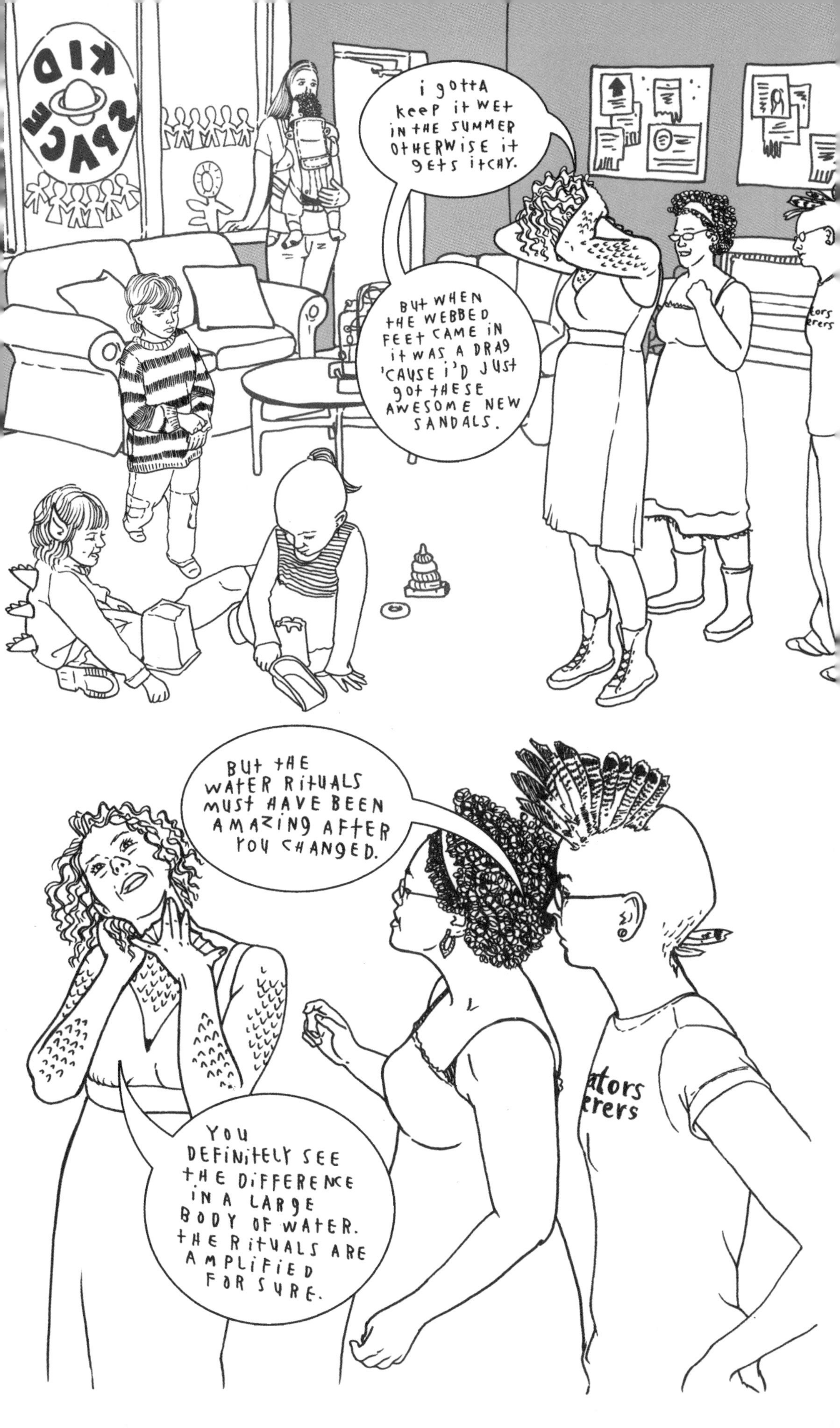
KID SPACE
i gotta keep it wet in the summer otherwise it gets itchy.
But when the webbed feet came in it was a drag 'cause i'd just got these awesome new sandals.
But the water rituals must have been amazing after you changed.
You definitely see the difference in a large body of water. the rituals are amplified for sure.

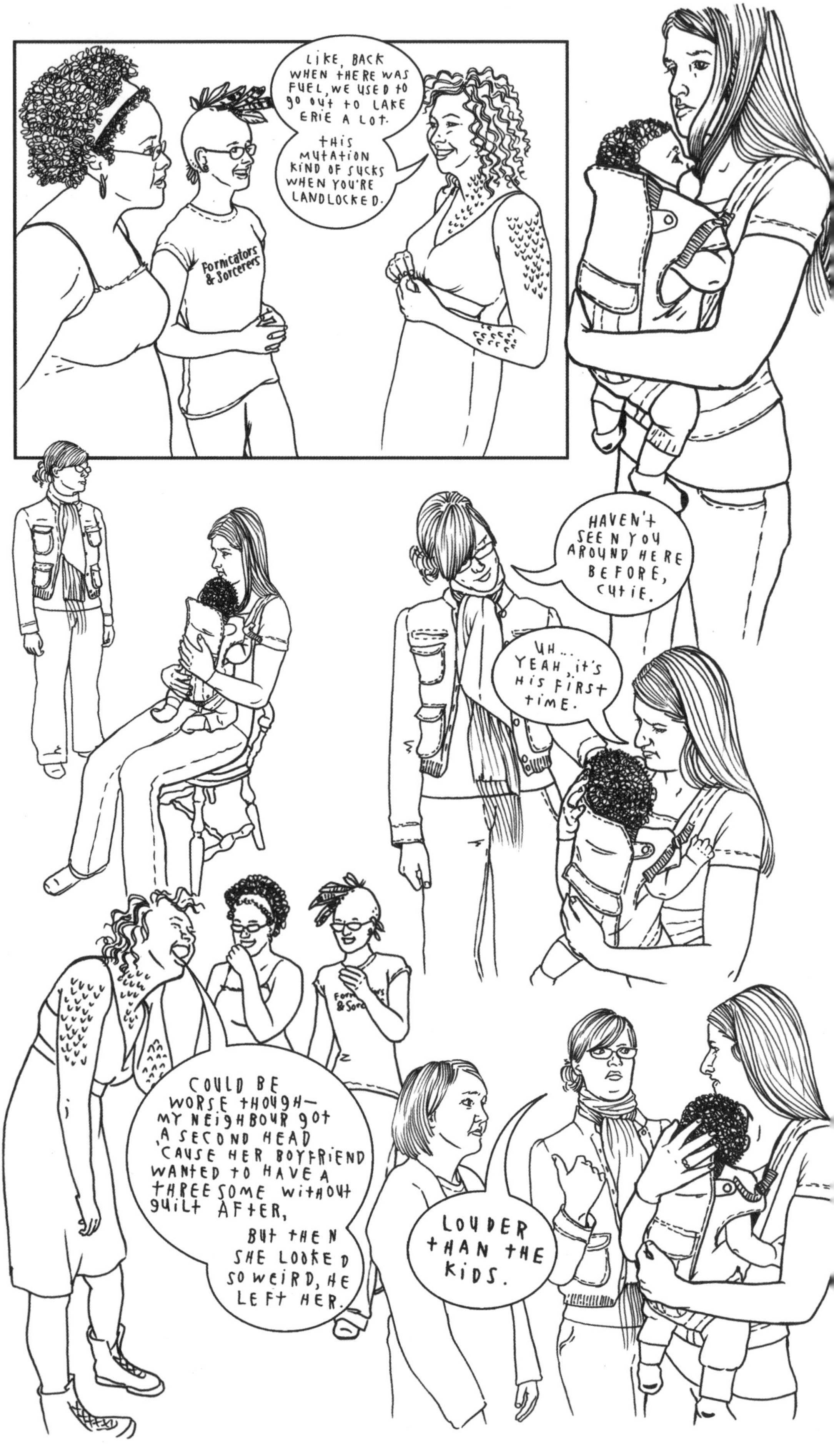
LIKE, BACK WHEN THERE WAS FUEL, WE USED TO GO OUT TO LAKE ERIE A LOT.
THIS MUTATION KIND OF SUCKS WHEN YOU'RE LANDLOCKED.
Fornicators & Sorcerers
HAVEN'T SEEN YOU AROUND HERE BEFORE, CUTIE.
UH... YEAH, IT'S HIS FIRST TIME.
COULD BE WORSE THOUGH— MY NEIGHBOUR GOT A SECOND HEAD 'CAUSE HER BOYFRIEND WANTED TO HAVE A THREESOME WITHOUT GUILT AFTER,
BUT THEN SHE LOOKED SO WEIRD, HE LEFT HER.
LOUDER THAN THE KIDS.

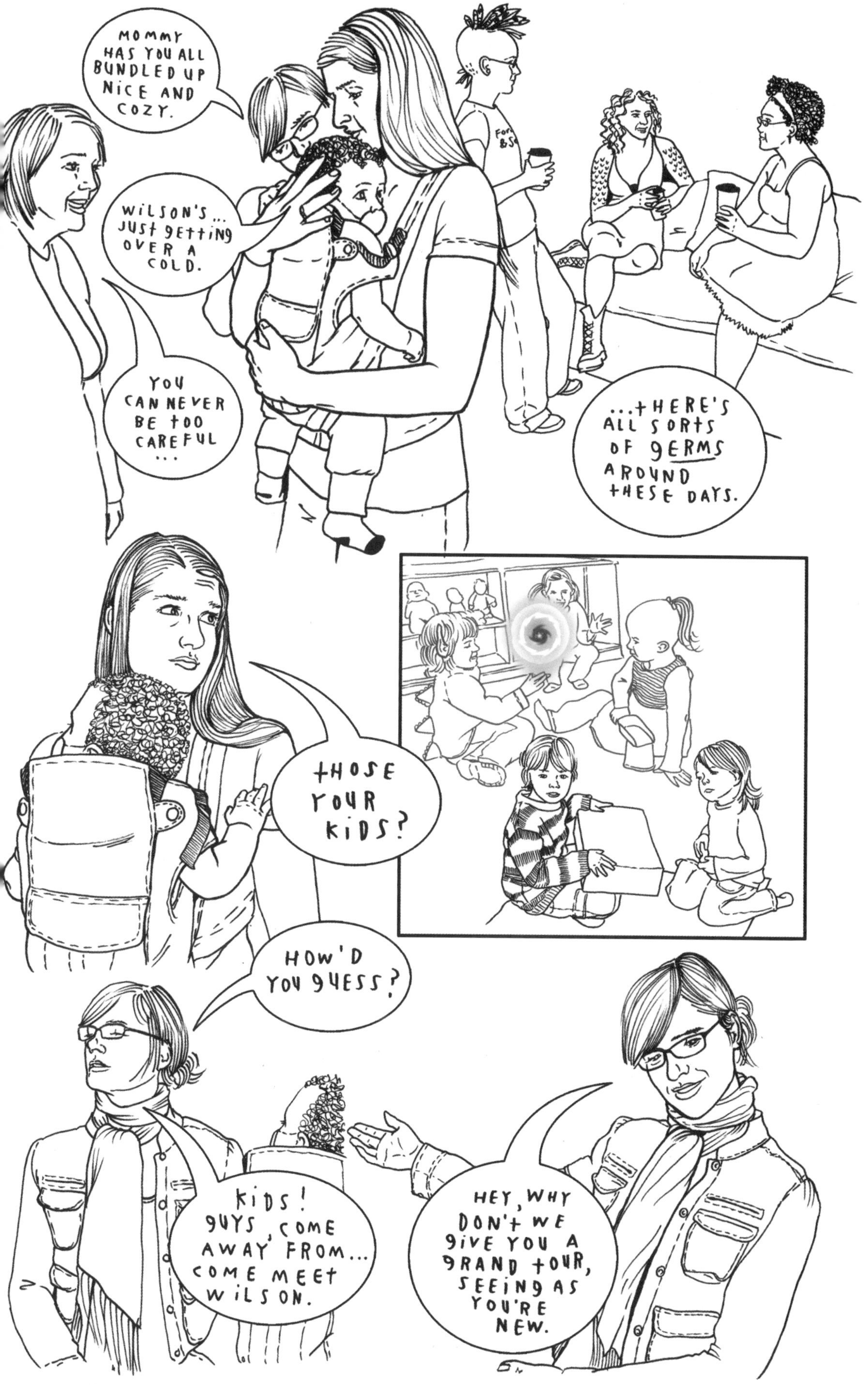
MOMMY HAS YOU ALL BUNDLED UP NICE AND COZY.
WILSON'S... JUST GETTING OVER A COLD.
YOU CAN NEVER BE TOO CAREFUL...
...THERE'S ALL SORTS OF GERMS AROUND THESE DAYS.
THOSE YOUR KIDS?
HOW'D YOU GUESS?
KIDS! GUYS, COME AWAY FROM... COME MEET WILSON.
HEY, WHY DON'T WE GIVE YOU A GRAND TOUR, SEEING AS YOU'RE NEW.

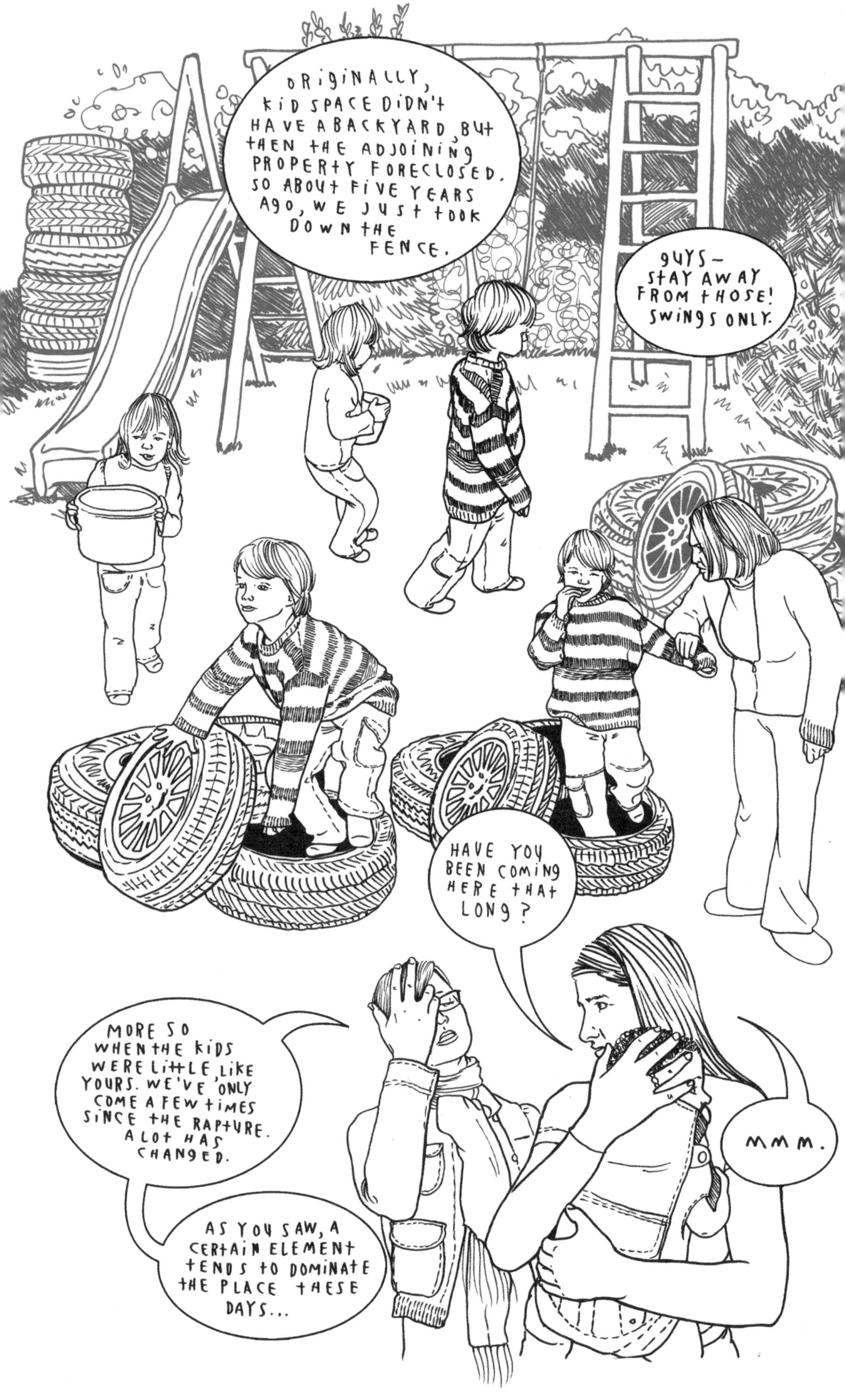
ORIGINALLY, KID SPACE DIDN'T HAVE A BACKYARD, BUT THEN THE ADJOINING PROPERTY FORECLOSED. SO ABOUT FIVE YEARS AGO, WE JUST TOOK DOWN THE FENCE.
GUYS— STAY AWAY FROM THOSE! SWINGS ONLY.
HAVE YOU BEEN COMING HERE THAT LONG?
MORE SO WHEN THE KIDS WERE LITTLE, LIKE YOURS. WE'VE ONLY COME A FEW TIMES SINCE THE RAPTURE. A LOT HAS CHANGED.
MMM.
AS YOU SAW, A CERTAIN ELEMENT TENDS TO DOMINATE THE PLACE THESE DAYS...

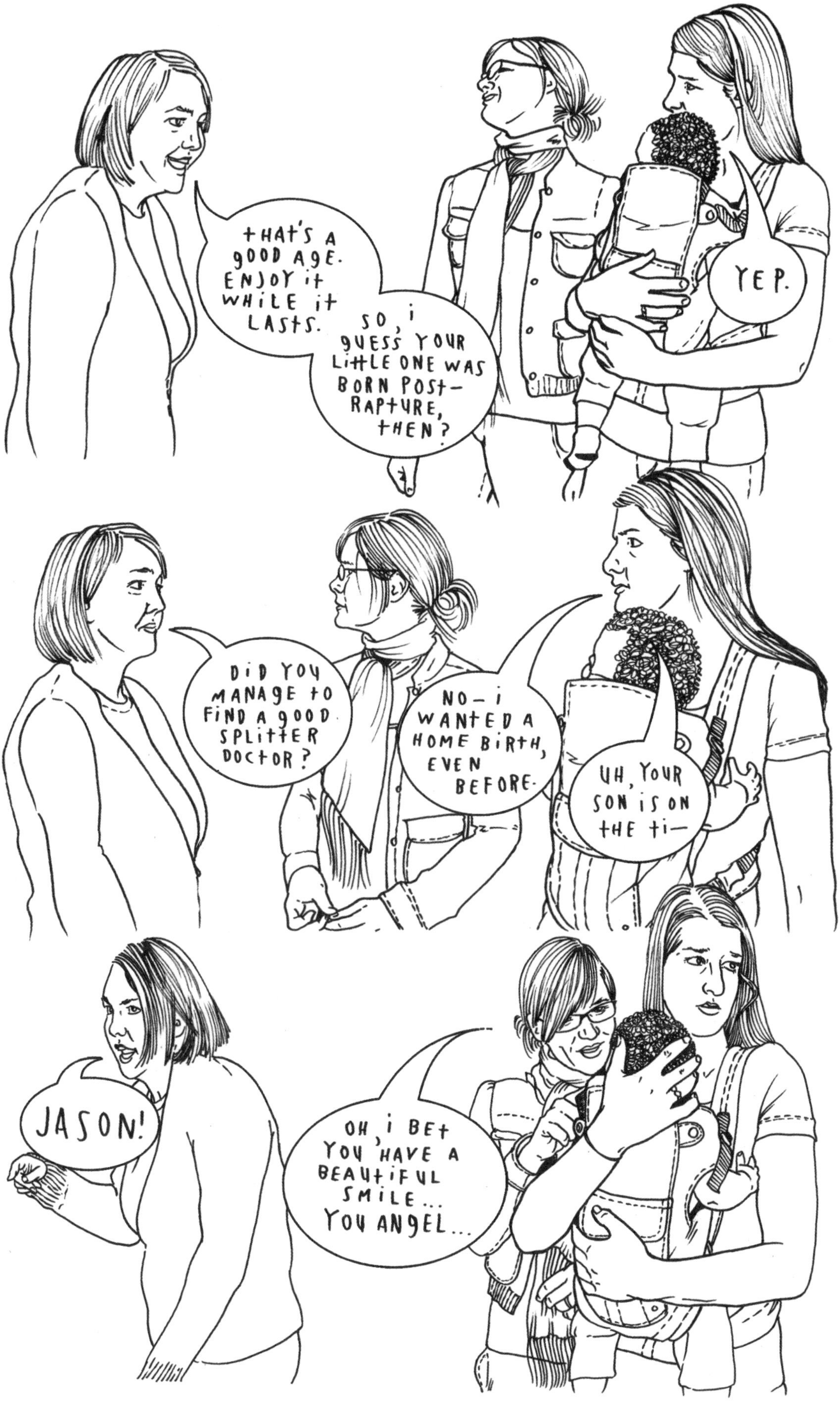
THAT'S A GOOD AGE. ENJOY IT WHILE IT LASTS.
YEP.
SO, I GUESS YOUR LITTLE ONE WAS BORN POST-RAPTURE, THEN?
DID YOU MANAGE TO FIND A GOOD SPLITTER DOCTOR?
NO— I WANTED A HOME BIRTH, EVEN BEFORE.
UH, YOUR SON IS ON THE TI—
JASON!
OH, I BET YOU HAVE A BEAUTIFUL SMILE... YOU ANGEL...

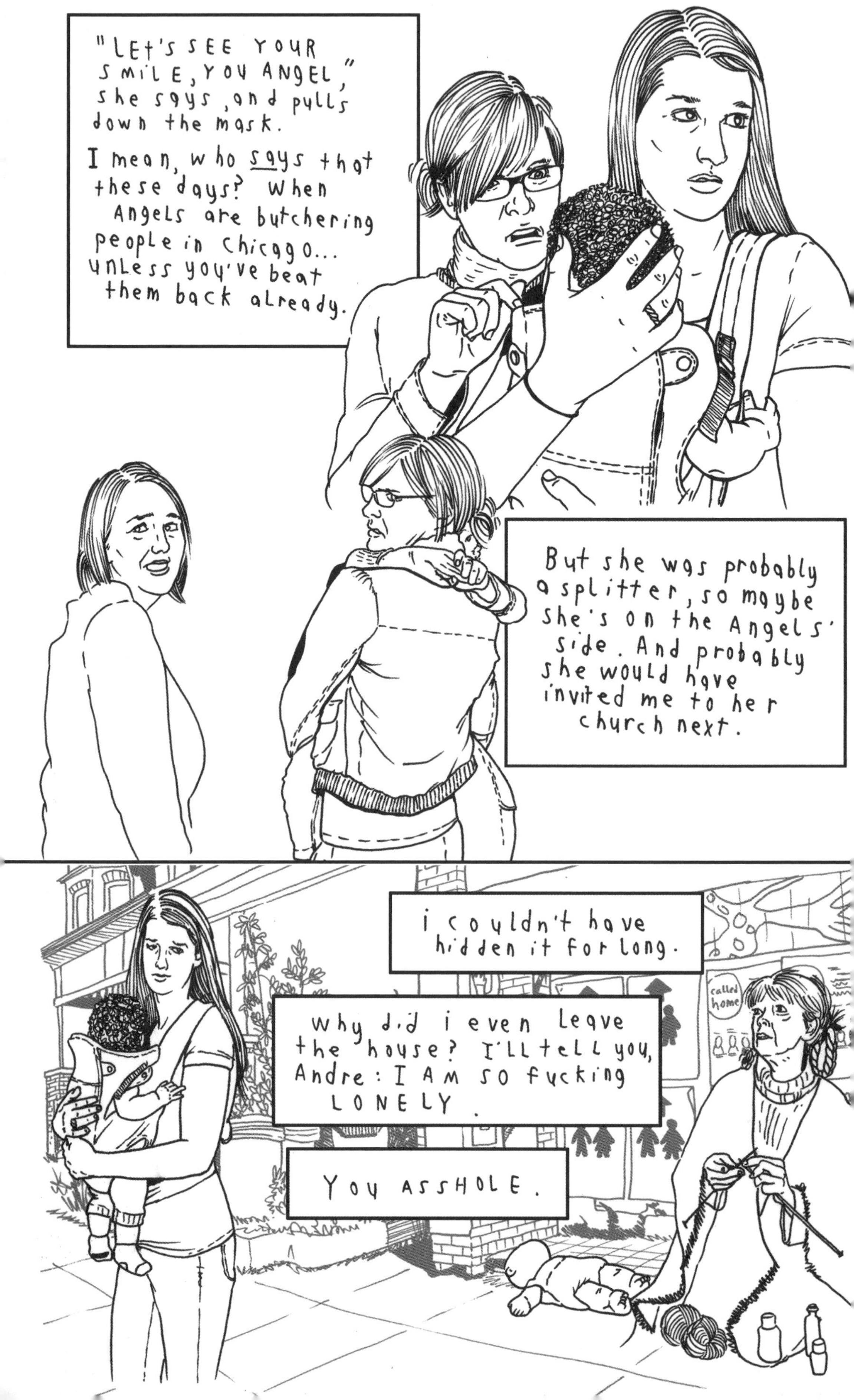
"LET'S SEE YOUR SMILE, YOU ANGEL," she says, and pulls down the mask.
I mean, who says that these days? When Angels are butchering people in Chicago... unless you've beat them back already.
But she was probably a splitter, so maybe she's on the Angels' side. And probably she would have invited me to her church next.
i couldn't have hidden it for long.
why did i even leave the house? I'LL tell you, Andre: I AM SO fucking LONELY.
YOU ASSHOLE.
called home

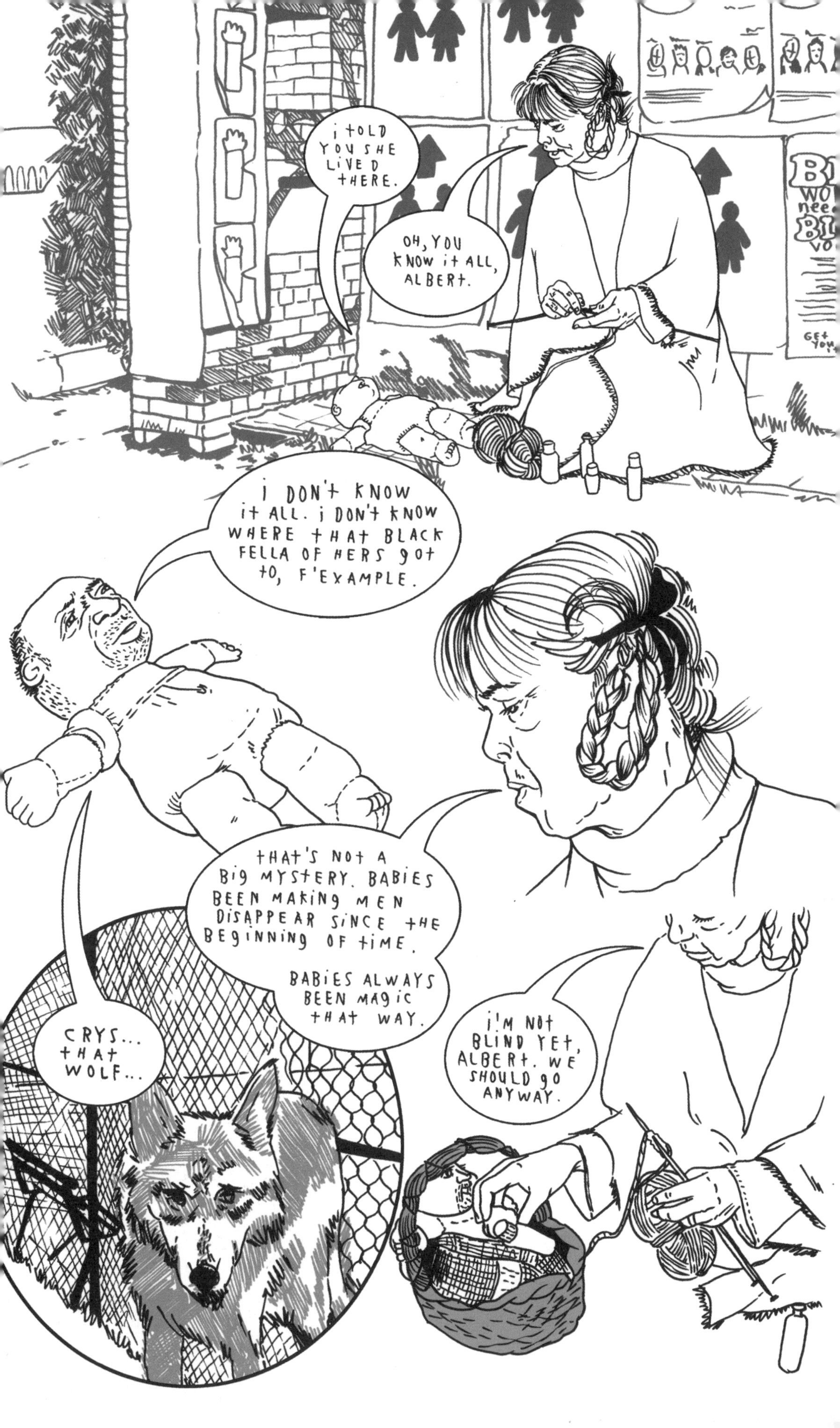
I TOLD YOU SHE LIVED THERE.
OH, YOU KNOW IT ALL, ALBERT.
I DON'T KNOW IT ALL. I DON'T KNOW WHERE THAT BLACK FELLA OF HERS GOT TO, F'EXAMPLE.
THAT'S NOT A BIG MYSTERY. BABIES BEEN MAKING MEN DISAPPEAR SINCE THE BEGINNING OF TIME.
BABIES ALWAYS BEEN MAGIC THAT WAY.
CRYS... THAT WOLF...
I'M NOT BLIND YET, ALBERT. WE SHOULD GO ANYWAY.

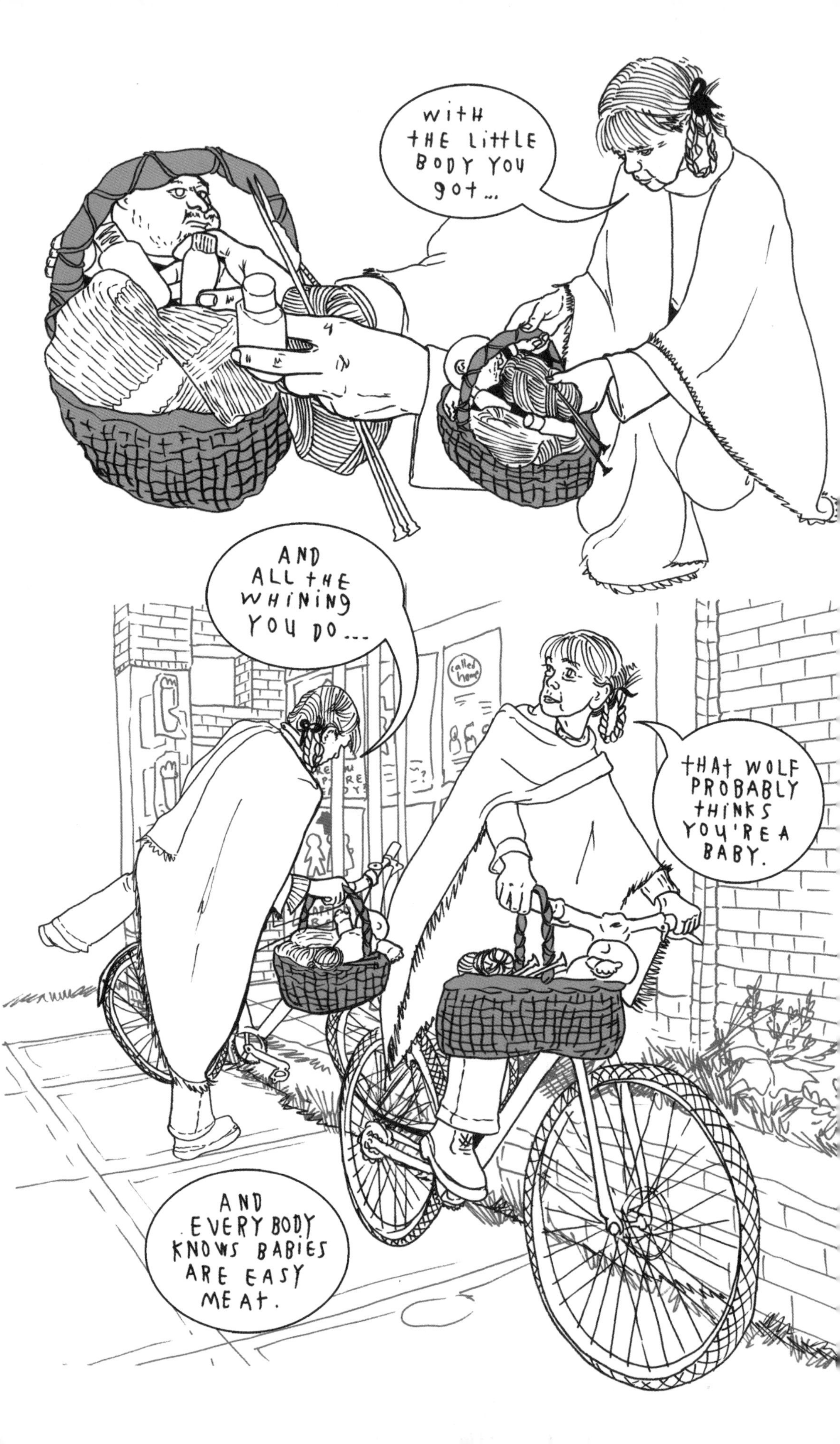
WITH THE LITTLE BODY YOU GOT...
AND ALL THE WHINING YOU DO...
THAT WOLF PROBABLY THINKS YOU'RE A BABY.
AND EVERYBODY KNOWS BABIES ARE EASY MEAT.

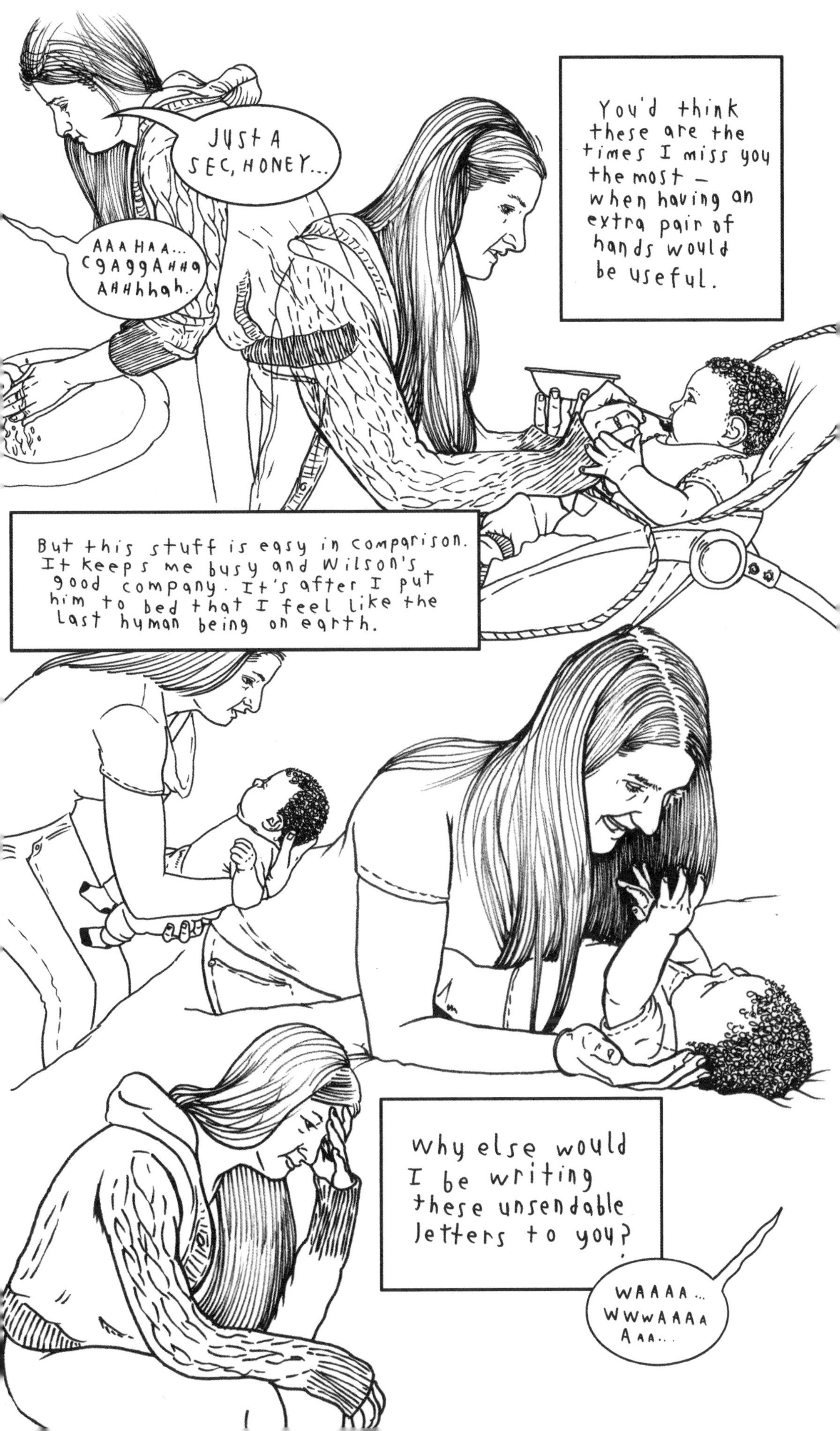

You'd think these are the times I miss you the most — when having an extra pair of hands would be useful.
JUST A SEC, HONEY...
AAAHAA... CGAGGAHHG AHHHhah..
But this stuff is easy in comparison. It keeps me busy and Wilson's good company. It's after I put him to bed that I feel like the last human being on earth.
Why else would I be writing these unsendable letters to you?
WAAAA... WWWAAAA AAA...

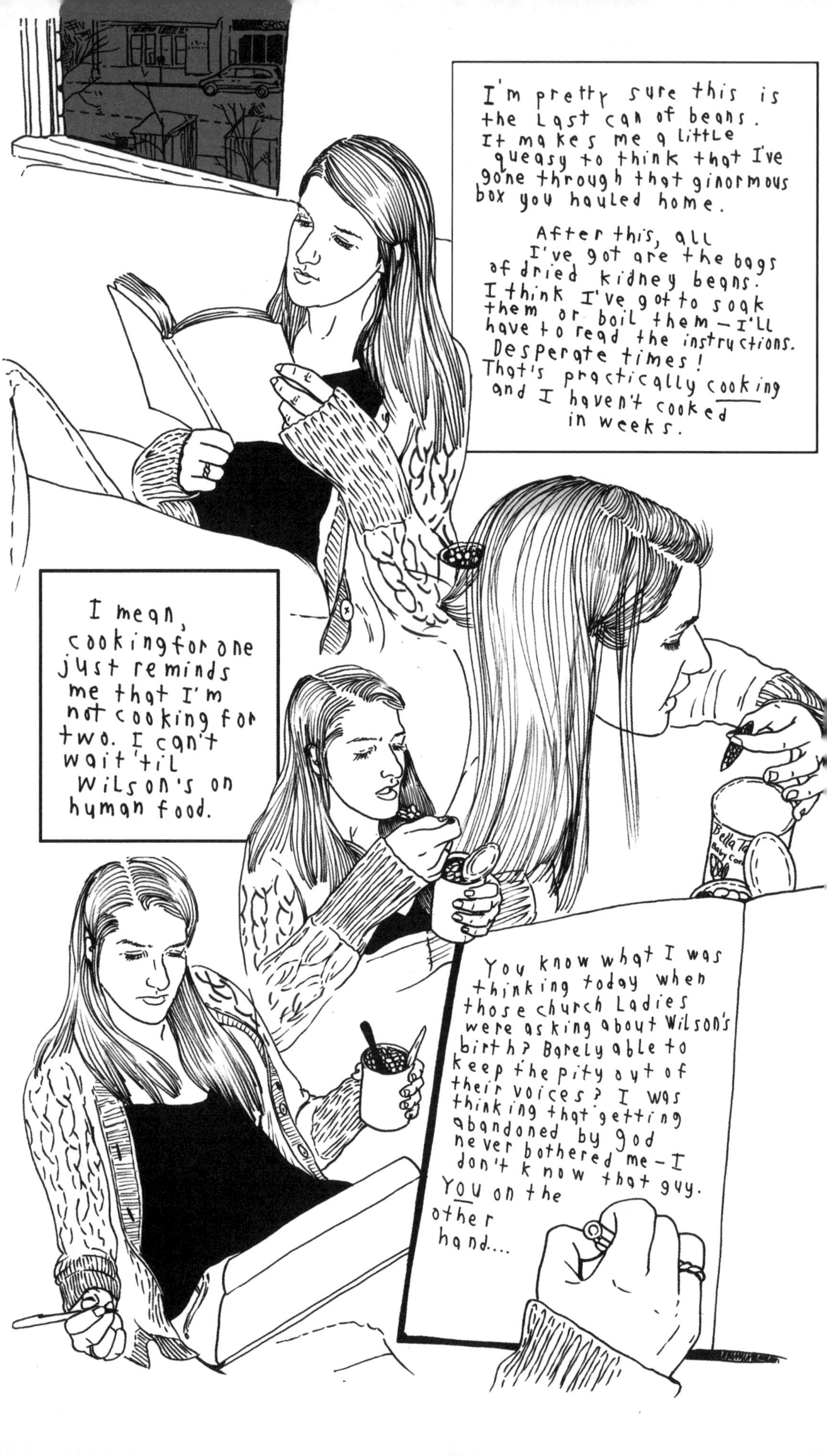
I'm pretty sure this is the last can of beans. It makes me a little queasy to think that I've gone through that ginormous box you hauled home.
After this, all I've got are the bags of dried kidney beans. I think I've got to soak them or boil them—I'll have to read the instructions. Desperate times! That's practically cooking and I haven't cooked in weeks.
I mean, cooking for one just reminds me that I'm not cooking for two. I can't wait 'til Wilson's on human food.
You know what I was thinking today when those church ladies were asking about Wilson's birth? Barely able to keep the pity out of their voices? I was thinking that getting abandoned by god never bothered me—I don't know that guy. YOU on the other hand....

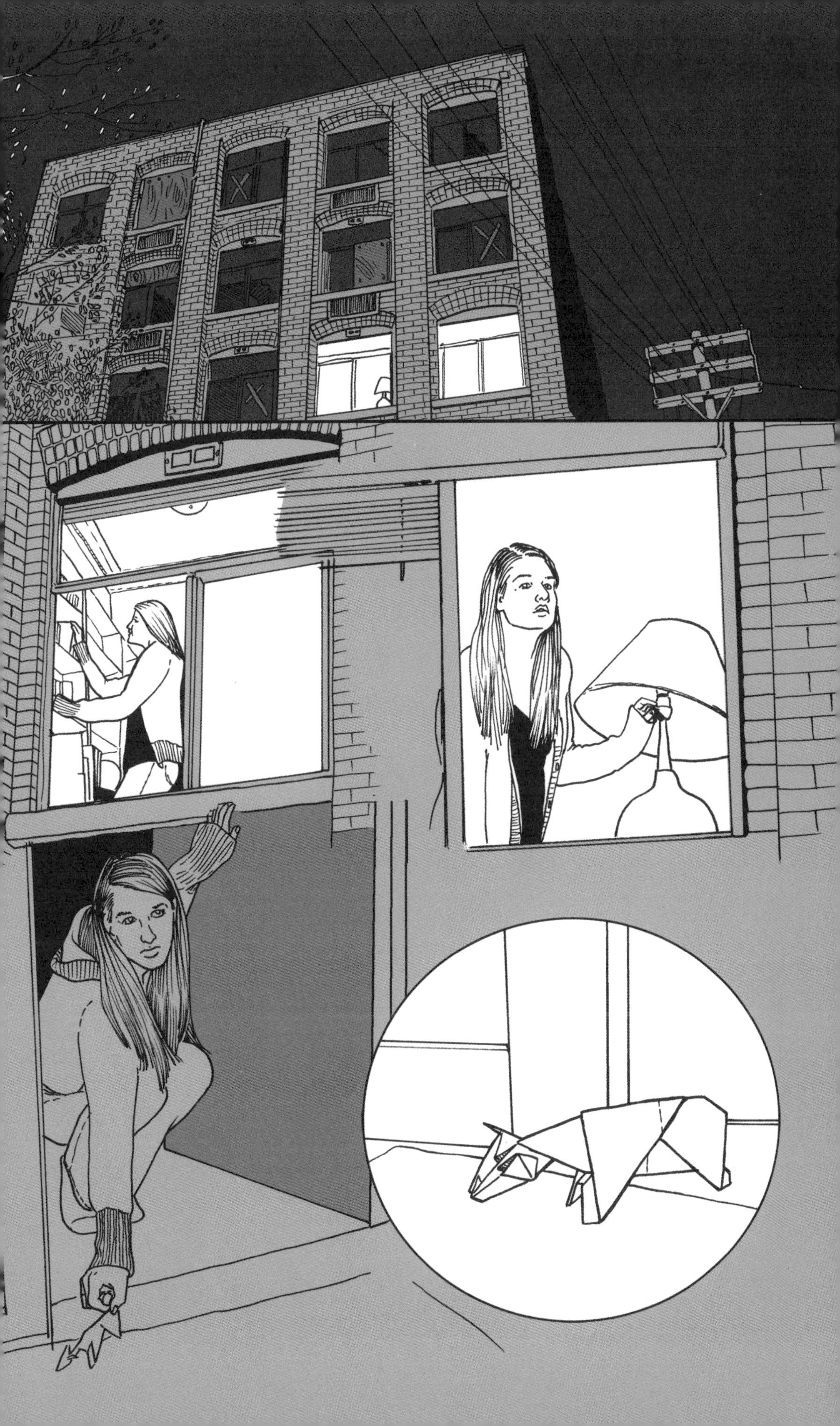

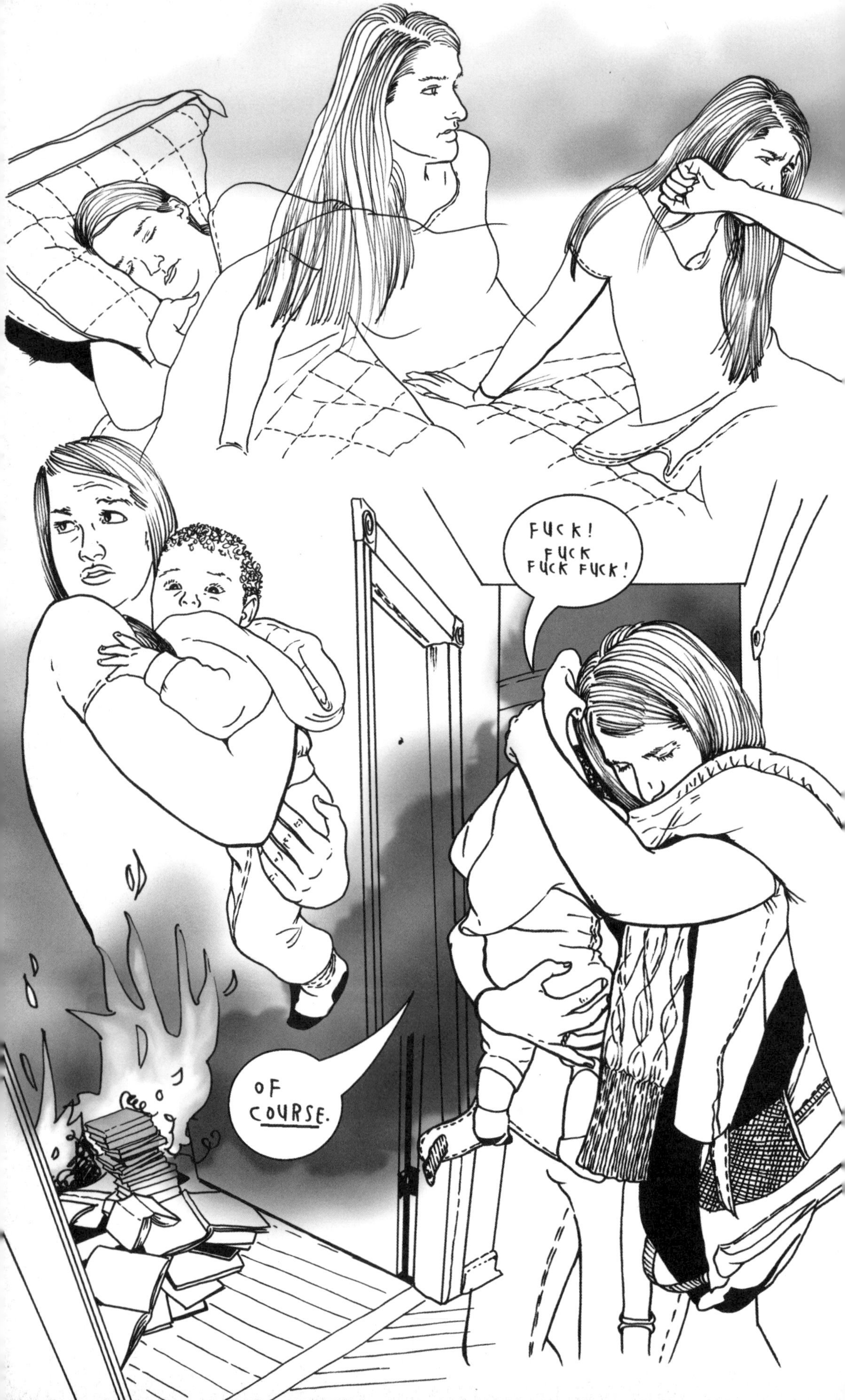
FUCK! FUCK FUCK FUCK!
OF COURSE.

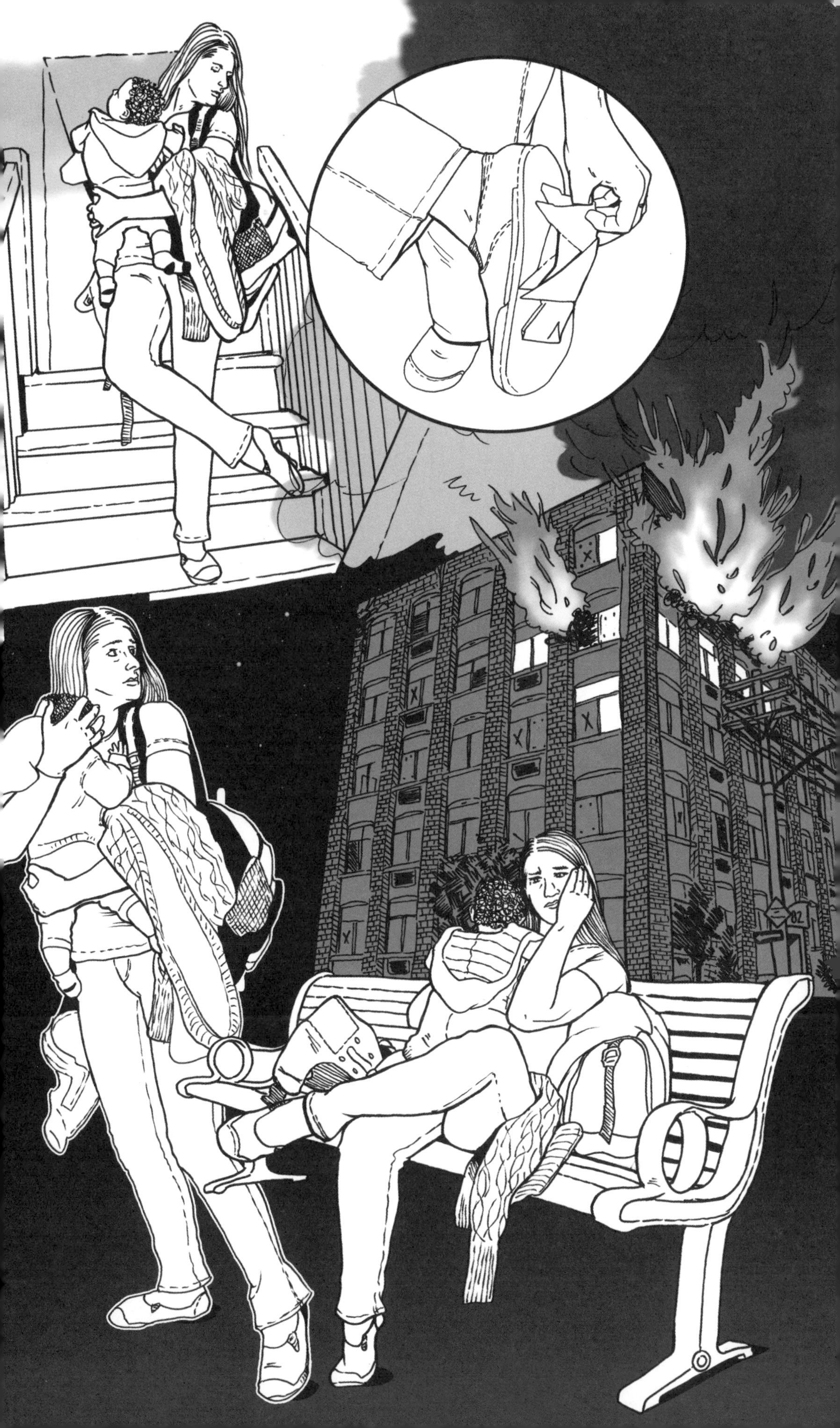
82

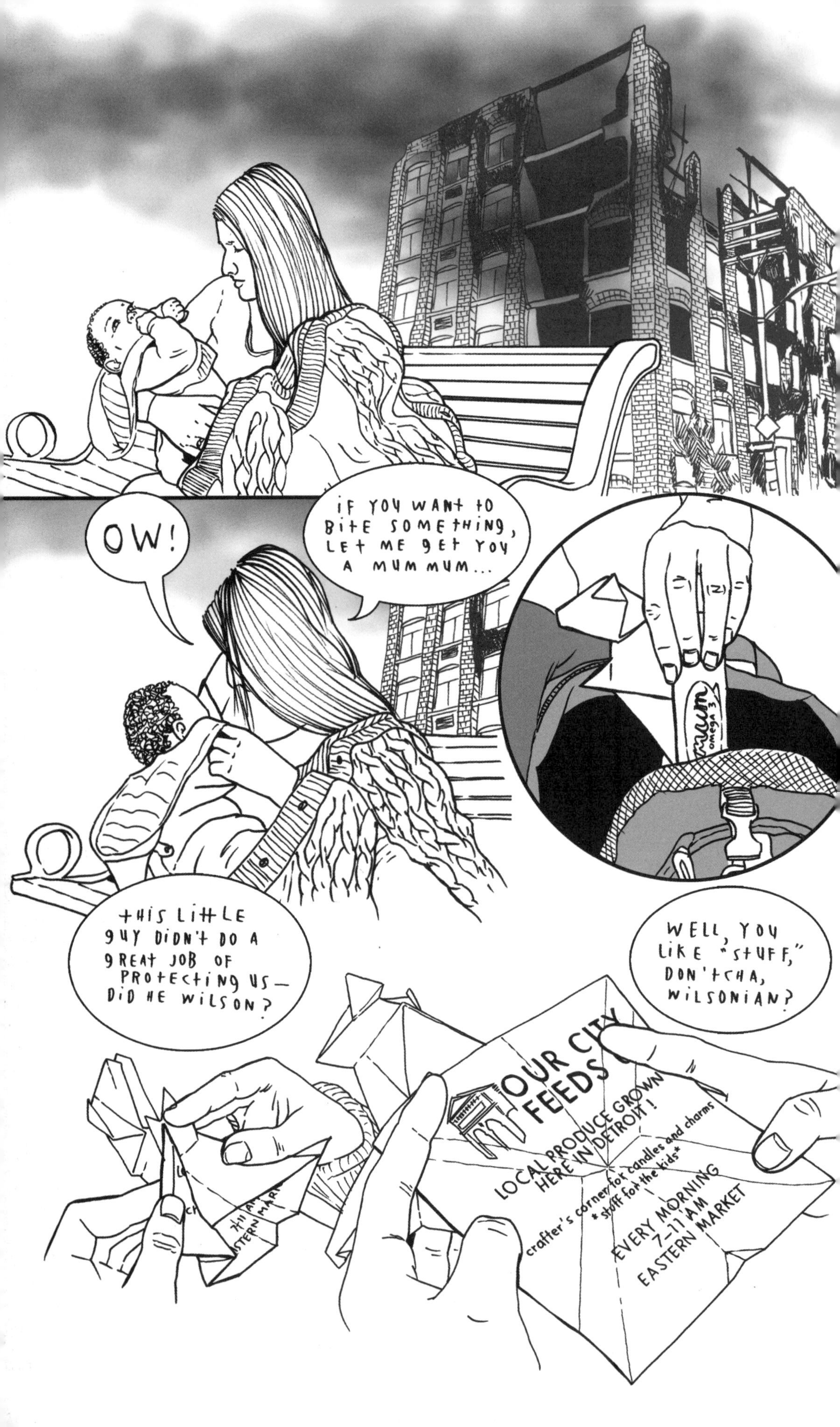
OW!
IF YOU WANT TO BITE SOMETHING, LET ME GET YOU A MUMMUM...
mum omega 3
THIS LITTLE GUY DIDN'T DO A GREAT JOB OF PROTECTING US— DID HE WILSON?
WELL, YOU LIKE "STUFF," DON'TCHA, WILSONIAN?
OUR CITY FEEDS
LOCAL PRODUCE GROWN HERE IN DETROIT!
crafter's corner for candles and charms
* stuff for the kids*
EVERY MORNING 7–11 AM
EASTERN MARKET

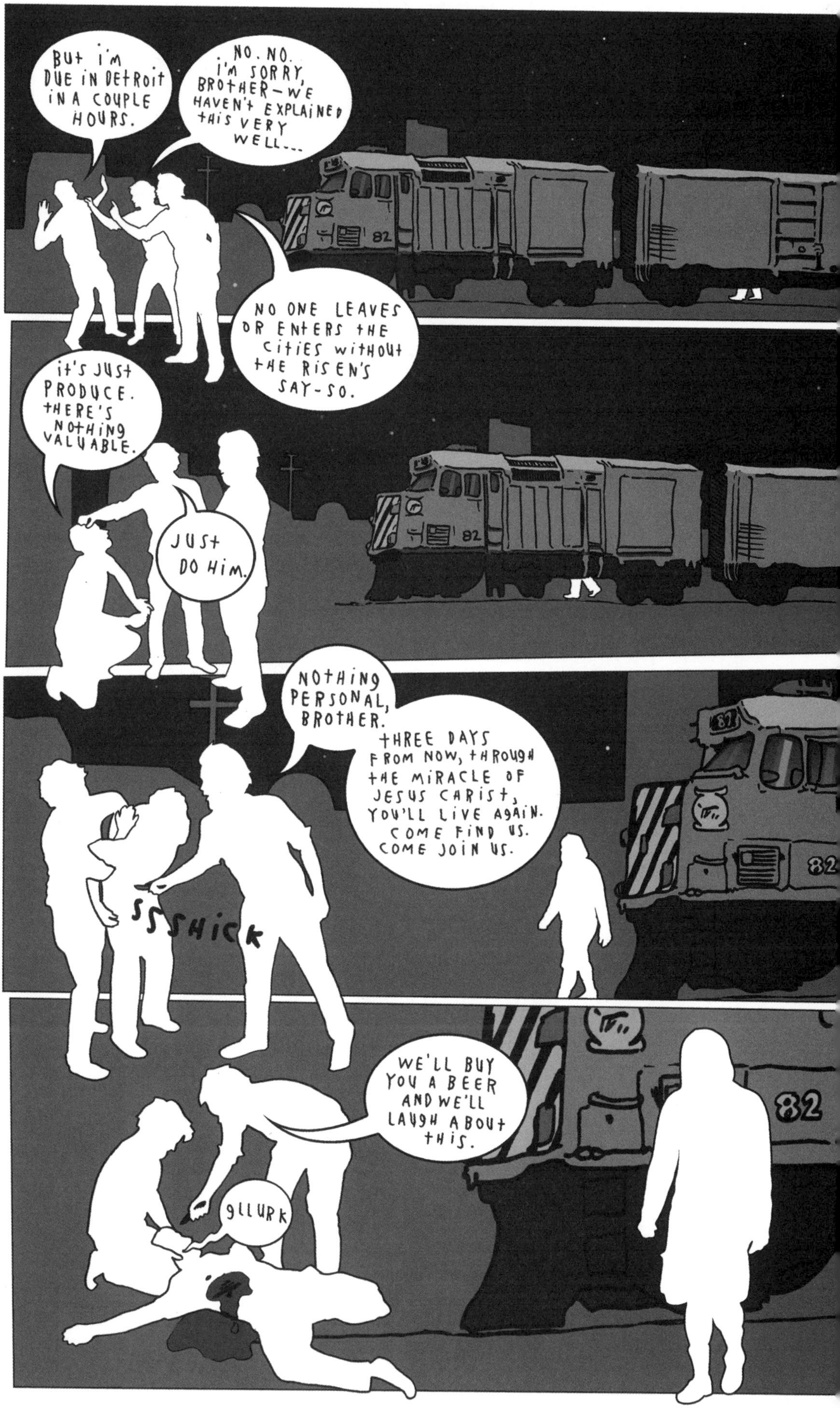

But i'm due in Detroit in a couple hours.
No. No. i'm sorry, brother—we haven't explained this very well...
No one leaves or enters the cities without the Risen's say-so.
it's just produce. there's nothing valuable.
Just do him.
Nothing personal, brother.
three days from now, through the miracle of Jesus Christ, you'll live again. Come find us. Come join us.
SSSHICK
We'll buy you a beer and we'll laugh about this.
gllurk

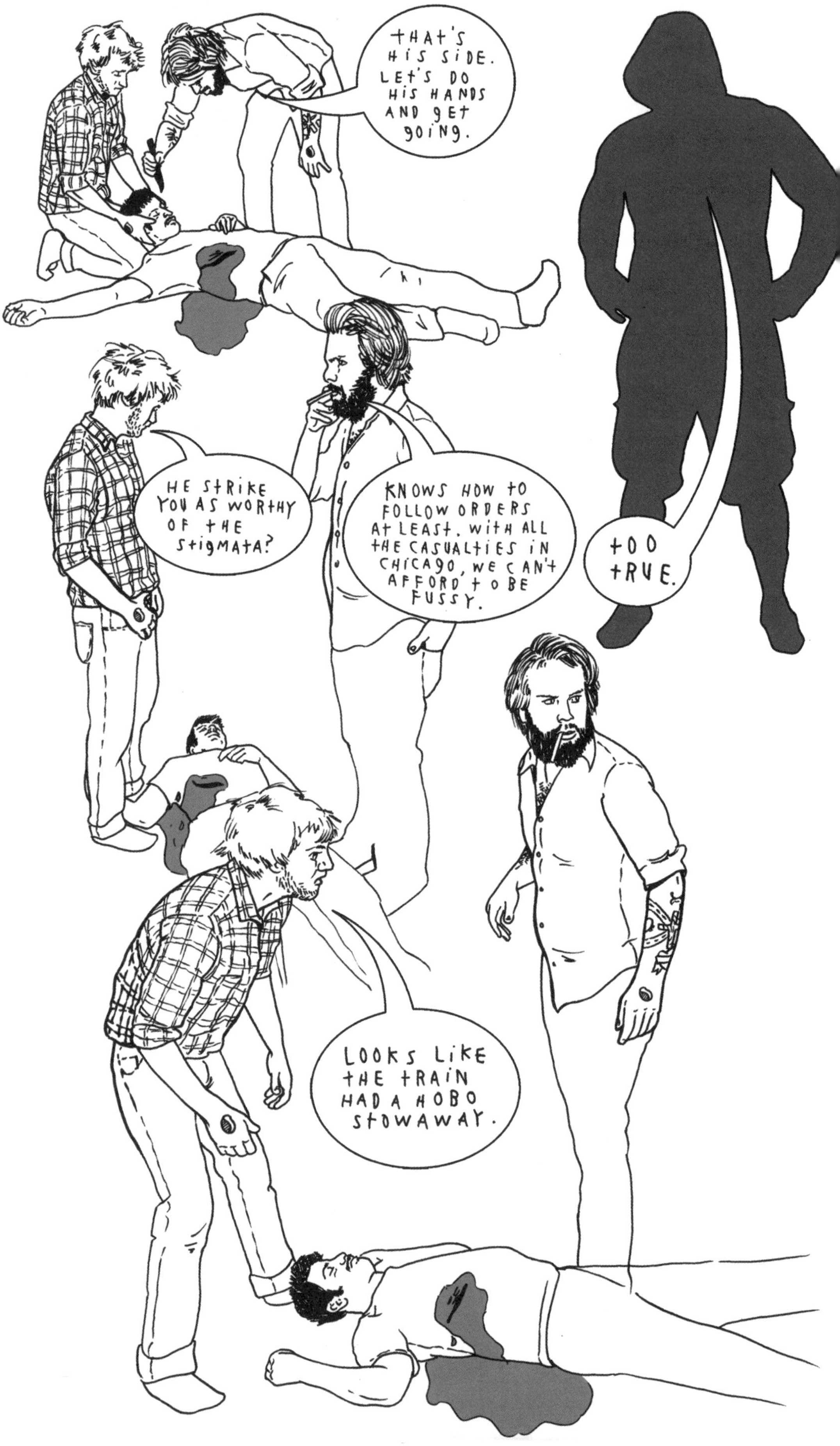
THAT'S HIS SIDE. LET'S DO HIS HANDS AND GET GOING.
HE STRIKE YOU AS WORTHY OF THE STIGMATA?
KNOWS HOW TO FOLLOW ORDERS AT LEAST. WITH ALL THE CASUALTIES IN CHICAGO, WE CAN'T AFFORD TO BE FUSSY.
TOO TRUE.
LOOKS LIKE THE TRAIN HAD A HOBO STOWAWAY.

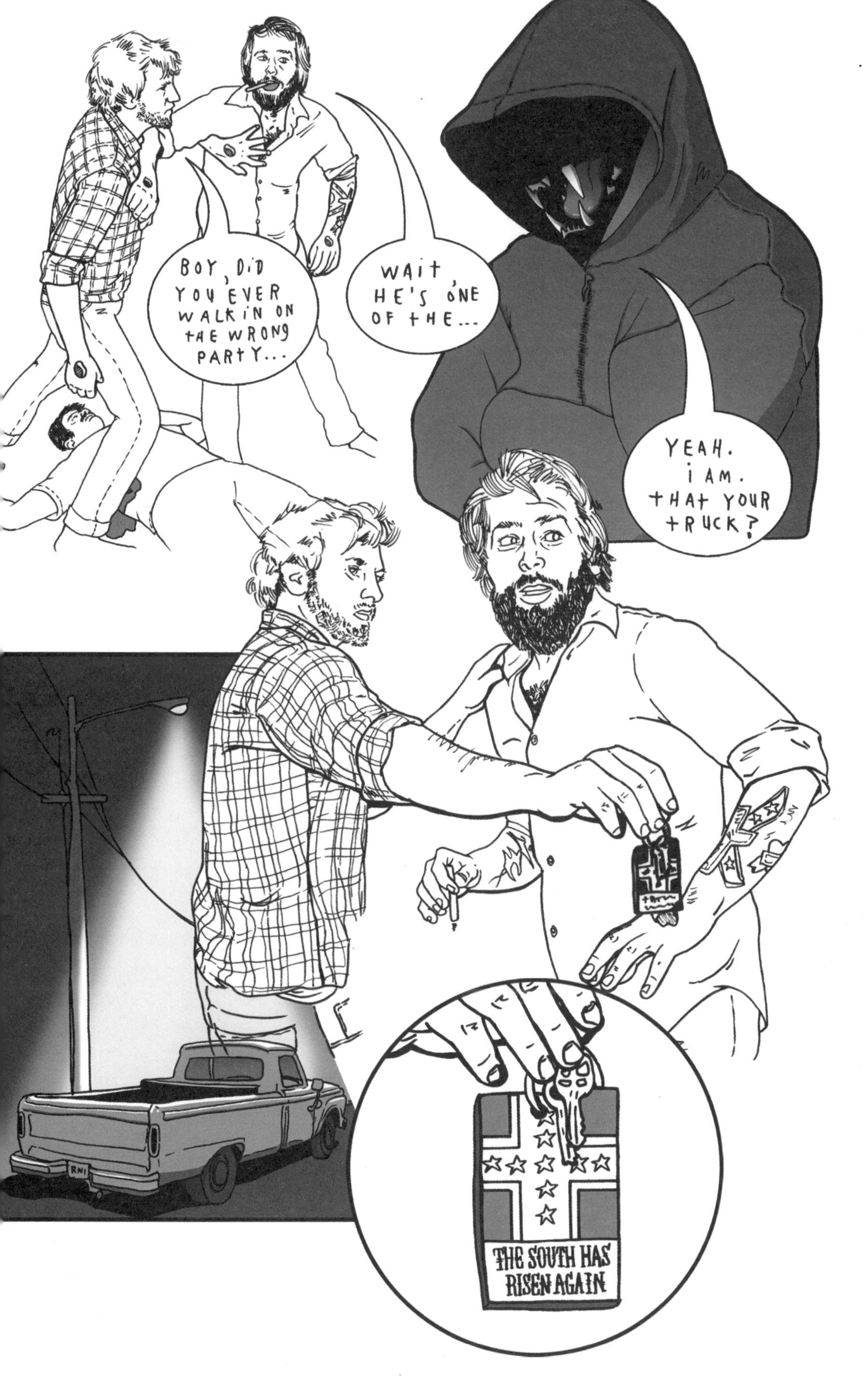
BOY, DID YOU EVER WALK IN ON THE WRONG PARTY...
WAIT, HE'S ONE OF THE...
YEAH. I AM. THAT YOUR TRUCK?
THE SOUTH HAS RISEN AGAIN

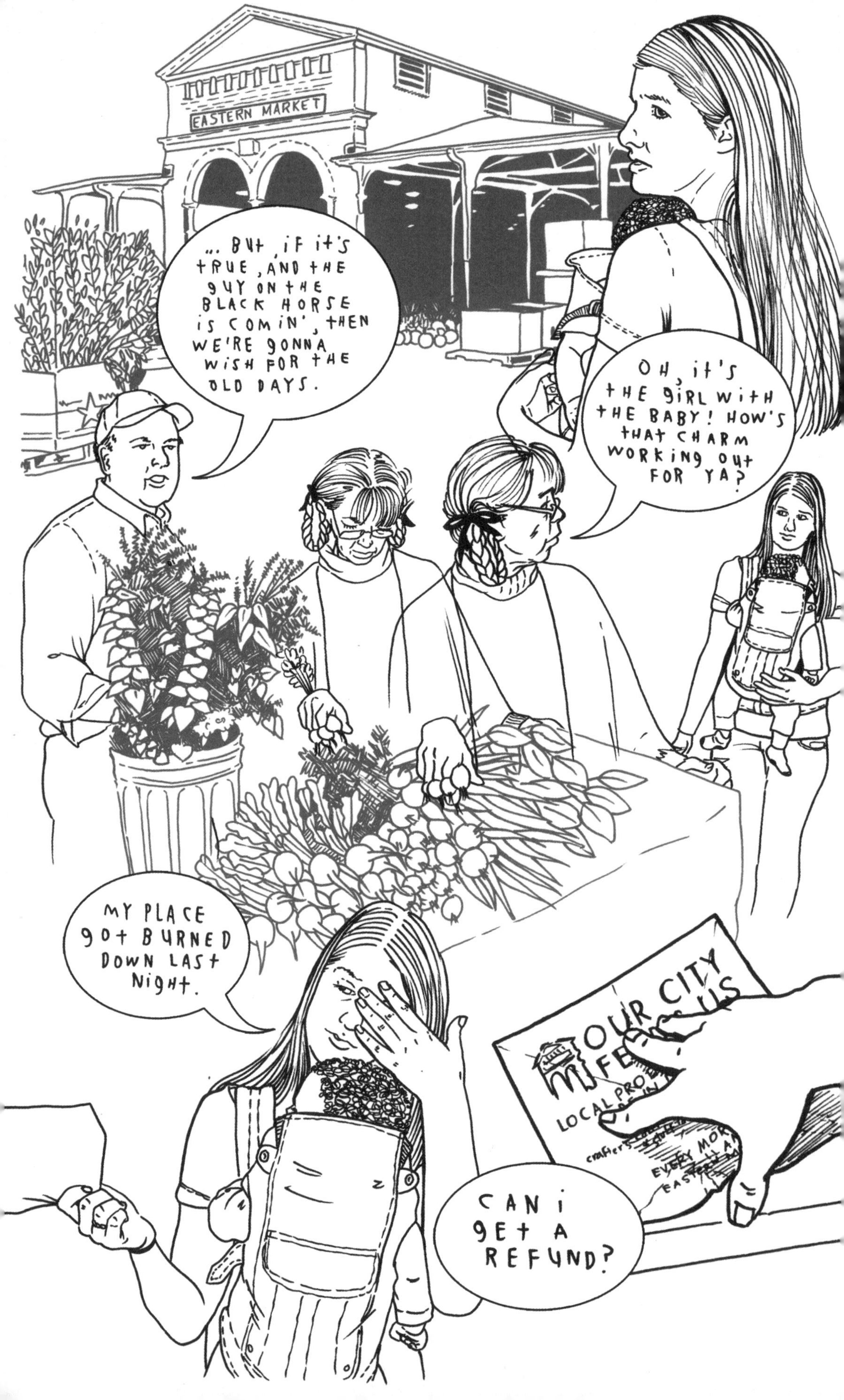
EASTERN MARKET
... BUT, IF IT'S TRUE, AND THE GUY ON THE BLACK HORSE IS COMIN', THEN WE'RE GONNA WISH FOR THE OLD DAYS.
OH, IT'S THE GIRL WITH THE BABY! HOW'S THAT CHARM WORKING OUT FOR YA?
MY PLACE GOT BURNED DOWN LAST NIGHT.
OUR CITY
CAN I GET A REFUND?

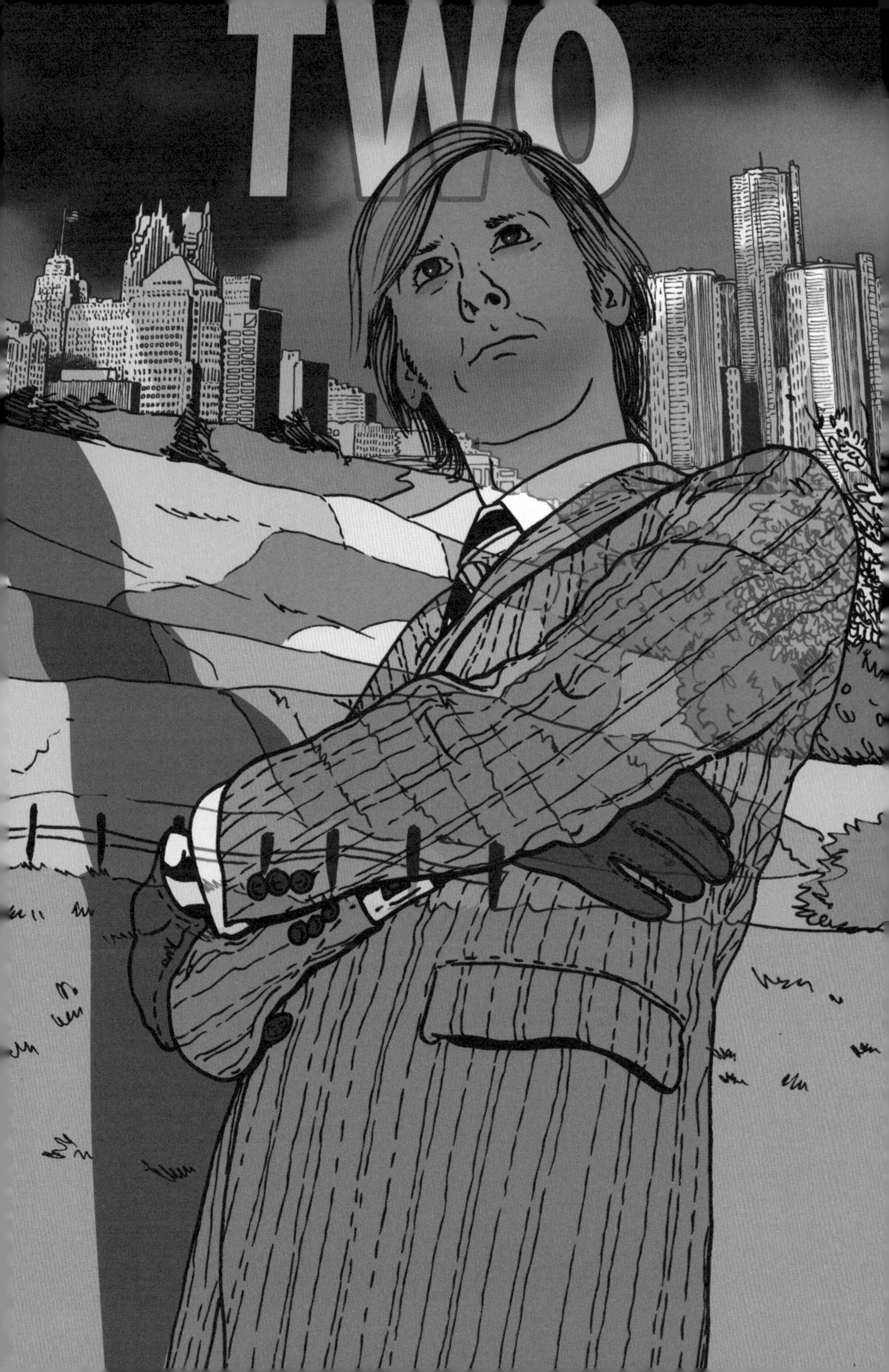
TWO

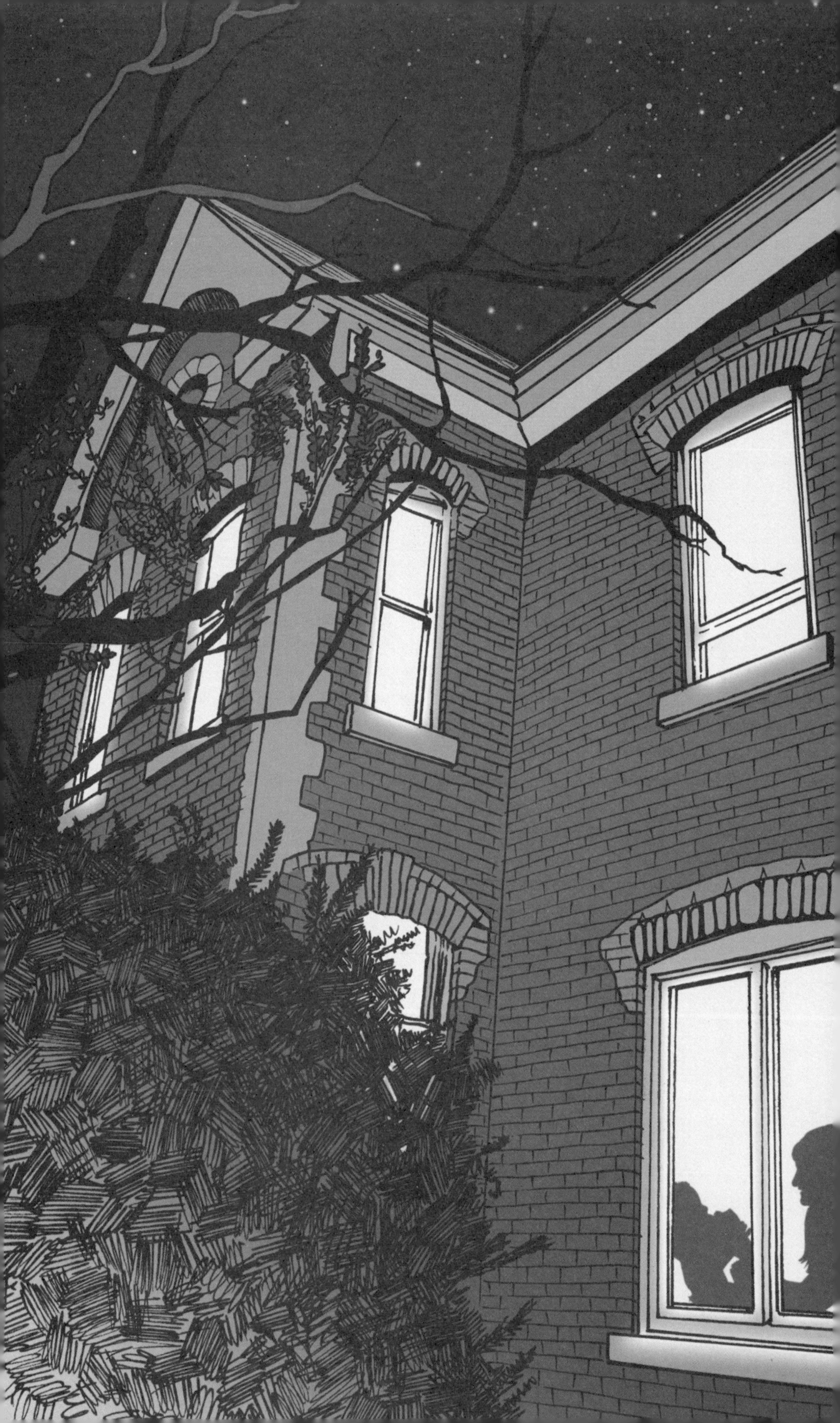

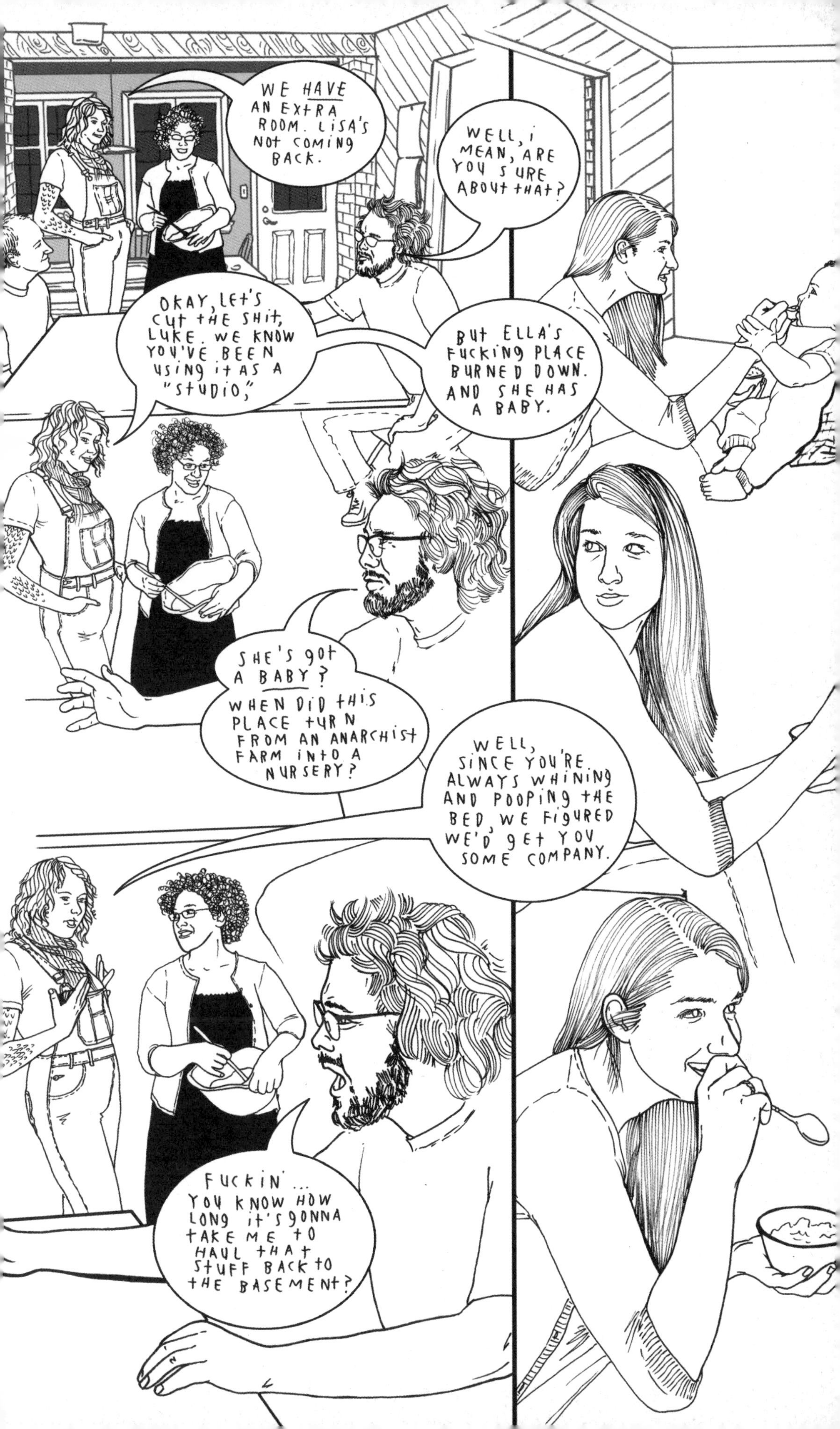
WE HAVE AN EXTRA ROOM. LISA'S NOT COMING BACK.
WELL, I MEAN, ARE YOU SURE ABOUT THAT?
OKAY, LET'S CUT THE SHIT, LUKE. WE KNOW YOU'VE BEEN USING IT AS A "STUDIO,"
BUT ELLA'S FUCKING PLACE BURNED DOWN. AND SHE HAS A BABY.
SHE'S GOT A BABY? WHEN DID THIS PLACE TURN FROM AN ANARCHIST FARM INTO A NURSERY?
WELL, SINCE YOU'RE ALWAYS WHINING AND POOPING THE BED, WE FIGURED WE'D GET YOU SOME COMPANY.
FUCKIN'... YOU KNOW HOW LONG IT'S GONNA TAKE ME TO HAUL THAT STUFF BACK TO THE BASEMENT?

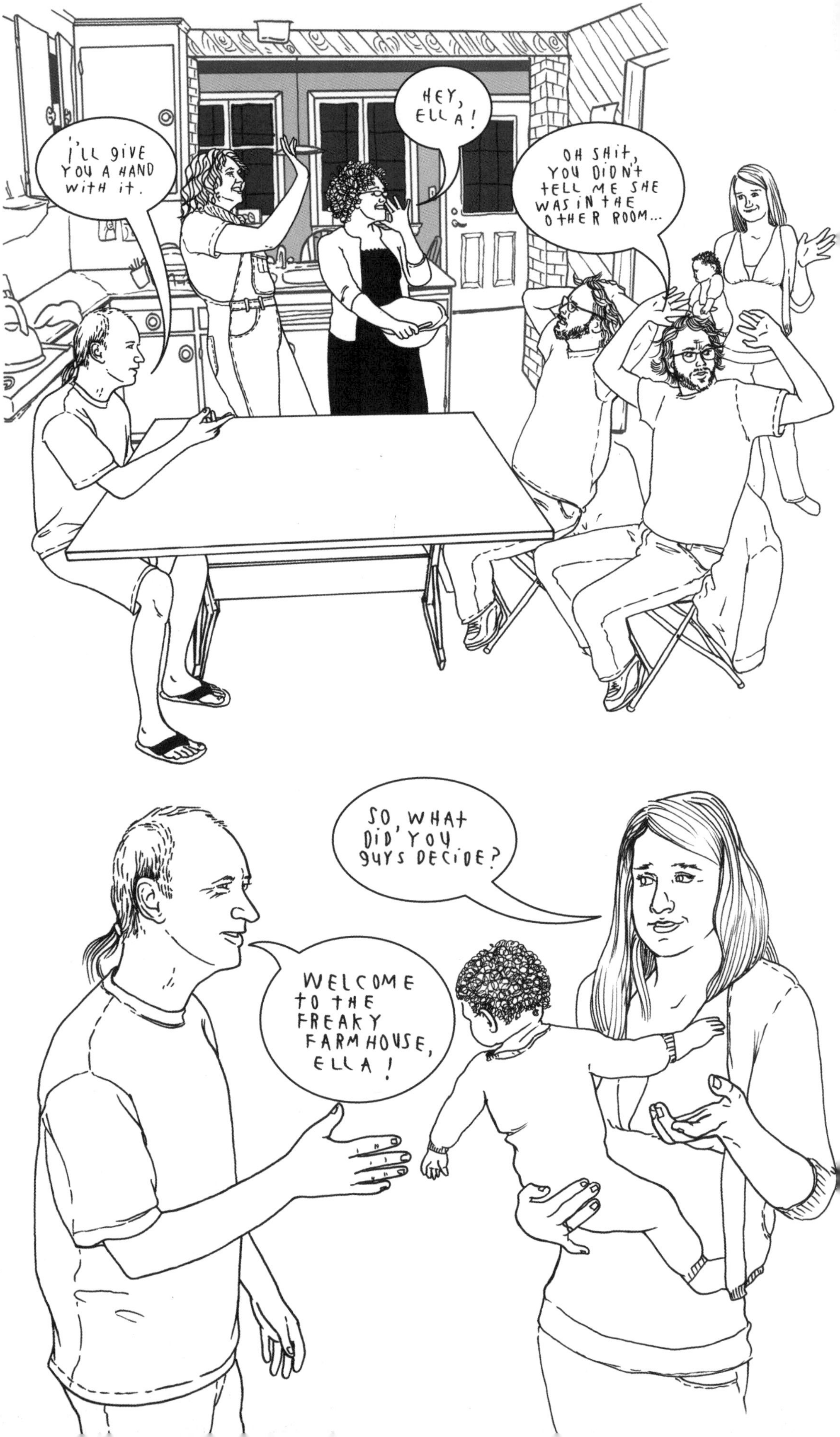
I'LL GIVE YOU A HAND WITH IT.
HEY, ELLA!
OH SHIT, YOU DIDN'T TELL ME SHE WAS IN THE OTHER ROOM...
SO, WHAT DID YOU GUYS DECIDE?
WELCOME TO THE FREAKY FARMHOUSE, ELLA!

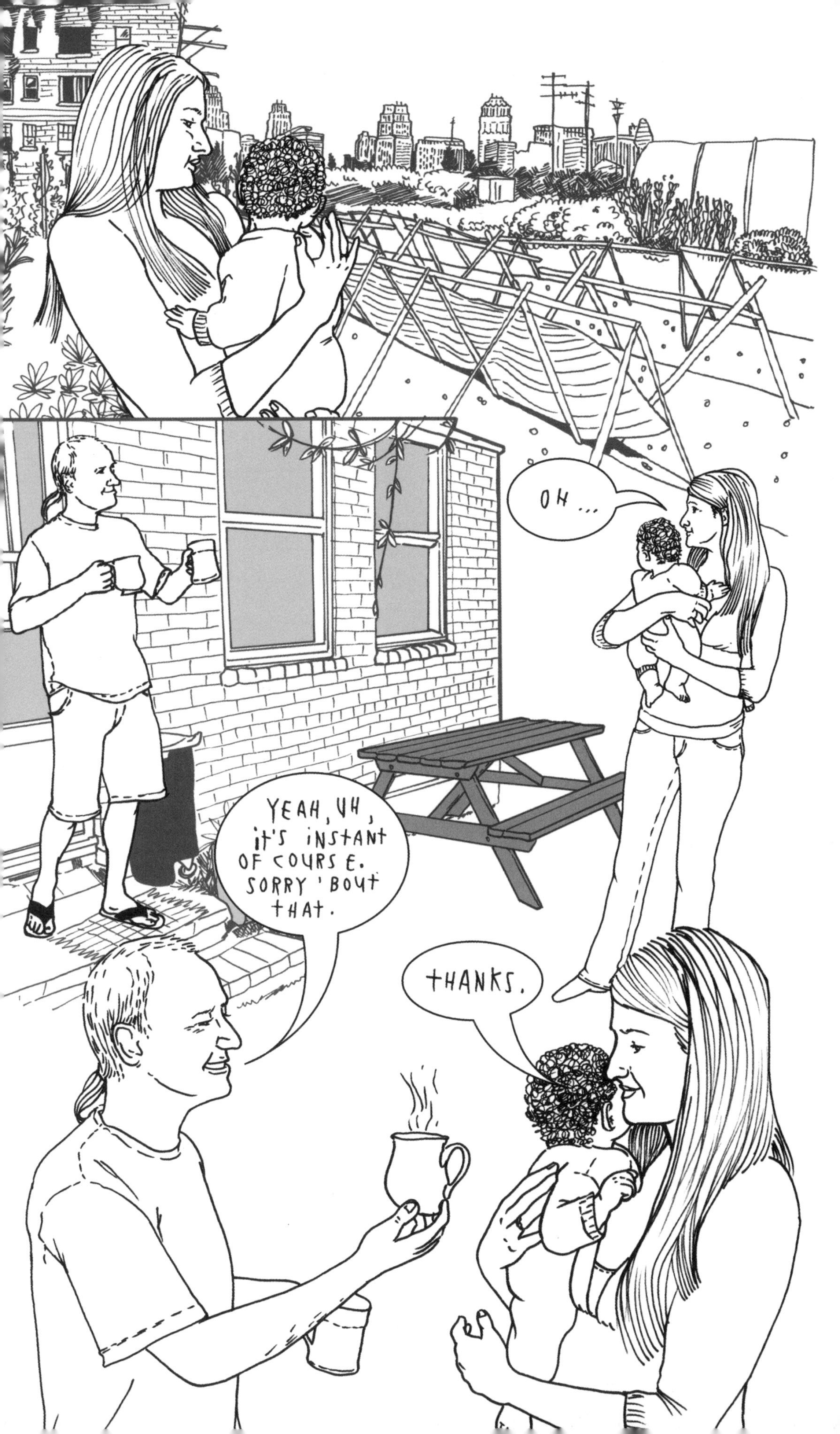
OH...
YEAH, UH, it's instant OF COURSE. SORRY 'BOUT THAT.
THANKS.

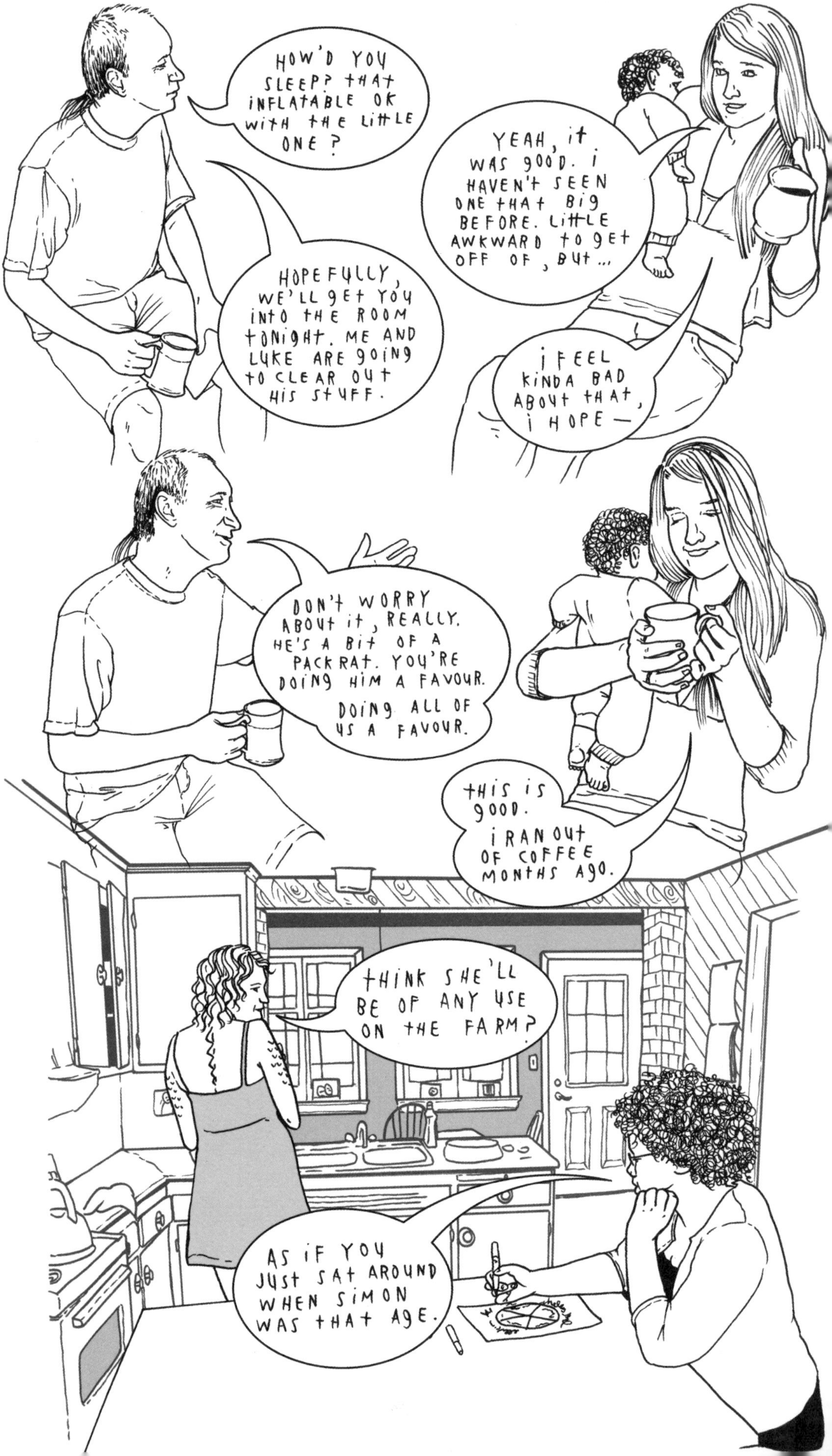

HOW'D YOU SLEEP? THAT INFLATABLE OK WITH THE LITTLE ONE?
YEAH, IT WAS GOOD. I HAVEN'T SEEN ONE THAT BIG BEFORE. LITTLE AWKWARD TO GET OFF OF, BUT...
HOPEFULLY, WE'LL GET YOU INTO THE ROOM TONIGHT. ME AND LUKE ARE GOING TO CLEAR OUT HIS STUFF.
I FEEL KINDA BAD ABOUT THAT, I HOPE—
DON'T WORRY ABOUT IT, REALLY. HE'S A BIT OF A PACKRAT. YOU'RE DOING HIM A FAVOUR.
DOING ALL OF US A FAVOUR.
THIS IS GOOD.
I RAN OUT OF COFFEE MONTHS AGO.
THINK SHE'LL BE OF ANY USE ON THE FARM?
AS IF YOU JUST SAT AROUND WHEN SIMON WAS THAT AGE.

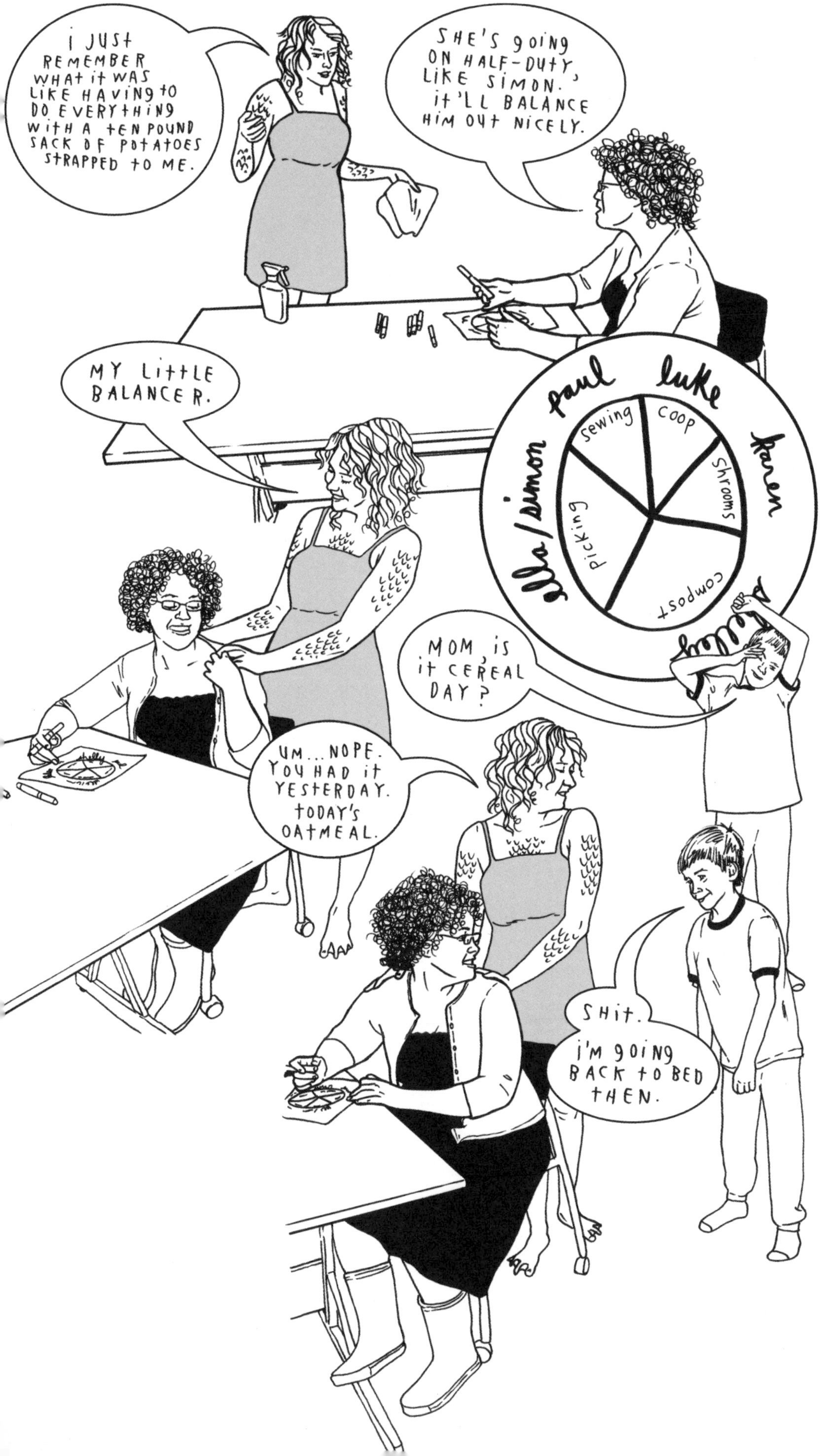
I JUST REMEMBER WHAT IT WAS LIKE HAVING TO DO EVERYTHING WITH A TEN POUND SACK OF POTATOES STRAPPED TO ME.
SHE'S GOING ON HALF-DUTY, LIKE SIMON. IT'LL BALANCE HIM OUT NICELY.
MY LITTLE BALANCER.
paul
luke
karen
ella/simon
sewing
coop
shrooms
compost
picking
MOM, IS IT CEREAL DAY?
UM... NOPE. YOU HAD IT YESTERDAY. TODAY'S OATMEAL.
SHIT.
I'M GOING BACK TO BED THEN.

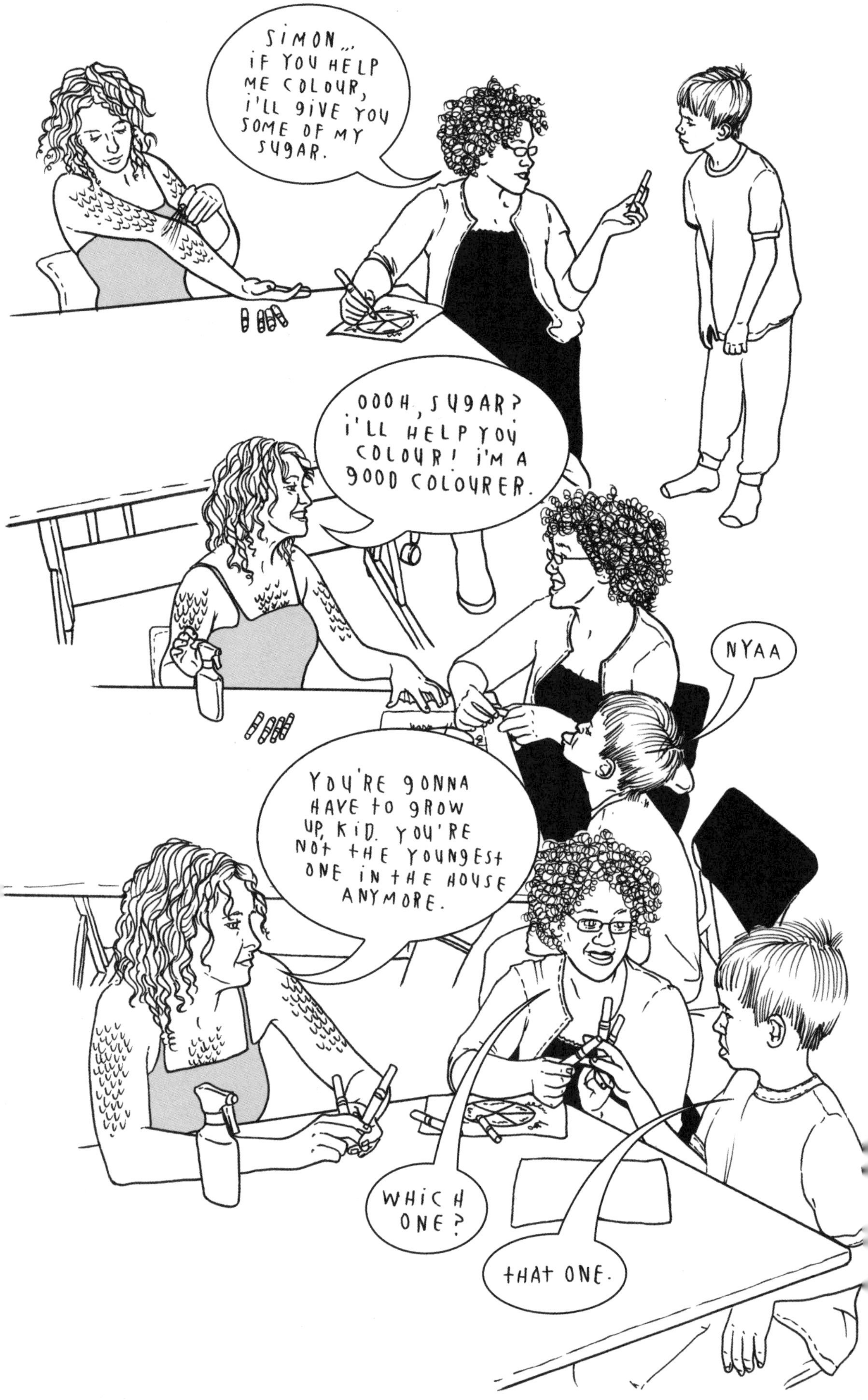
SIMON... IF YOU HELP ME COLOUR, I'LL GIVE YOU SOME OF MY SUGAR.
OOOH, SUGAR? I'LL HELP YOU COLOUR! I'M A GOOD COLOURER.
NYAA
YOU'RE GONNA HAVE TO GROW UP, KID. YOU'RE NOT THE YOUNGEST ONE IN THE HOUSE ANYMORE.
WHICH ONE?
THAT ONE.

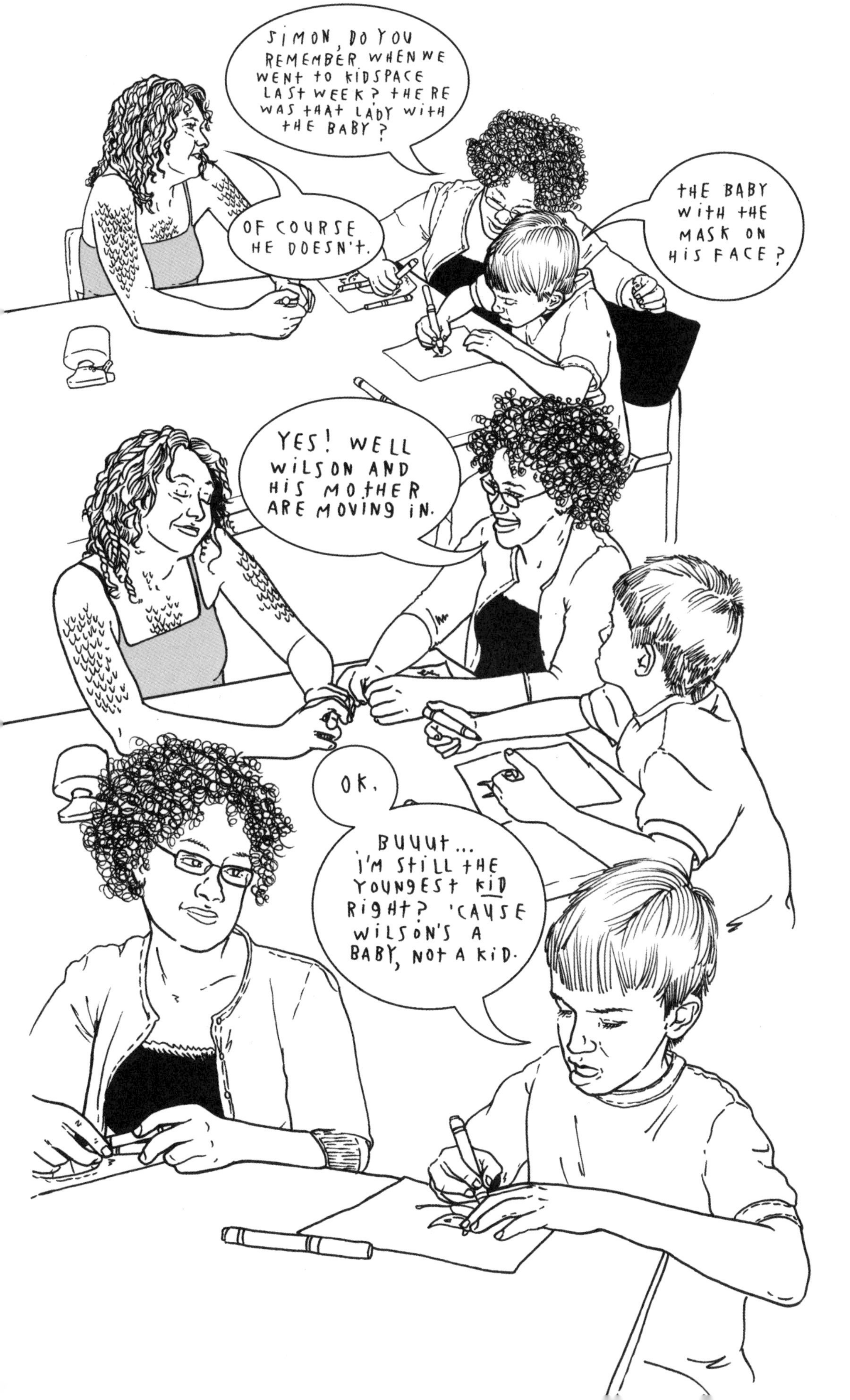
SIMON, DO YOU REMEMBER WHEN WE WENT TO KIDSPACE LAST WEEK? THERE WAS THAT LADY WITH THE BABY?
OF COURSE HE DOESN'T.
THE BABY WITH THE MASK ON HIS FACE?
YES! WELL WILSON AND HIS MOTHER ARE MOVING IN.
OK.
BUUUT... I'M STILL THE YOUNGEST KID RIGHT? 'CAUSE WILSON'S A BABY, NOT A KID.

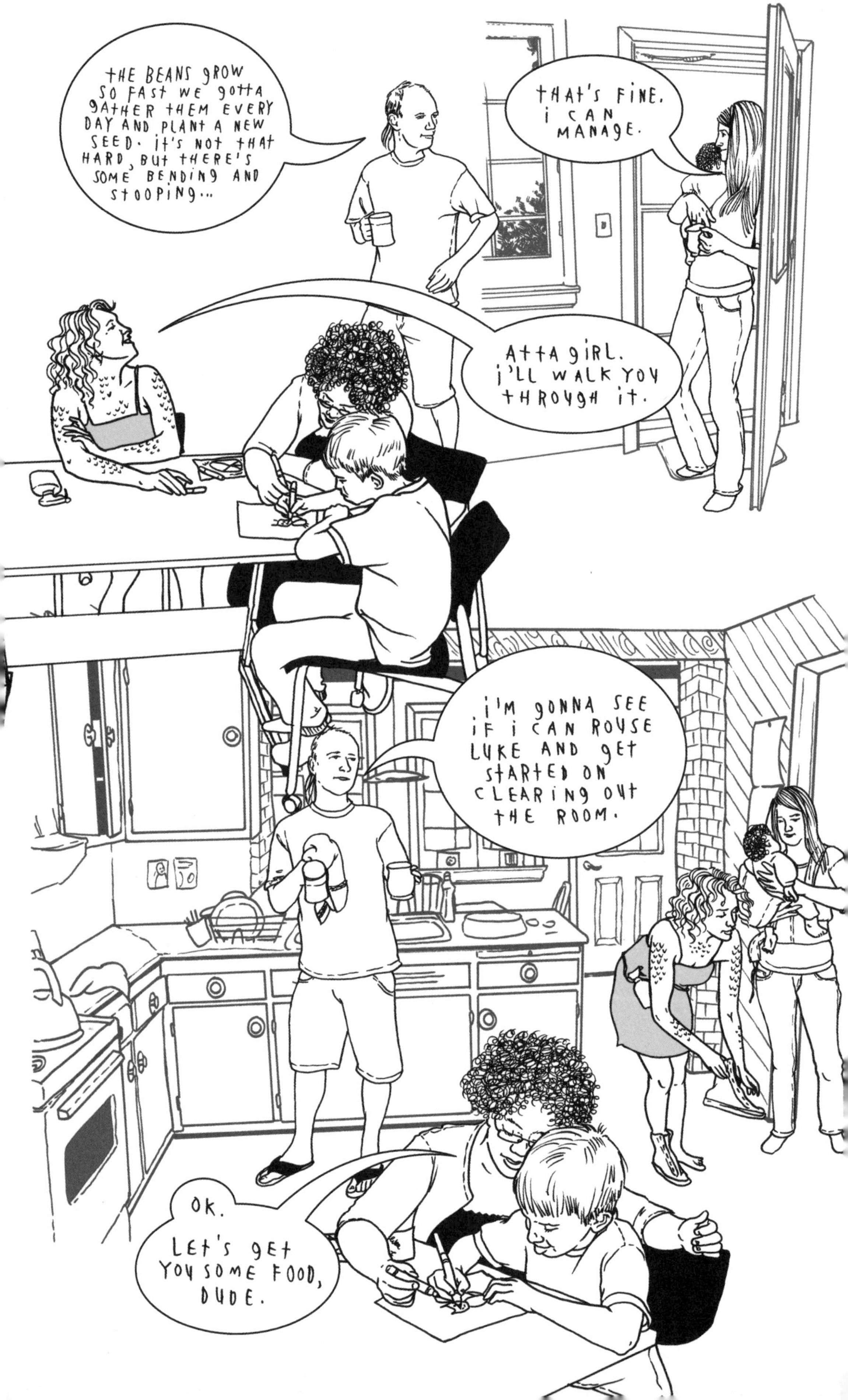
THE BEANS GROW SO FAST WE GOTTA GATHER THEM EVERY DAY AND PLANT A NEW SEED. IT'S NOT THAT HARD, BUT THERE'S SOME BENDING AND STOOPING...
THAT'S FINE. I CAN MANAGE.
ATTA GIRL. I'LL WALK YOU THROUGH IT.
I'M GONNA SEE IF I CAN ROUSE LUKE AND GET STARTED ON CLEARING OUT THE ROOM.
OK.
LET'S GET YOU SOME FOOD, DUDE.

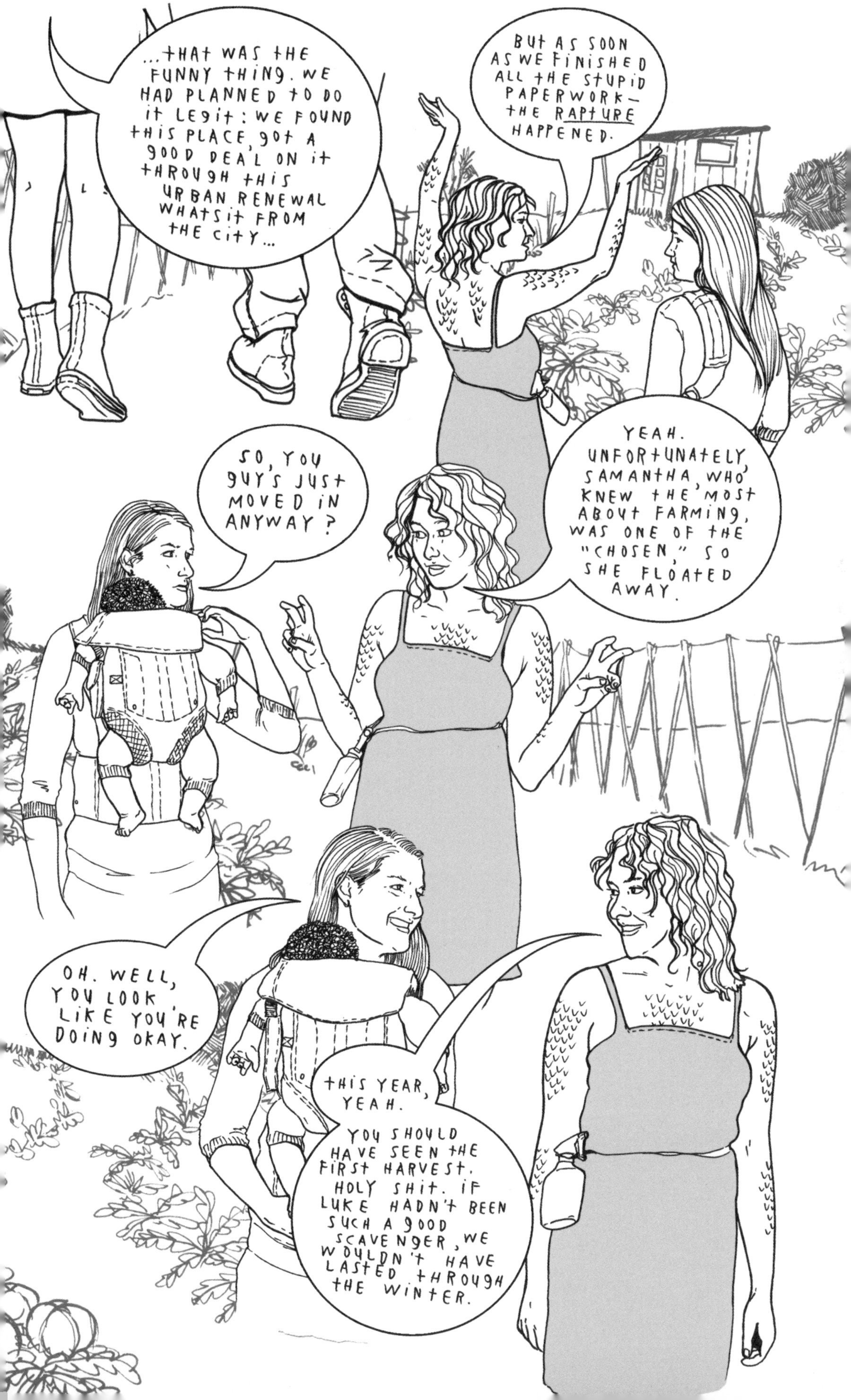
...THAT WAS THE FUNNY THING. WE HAD PLANNED TO DO IT LEGIT: WE FOUND THIS PLACE, GOT A GOOD DEAL ON IT THROUGH THIS URBAN RENEWAL WHATSIT FROM THE CITY...
BUT AS SOON AS WE FINISHED ALL THE STUPID PAPERWORK— THE RAPTURE HAPPENED.
SO, YOU GUY'S JUST MOVED IN ANYWAY?
YEAH. UNFORTUNATELY, SAMANTHA, WHO KNEW THE MOST ABOUT FARMING, WAS ONE OF THE "CHOSEN," SO SHE FLOATED AWAY.
OH. WELL, YOU LOOK LIKE YOU'RE DOING OKAY.
THIS YEAR, YEAH.
YOU SHOULD HAVE SEEN THE FIRST HARVEST. HOLY SHIT. IF LUKE HADN'T BEEN SUCH A GOOD SCAVENGER, WE WOULDN'T HAVE LASTED THROUGH THE WINTER.

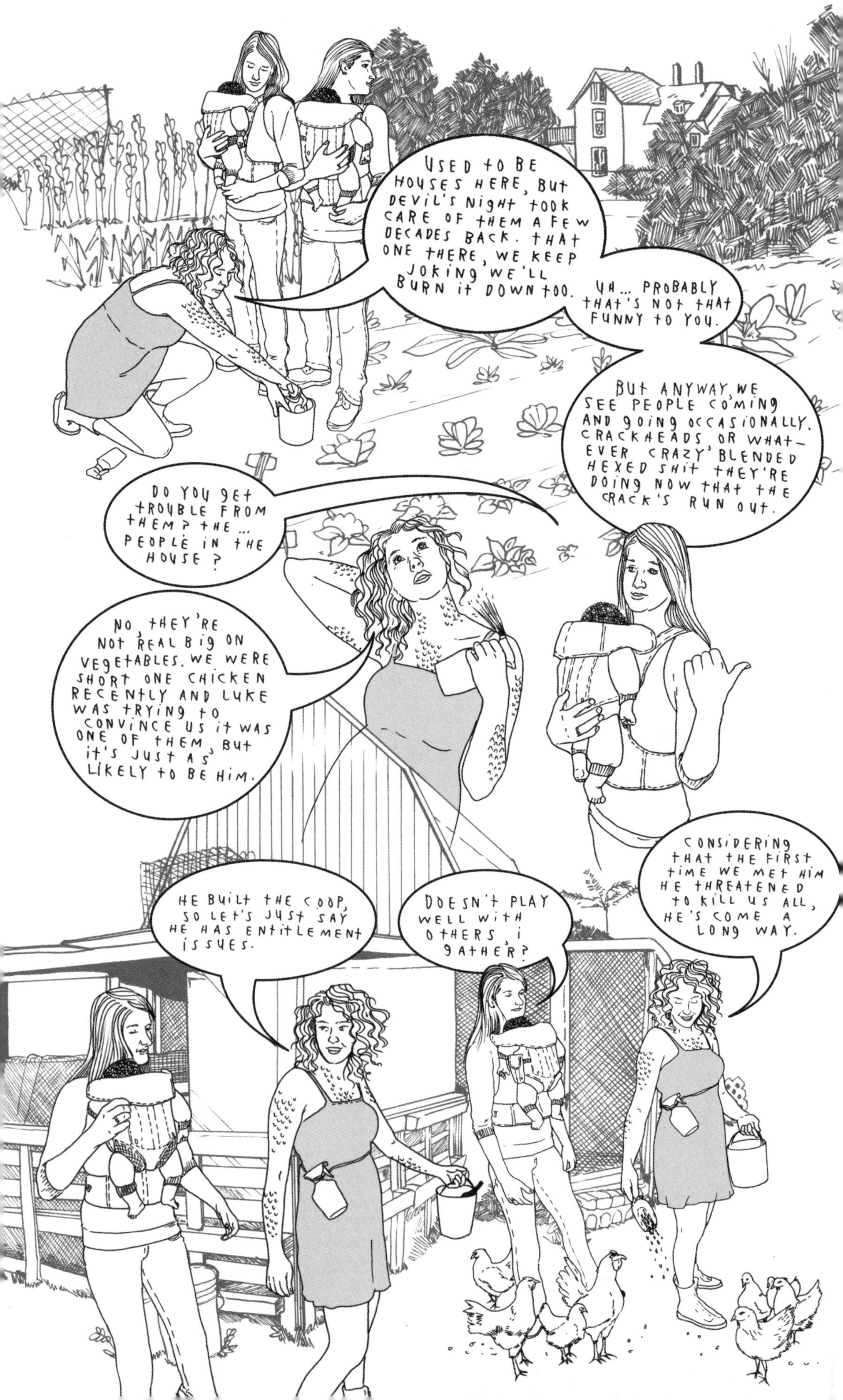
USED TO BE HOUSES HERE, BUT DEVIL'S NIGHT TOOK CARE OF THEM A FEW DECADES BACK. THAT ONE THERE, WE KEEP JOKING WE'LL BURN IT DOWN TOO.
UH... PROBABLY THAT'S NOT THAT FUNNY TO YOU.
BUT ANYWAY, WE SEE PEOPLE COMING AND GOING OCCASIONALLY. CRACKHEADS, OR WHATEVER CRAZY BLENDED HEXED SHIT THEY'RE DOING NOW THAT THE CRACK'S RUN OUT.
DO YOU GET TROUBLE FROM THEM? THE... PEOPLE IN THE HOUSE?
NO, THEY'RE NOT REAL BIG ON VEGETABLES. WE WERE SHORT ONE CHICKEN RECENTLY AND LUKE WAS TRYING TO CONVINCE US IT WAS ONE OF THEM, BUT IT'S JUST AS LIKELY TO BE HIM.
HE BUILT THE COOP, SO LET'S JUST SAY HE HAS ENTITLEMENT ISSUES.
DOESN'T PLAY WELL WITH OTHERS, I GATHER?
CONSIDERING THAT THE FIRST TIME WE MET HIM HE THREATENED TO KILL US ALL, HE'S COME A LONG WAY.

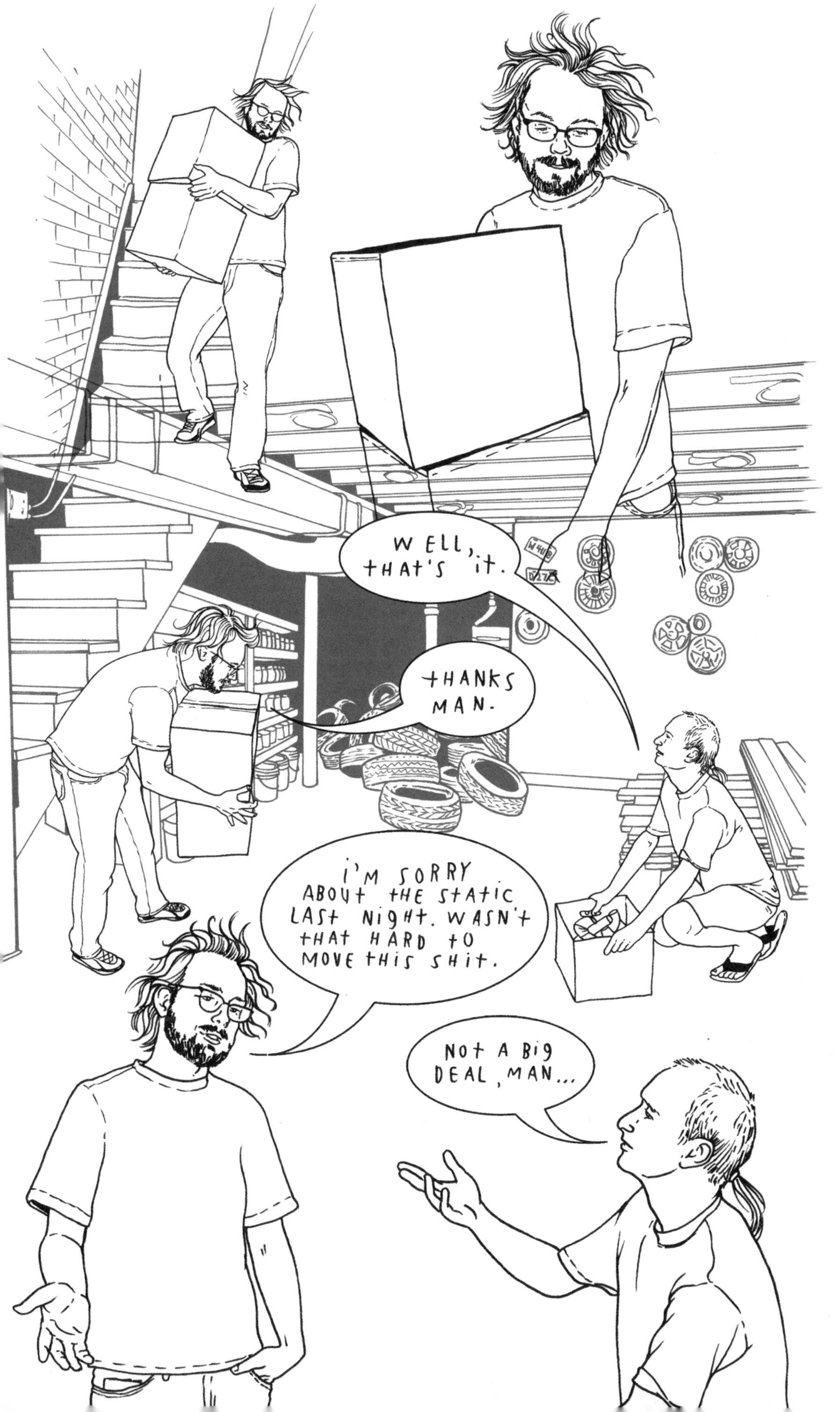

WELL, THAT'S IT.
THANKS MAN.
I'M SORRY ABOUT THE STATIC LAST NIGHT. WASN'T THAT HARD TO MOVE THIS SHIT.
NOT A BIG DEAL, MAN...

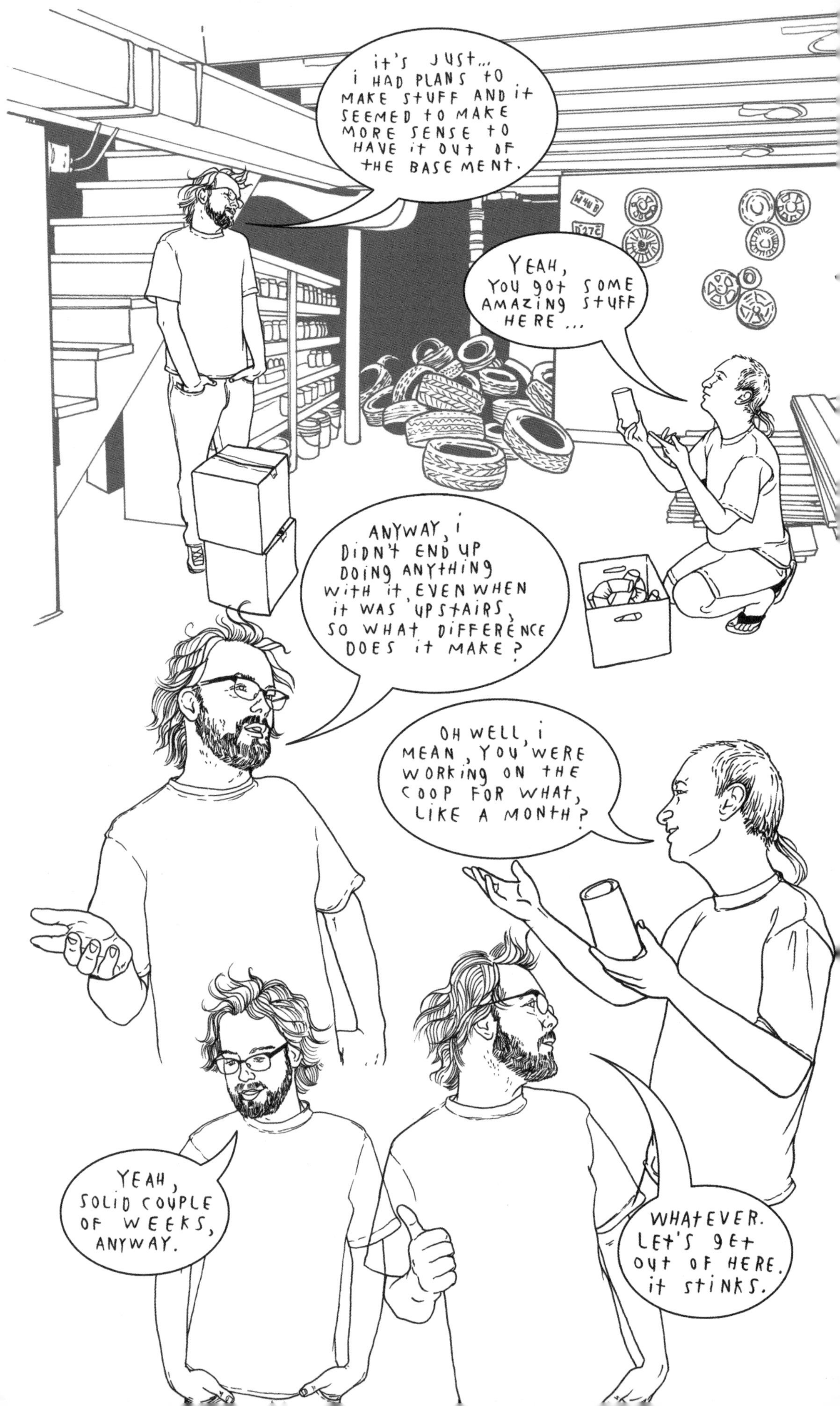
it's just... i had plans to make stuff and it seemed to make more sense to have it out of the basement.
Yeah, you got some amazing stuff here...
Anyway, i didn't end up doing anything with it, even when it was upstairs, so what difference does it make?
Oh well, i mean, you were working on the coop for what, like a month?
Yeah, solid couple of weeks, anyway.
Whatever. Let's get out of here. it stinks.

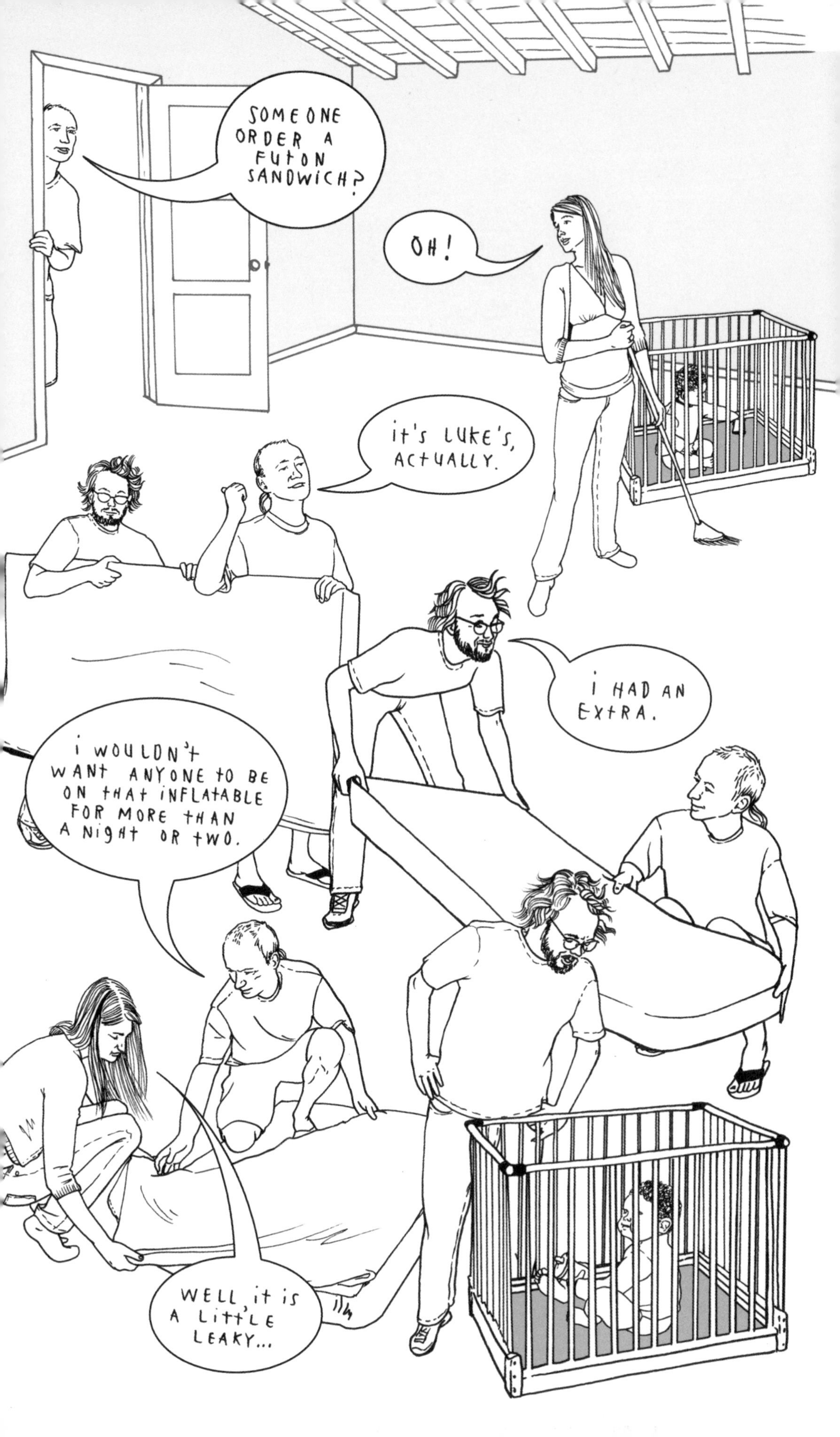
SOMEONE ORDER A FUTON SANDWICH?
OH!
IT'S LUKE'S, ACTUALLY.
I HAD AN EXTRA.
I WOULDN'T WANT ANYONE TO BE ON THAT INFLATABLE FOR MORE THAN A NIGHT OR TWO.
WELL, IT IS A LITTLE LEAKY...

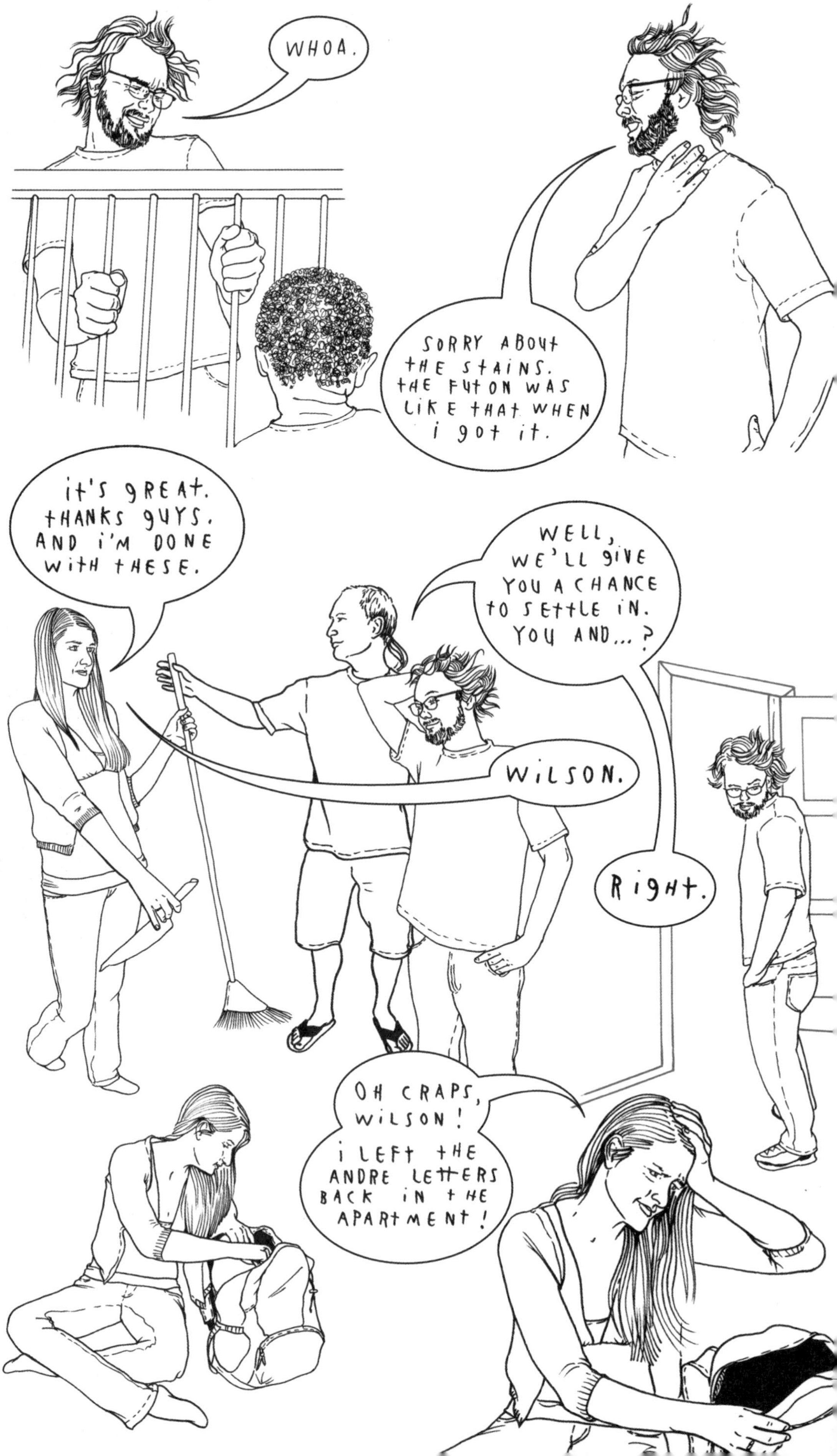
WHOA.
SORRY ABOUT THE STAINS. THE FUTON WAS LIKE THAT WHEN I GOT IT.
IT'S GREAT. THANKS GUYS. AND I'M DONE WITH THESE.
WELL, WE'LL GIVE YOU A CHANCE TO SETTLE IN. YOU AND...?
WILSON.
RIGHT.
OH CRAPS, WILSON!
I LEFT THE ANDRE LETTERS BACK IN THE APARTMENT!

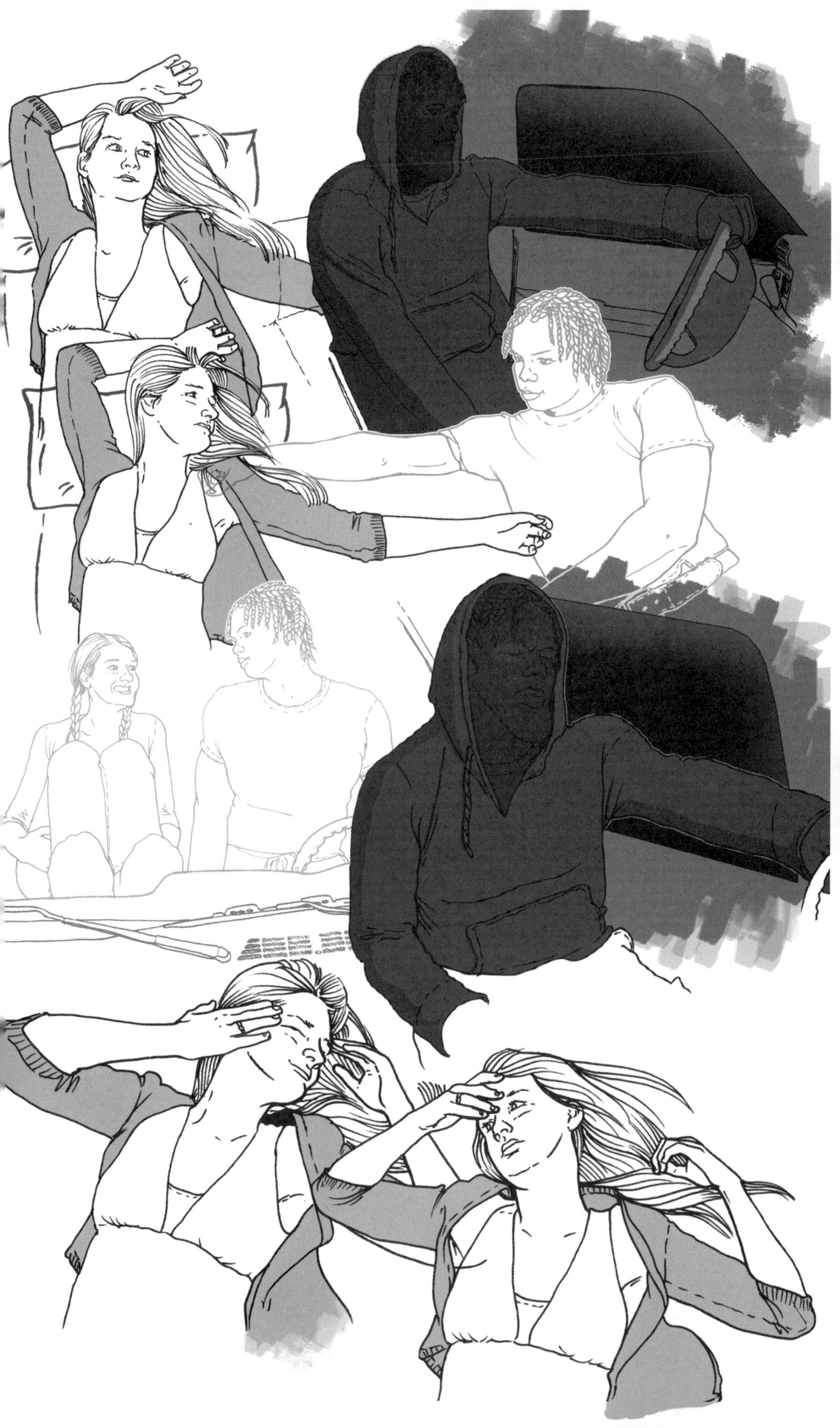

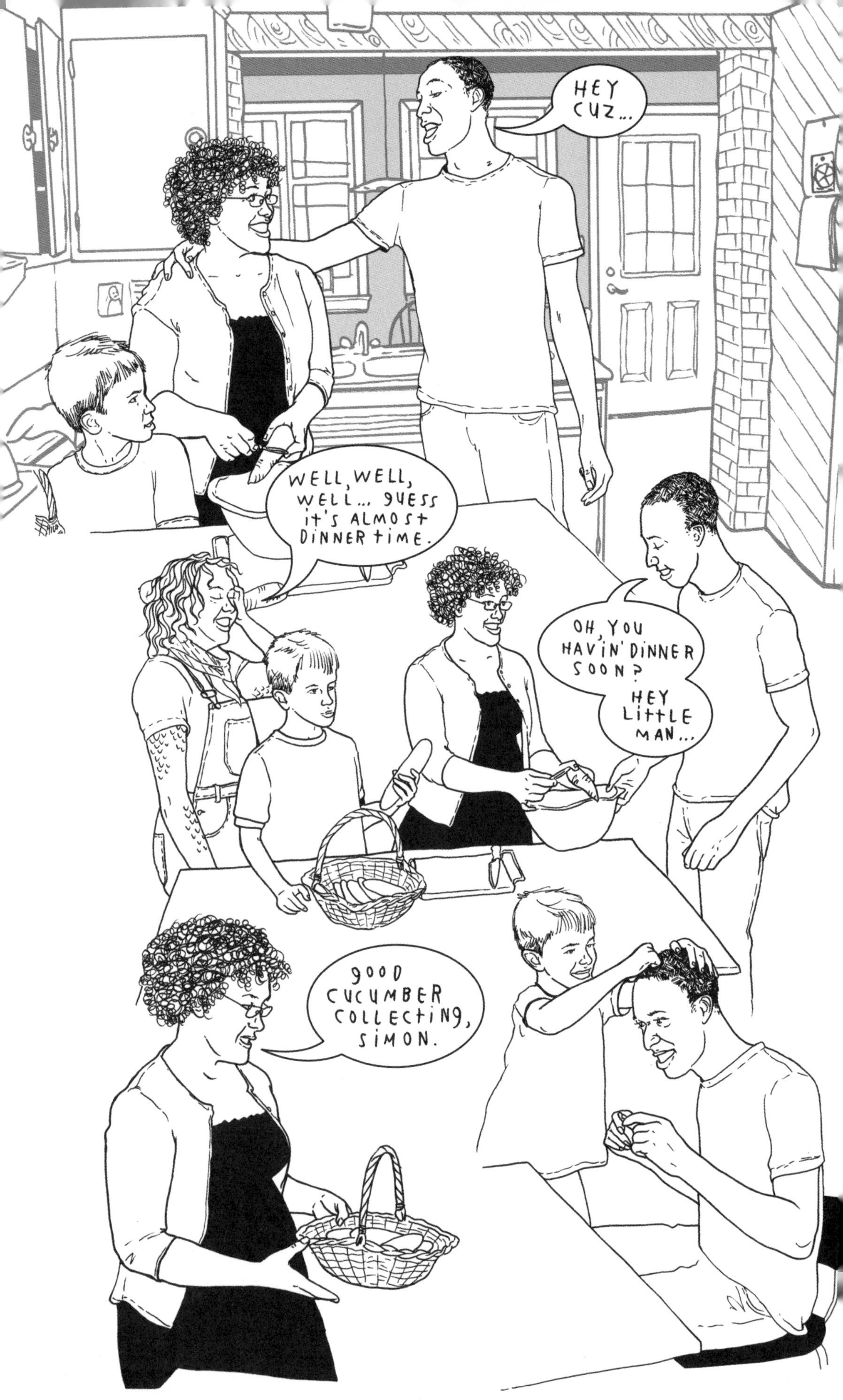
HEY CUZ...
WELL, WELL, WELL... GUESS IT'S ALMOST DINNER TIME.
OH, YOU HAVIN' DINNER SOON?
HEY LITTLE MAN...
GOOD CUCUMBER COLLECTING, SIMON.

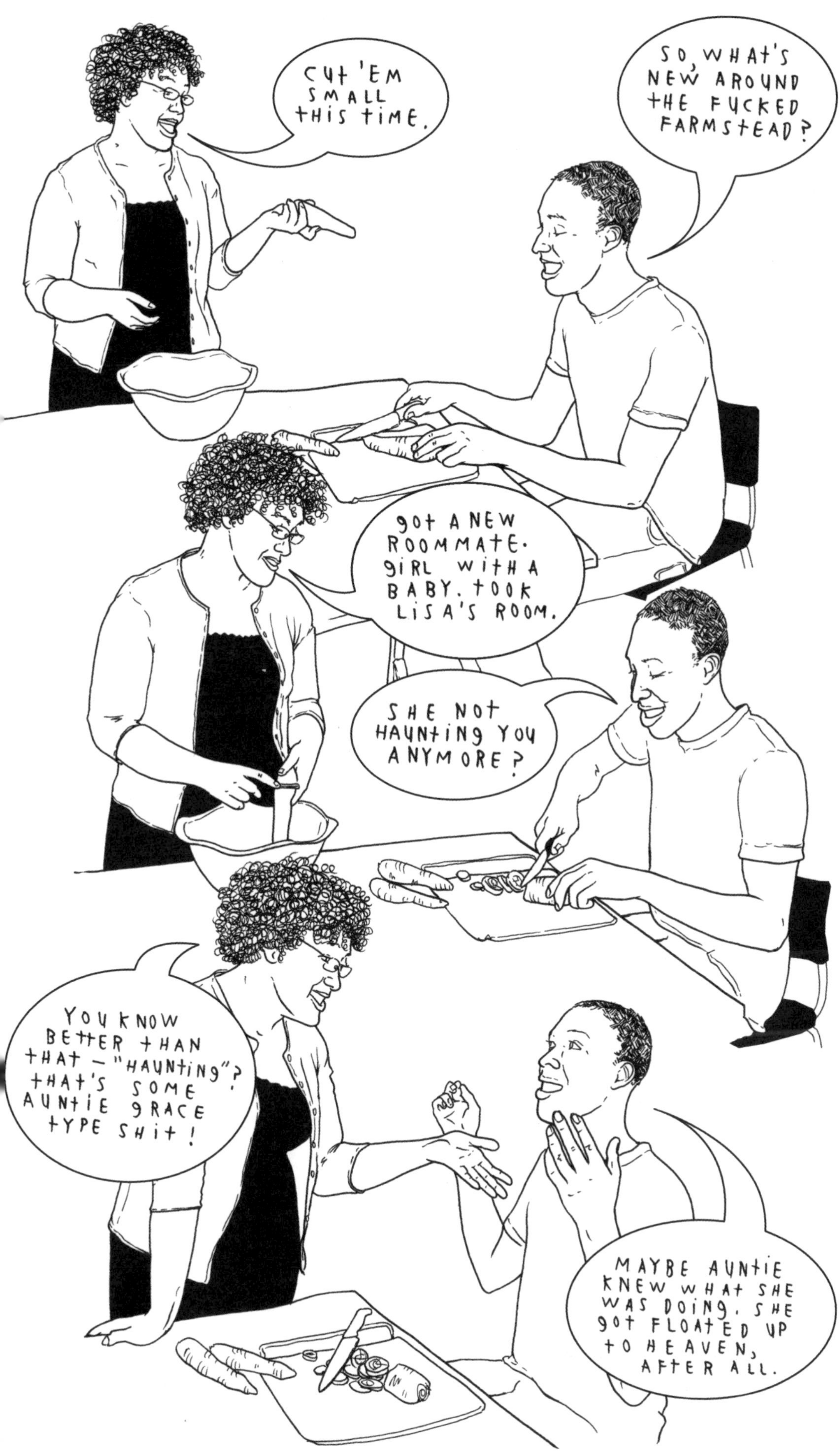
CUT 'EM SMALL THIS TIME.
SO, WHAT'S NEW AROUND THE FUCKED FARMSTEAD?
GOT A NEW ROOMMATE. GIRL WITH A BABY. TOOK LISA'S ROOM.
SHE NOT HAUNTING YOU ANYMORE?
YOU KNOW BETTER THAN THAT — "HAUNTING"? THAT'S SOME AUNTIE GRACE TYPE SHIT!
MAYBE AUNTIE KNEW WHAT SHE WAS DOING. SHE GOT FLOATED UP TO HEAVEN, AFTER ALL.

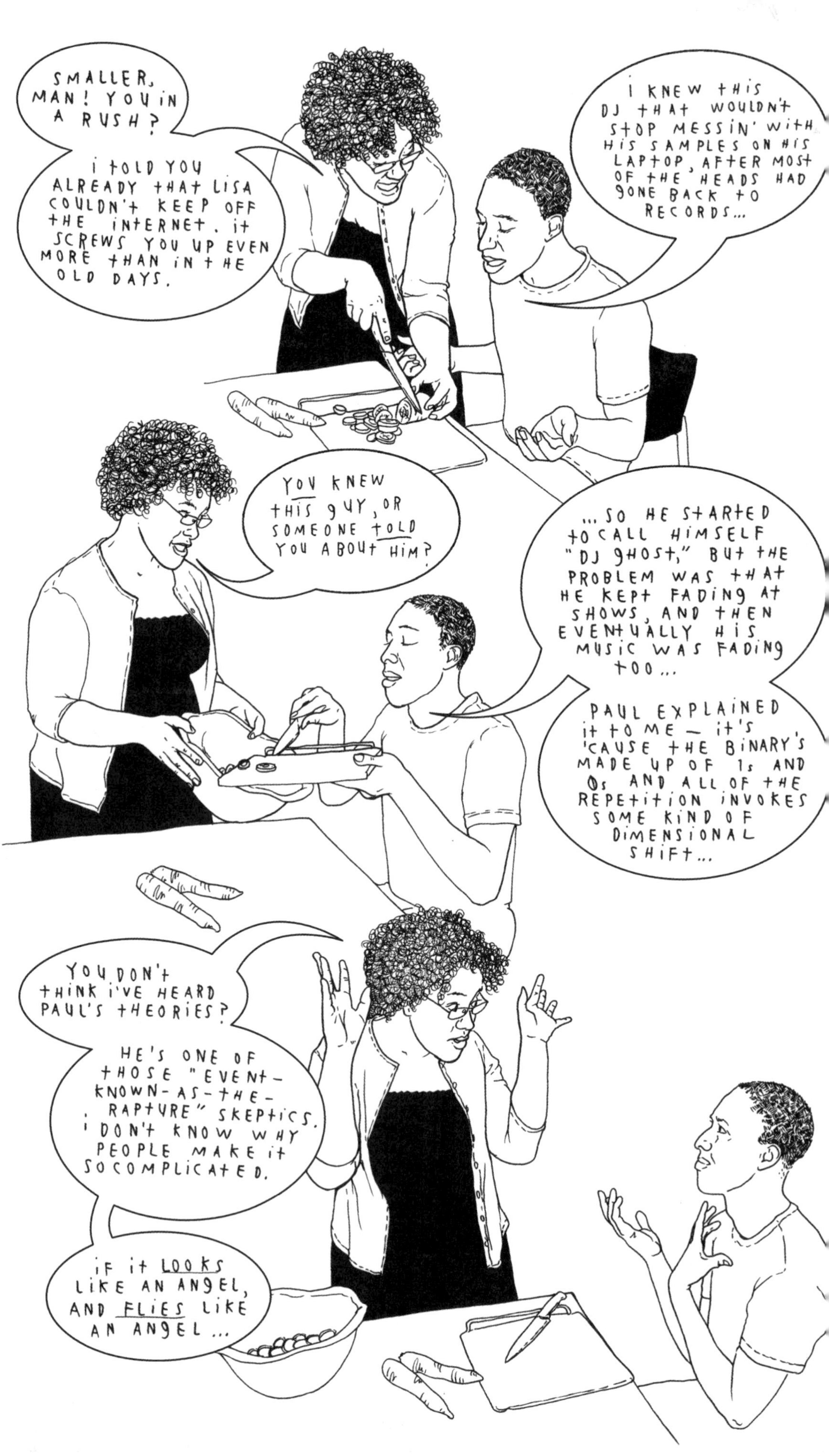
SMALLER, MAN! YOU IN A RUSH?
I TOLD YOU ALREADY THAT LISA COULDN'T KEEP OFF THE INTERNET. IT SCREWS YOU UP EVEN MORE THAN IN THE OLD DAYS.
I KNEW THIS DJ THAT WOULDN'T STOP MESSIN' WITH HIS SAMPLES ON HIS LAPTOP, AFTER MOST OF THE HEADS HAD GONE BACK TO RECORDS...
YOU KNEW THIS GUY, OR SOMEONE TOLD YOU ABOUT HIM?
...SO HE STARTED TO CALL HIMSELF "DJ GHOST," BUT THE PROBLEM WAS THAT HE KEPT FADING AT SHOWS, AND THEN EVENTUALLY HIS MUSIC WAS FADING TOO...
PAUL EXPLAINED IT TO ME — IT'S 'CAUSE THE BINARY'S MADE UP OF 1s AND 0s AND ALL OF THE REPETITION INVOKES SOME KIND OF DIMENSIONAL SHIFT...
YOU DON'T THINK I'VE HEARD PAUL'S THEORIES?
HE'S ONE OF THOSE "EVENT-KNOWN-AS-THE-RAPTURE" SKEPTICS. I DON'T KNOW WHY PEOPLE MAKE IT SO COMPLICATED.
IF IT LOOKS LIKE AN ANGEL, AND FLIES LIKE AN ANGEL...

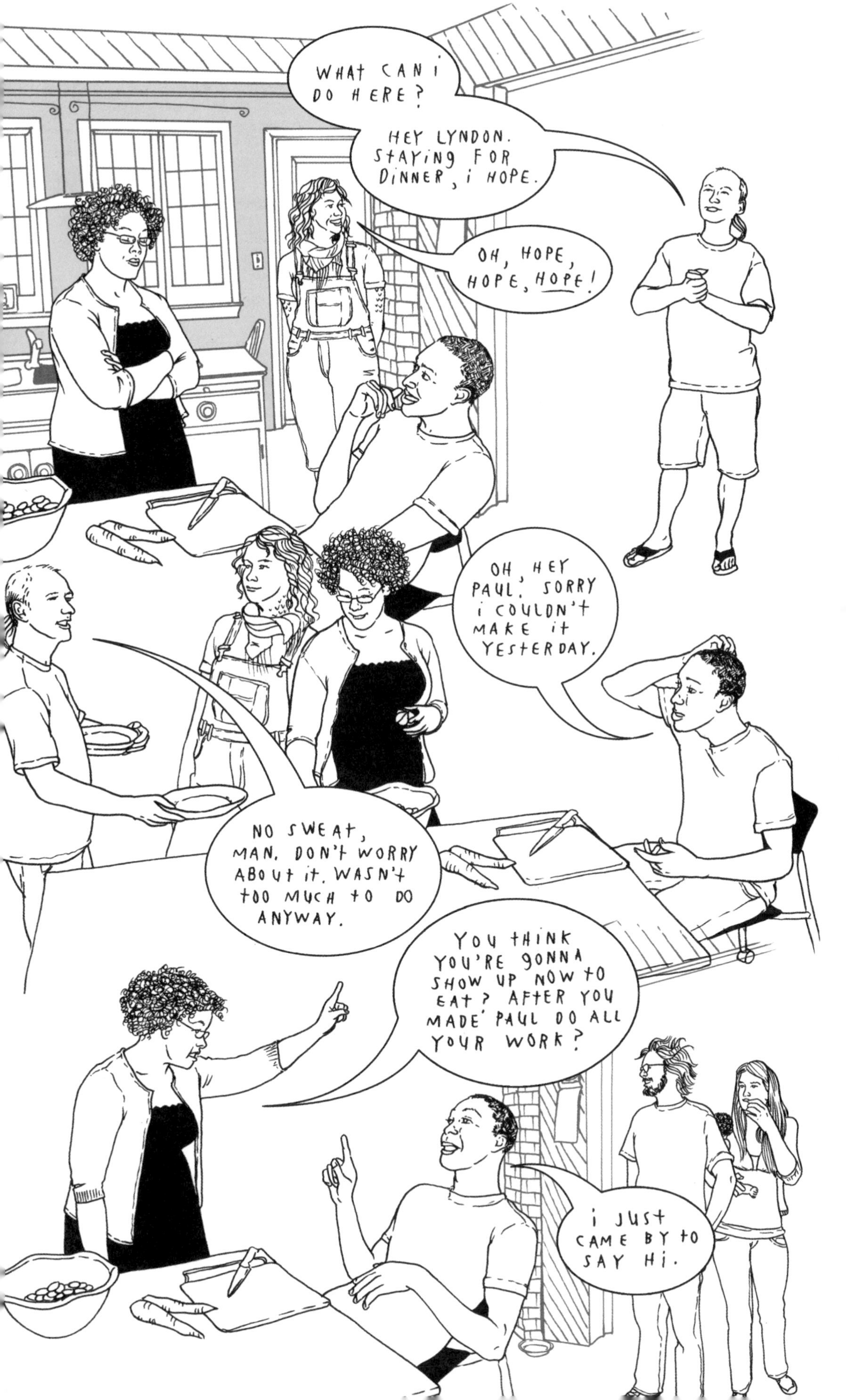
WHAT CAN I DO HERE?
HEY LYNDON. STAYING FOR DINNER, I HOPE.
OH, HOPE, HOPE, HOPE!
OH, HEY PAUL. SORRY I COULDN'T MAKE IT YESTERDAY.
NO SWEAT, MAN. DON'T WORRY ABOUT IT. WASN'T TOO MUCH TO DO ANYWAY.
YOU THINK YOU'RE GONNA SHOW UP NOW TO EAT? AFTER YOU MADE PAUL DO ALL YOUR WORK?
I JUST CAME BY TO SAY HI.

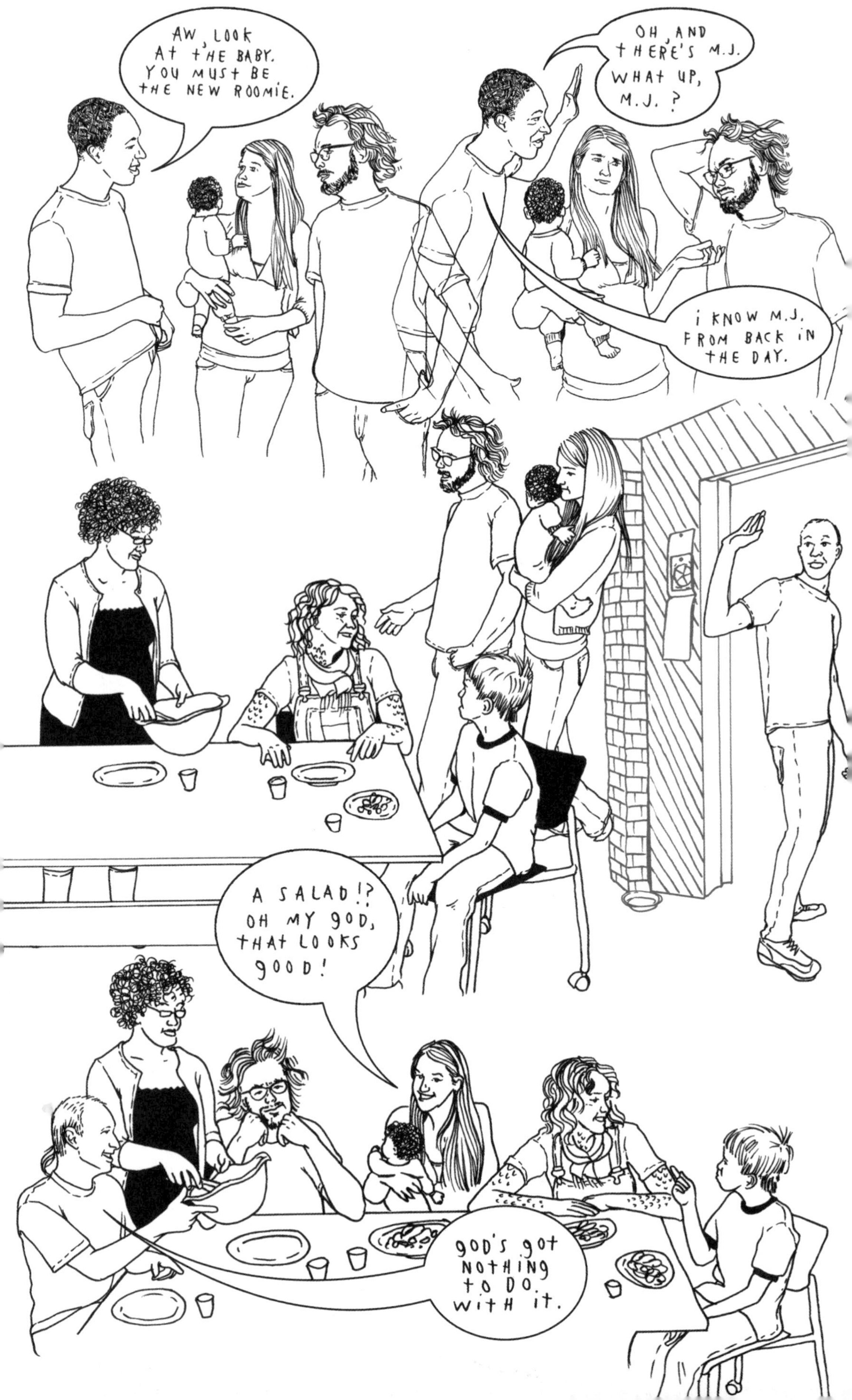
AW, LOOK AT THE BABY. YOU MUST BE THE NEW ROOMIE.
OH, AND THERE'S M.J. WHAT UP, M.J.?
i KNOW M.J. FROM BACK IN THE DAY.
A SALAD!? OH MY GOD, THAT LOOKS GOOD!
GOD'S GOT NOTHING TO DO WITH IT.

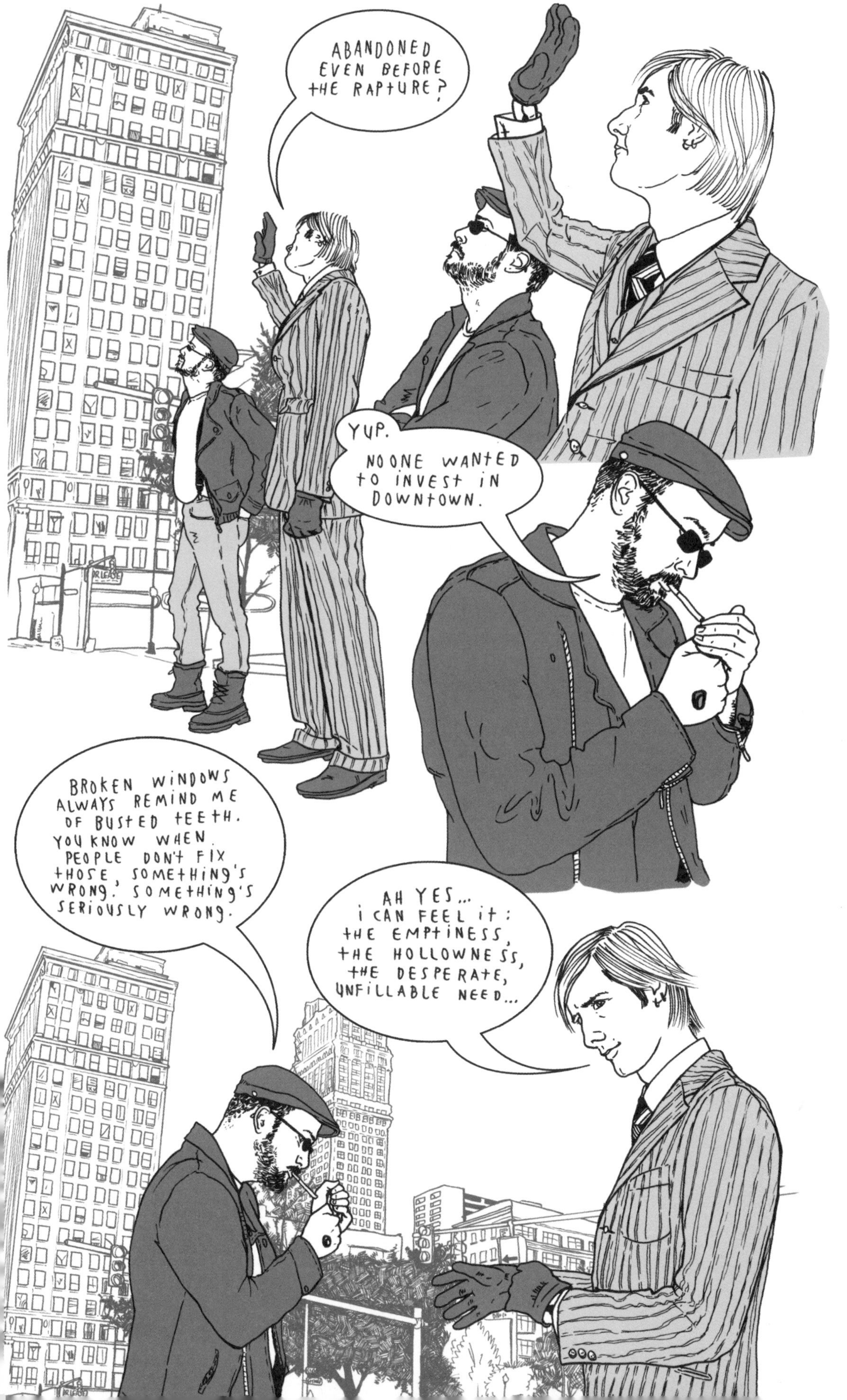
ABANDONED EVEN BEFORE THE RAPTURE?
YUP.
NO ONE WANTED TO INVEST IN DOWNTOWN.
BROKEN WINDOWS ALWAYS REMIND ME OF BUSTED TEETH. YOU KNOW WHEN PEOPLE DON'T FIX THOSE, SOMETHING'S WRONG. SOMETHING'S SERIOUSLY WRONG.
AH YES... I CAN FEEL IT: THE EMPTINESS, THE HOLLOWNESS, THE DESPERATE, UNFILLABLE NEED...

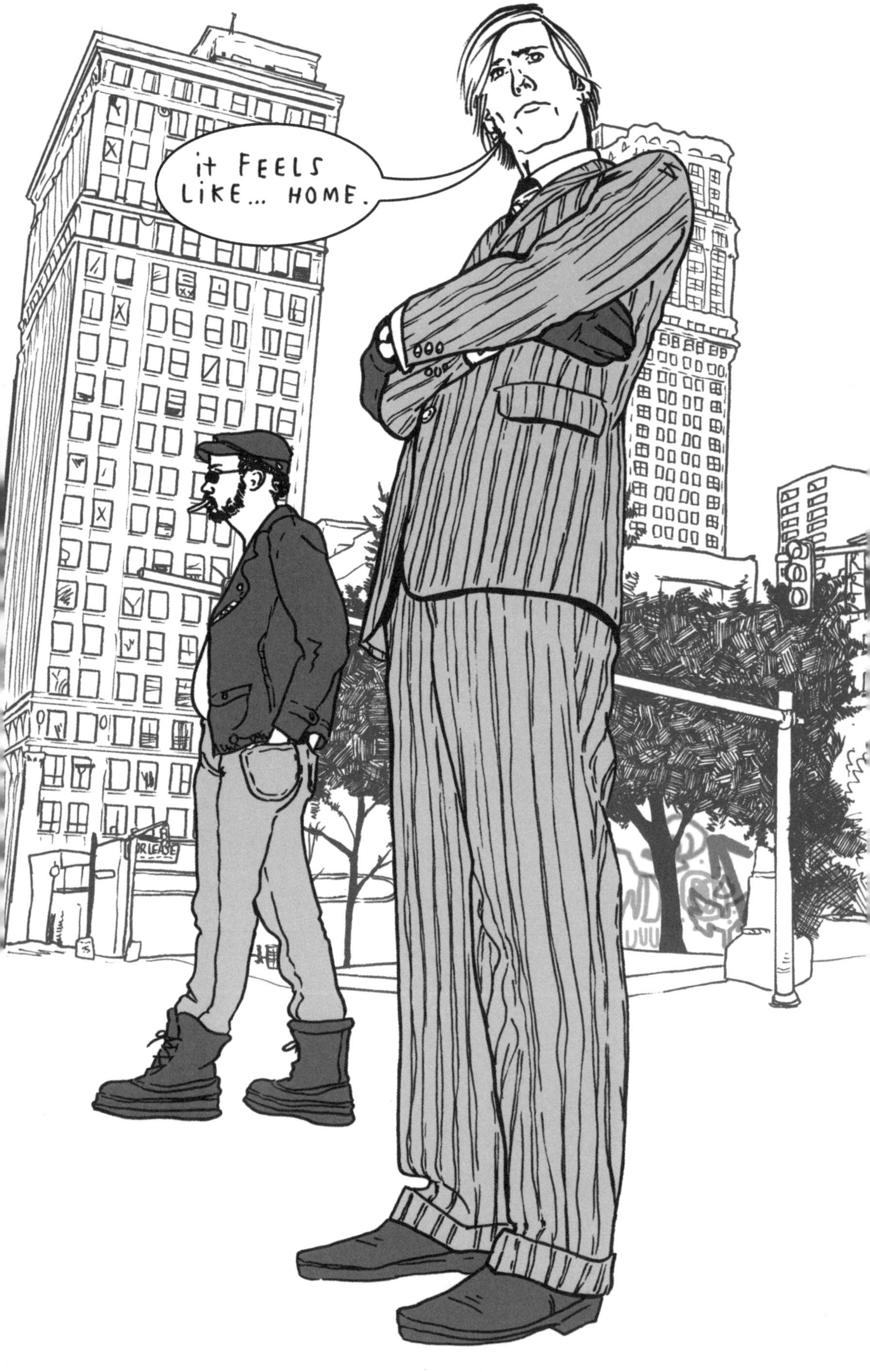
it FEELS LIKE... HOME.

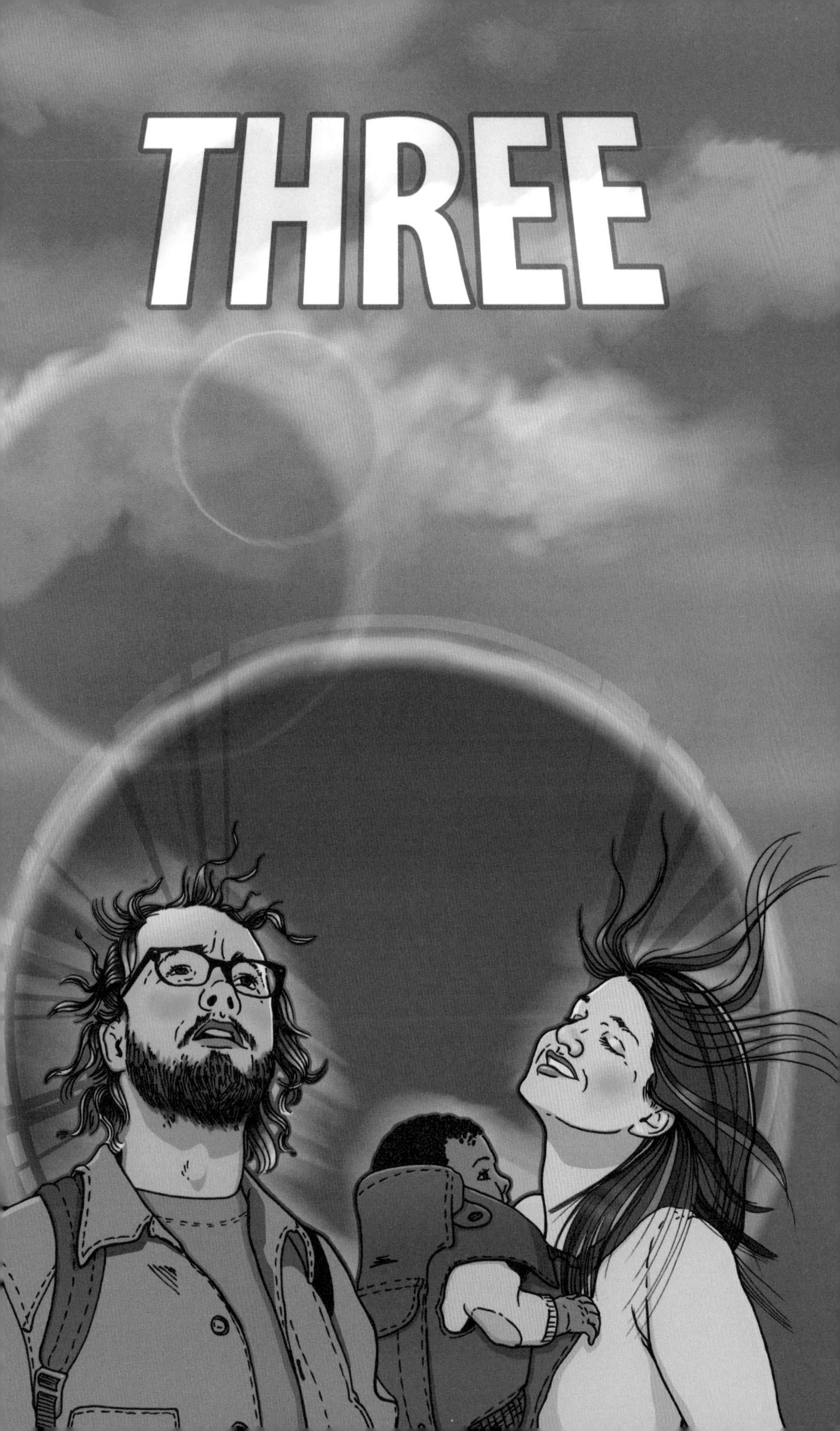
THREE

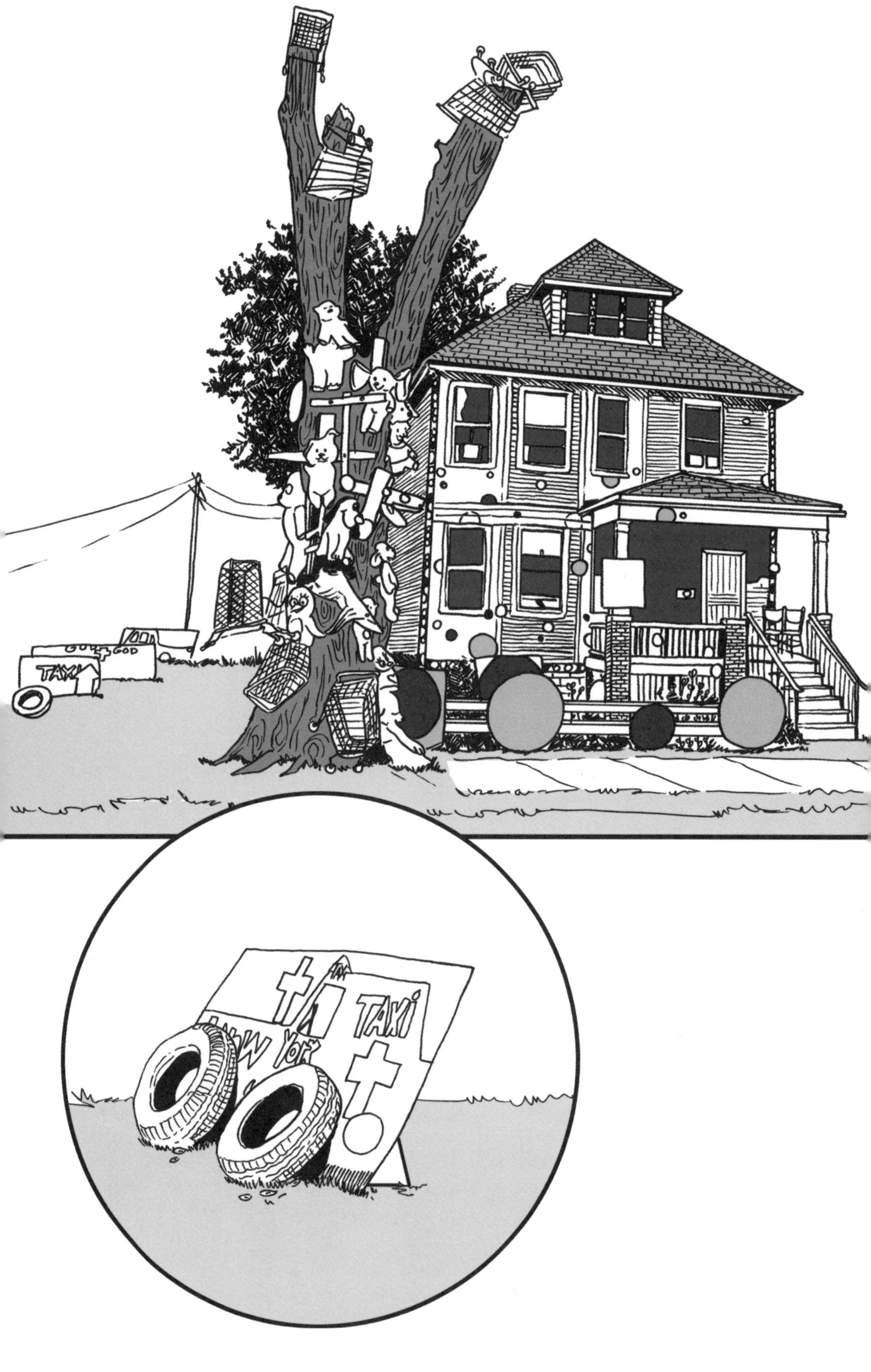
TAXI
GOD
TAXI
YORK

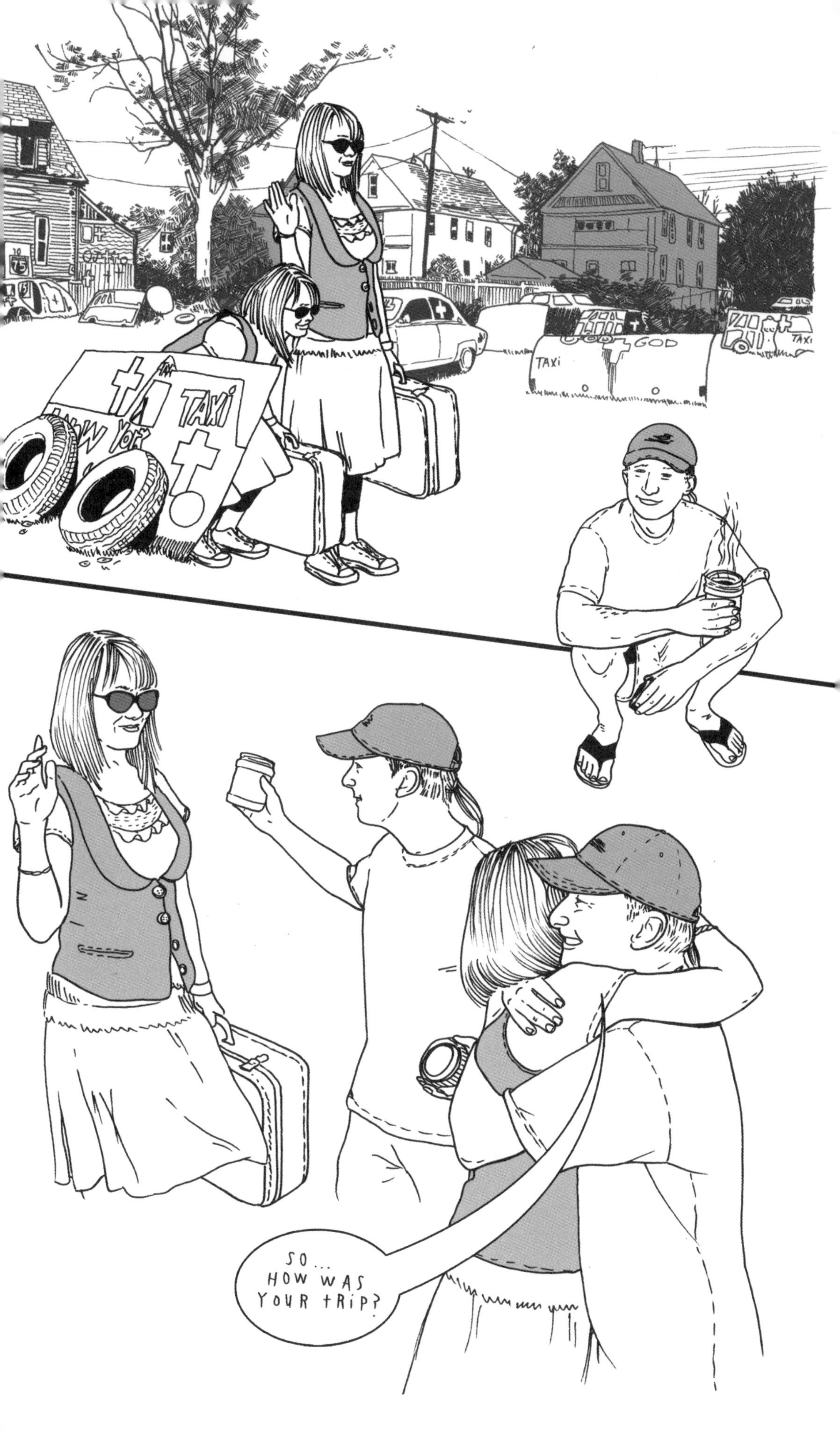

TAXI
NEW YORK
TAXI
GOD
GOD
TAXI
TAXI
SO...
HOW WAS
YOUR TRIP?

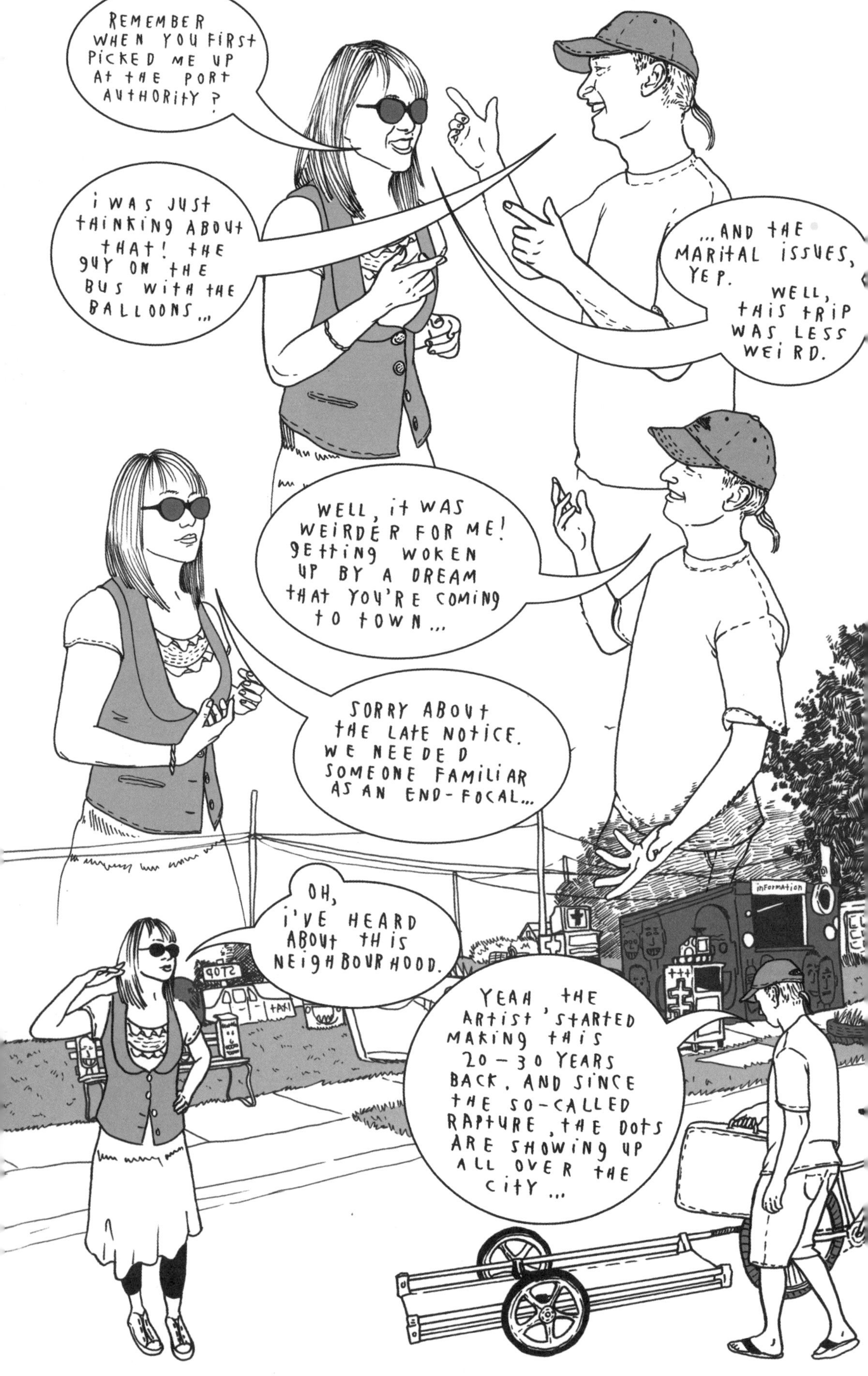
REMEMBER WHEN YOU FIRST PICKED ME UP AT THE PORT AUTHORITY?
I WAS JUST THINKING ABOUT THAT! THE GUY ON THE BUS WITH THE BALLOONS...
...AND THE MARITAL ISSUES, YEP. WELL, THIS TRIP WAS LESS WEIRD.
WELL, IT WAS WEIRDER FOR ME! GETTING WOKEN UP BY A DREAM THAT YOU'RE COMING TO TOWN...
SORRY ABOUT THE LATE NOTICE. WE NEEDED SOMEONE FAMILIAR AS AN END-FOCAL...
OH, I'VE HEARD ABOUT THIS NEIGHBOURHOOD.
YEAH, THE ARTIST STARTED MAKING THIS 20-30 YEARS BACK, AND SINCE THE SO-CALLED RAPTURE, THE DOTS ARE SHOWING UP ALL OVER THE CITY...
INFORMATION
STOP
TAXI

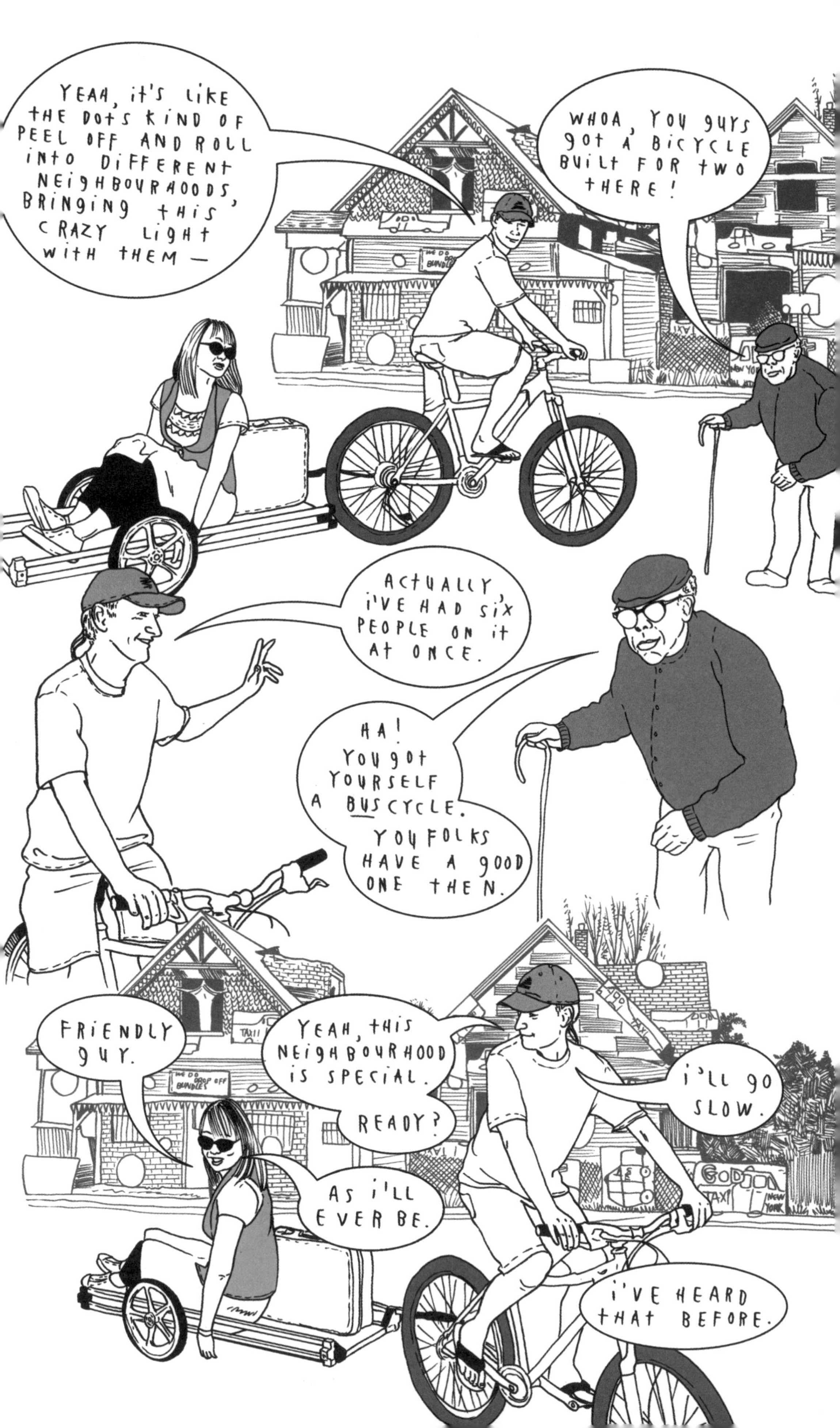
YEAH, it's LIKE THE DOTS KIND OF PEEL OFF AND ROLL INTO DIFFERENT NEIGHBOURHOODS, BRINGING THIS CRAZY LIGHT WITH THEM —
WHOA, YOU GUYS GOT A BICYCLE BUILT FOR TWO THERE!
ACTUALLY, I'VE HAD SIX PEOPLE ON IT AT ONCE.
HA! YOU GOT YOURSELF A BUSCYCLE.
YOU FOLKS HAVE A GOOD ONE THEN.
FRIENDLY GUY.
YEAH, THIS NEIGHBOURHOOD IS SPECIAL.
READY?
I'LL GO SLOW.
AS I'LL EVER BE.
I'VE HEARD THAT BEFORE.

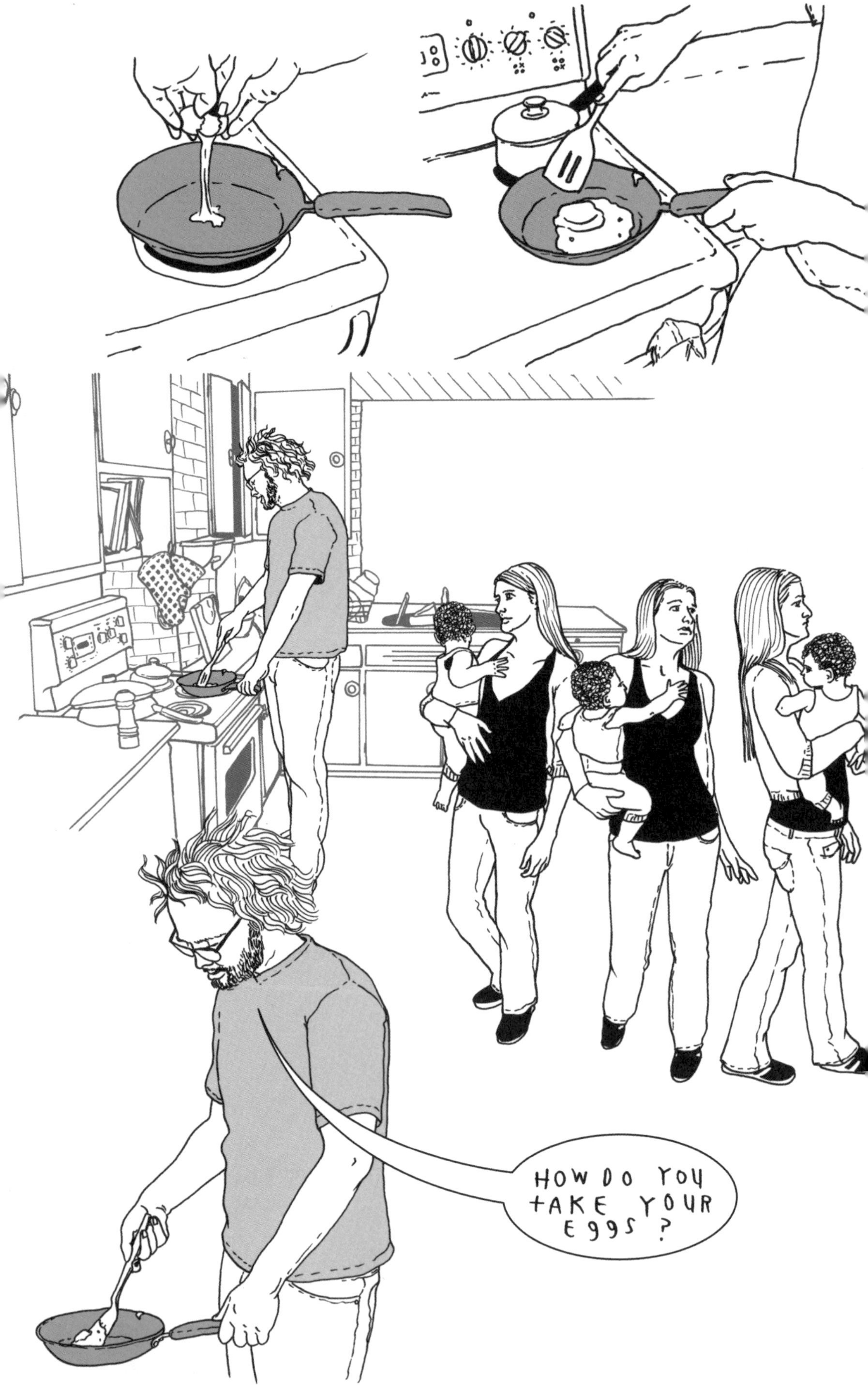
HOW DO YOU TAKE YOUR EGGS?

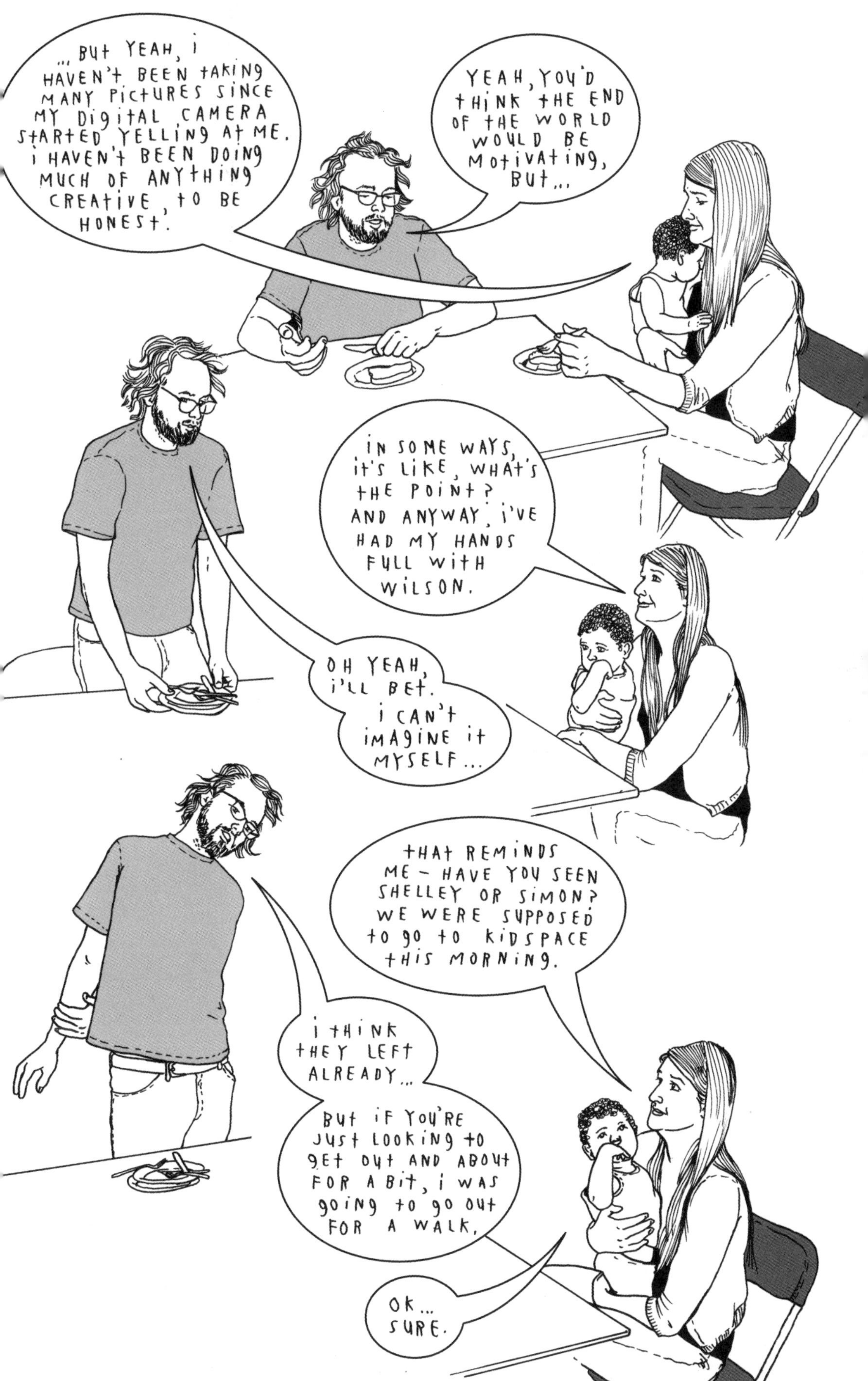
...BUT YEAH, I HAVEN'T BEEN TAKING MANY PICTURES SINCE MY DIGITAL CAMERA STARTED YELLING AT ME. I HAVEN'T BEEN DOING MUCH OF ANYTHING CREATIVE, TO BE HONEST.
YEAH, YOU'D THINK THE END OF THE WORLD WOULD BE MOTIVATING, BUT...
IN SOME WAYS, IT'S LIKE, WHAT'S THE POINT? AND ANYWAY, I'VE HAD MY HANDS FULL WITH WILSON.
OH YEAH, I'LL BET. I CAN'T IMAGINE IT MYSELF...
THAT REMINDS ME- HAVE YOU SEEN SHELLEY OR SIMON? WE WERE SUPPOSED TO GO TO KIDSPACE THIS MORNING.
I THINK THEY LEFT ALREADY...
BUT IF YOU'RE JUST LOOKING TO GET OUT AND ABOUT FOR A BIT, I WAS GOING TO GO OUT FOR A WALK.
OK... SURE.

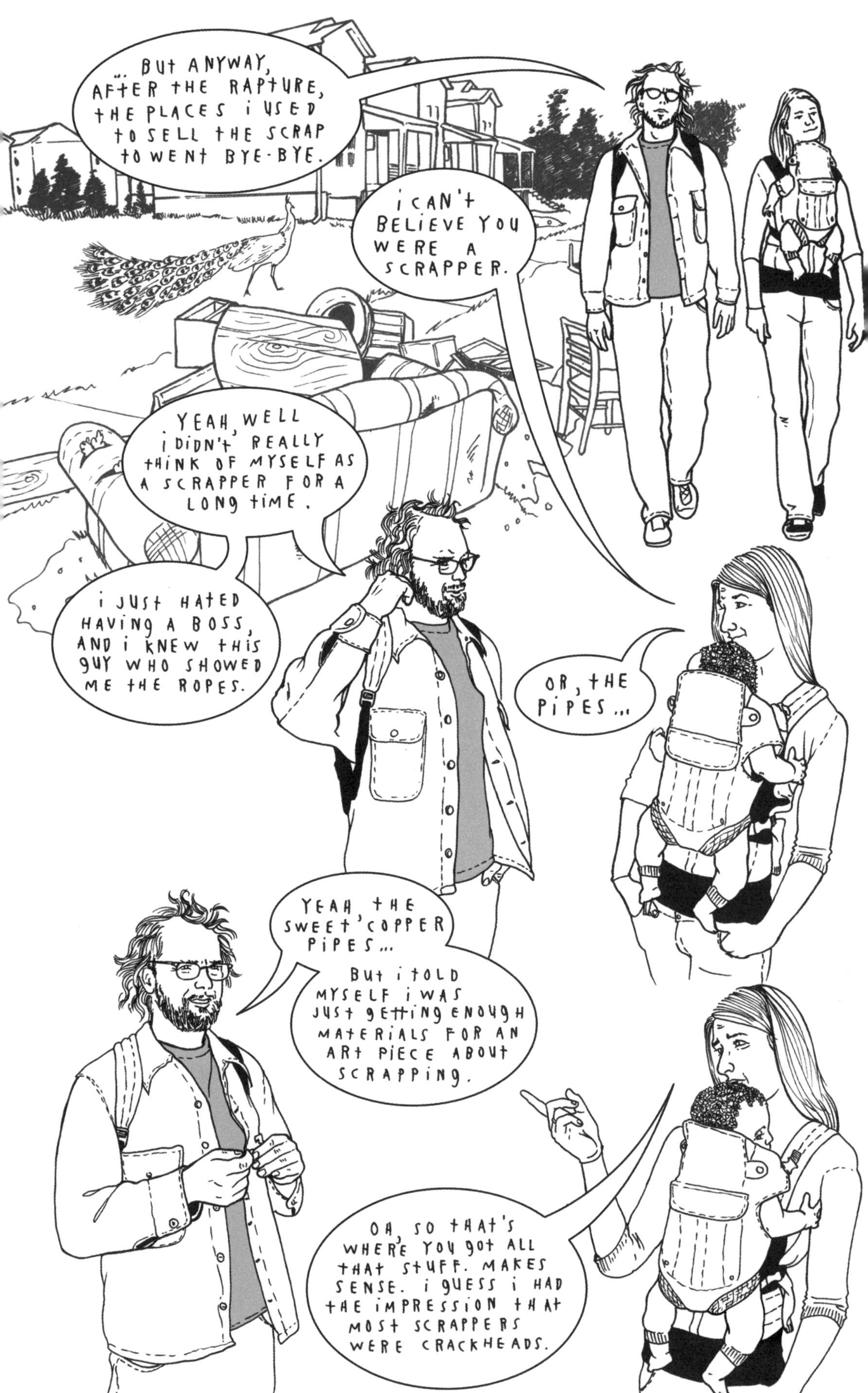
... BUT ANYWAY, AFTER THE RAPTURE, THE PLACES I USED TO SELL THE SCRAP TO WENT BYE-BYE.
I CAN'T BELIEVE YOU WERE A SCRAPPER.
YEAH, WELL I DIDN'T REALLY THINK OF MYSELF AS A SCRAPPER FOR A LONG TIME.
I JUST HATED HAVING A BOSS, AND I KNEW THIS GUY WHO SHOWED ME THE ROPES.
OR, THE PIPES...
YEAH, THE SWEET COPPER PIPES...
BUT I TOLD MYSELF I WAS JUST GETTING ENOUGH MATERIALS FOR AN ART PIECE ABOUT SCRAPPING.
OH, SO THAT'S WHERE YOU GOT ALL THAT STUFF. MAKES SENSE. I GUESS I HAD THE IMPRESSION THAT MOST SCRAPPERS WERE CRACKHEADS.

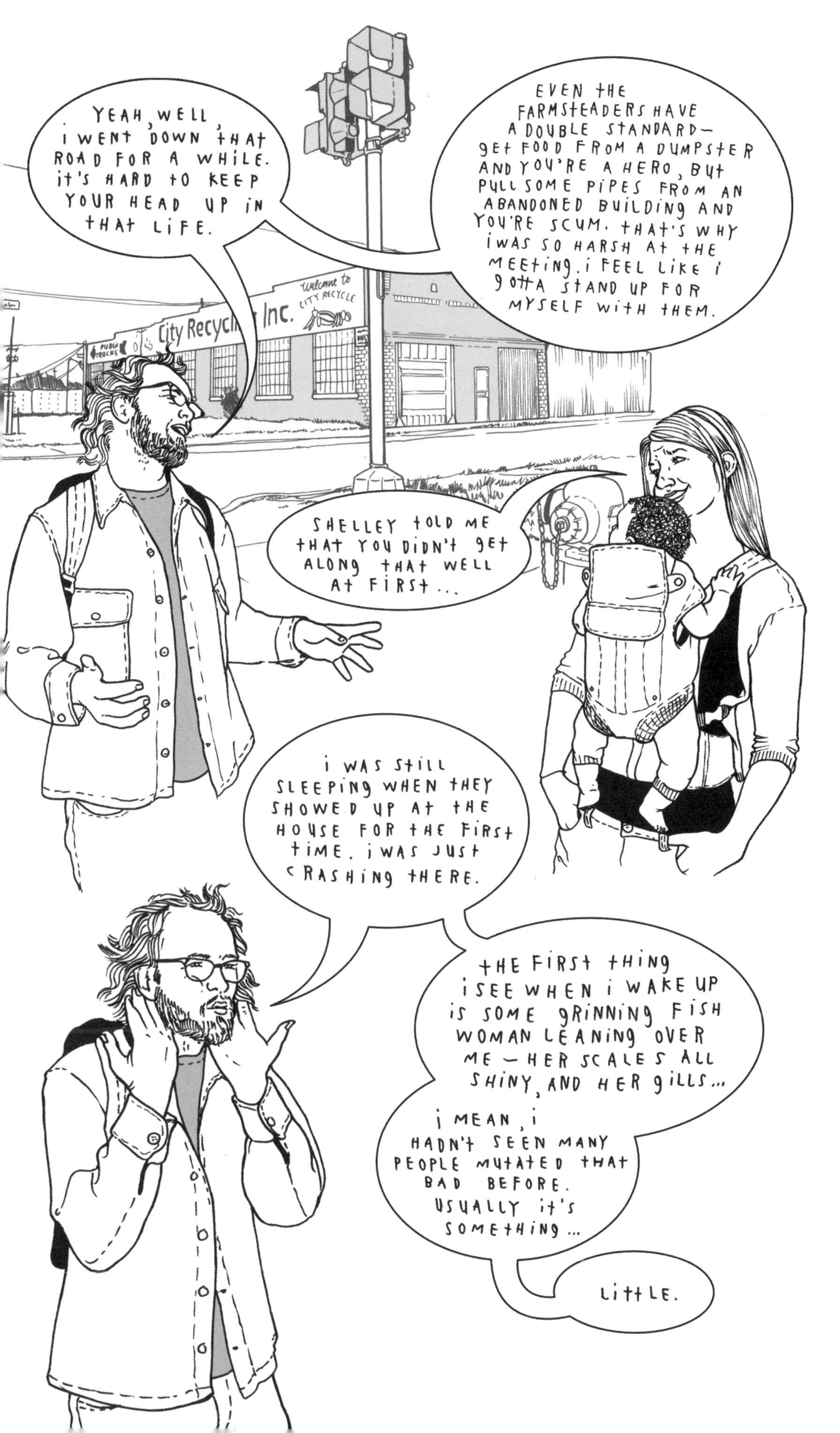

YEAH, WELL, i WENT DOWN THAT ROAD FOR A WHILE. it'S HARD TO KEEP YOUR HEAD UP iN THAT LiFE.
EVEN THE FARMSTEADERS HAVE A DOUBLE STANDARD— GET FOOD FROM A DUMPSTER AND YOU'RE A HERO, BUT PULL SOME PIPES FROM AN ABANDONED BUILDING AND YOU'RE SCUM. THAT'S WHY i WAS SO HARSH AT THE MEETING. i FEEL LIKE i GOTTA STAND UP FOR MYSELF WITH THEM.
Welcome to CITY RECYCLE
City Recycl Inc.
PUBLIC TRUCKS
SHELLEY TOLD ME THAT YOU DIDN'T GET ALONG THAT WELL AT FIRST...
i WAS STiLL SLEEPiNG WHEN THEY SHOWED UP AT THE HOUSE FOR THE FiRST TiME. i WAS JUST CRASHiNG THERE.
THE FiRST THiNG i SEE WHEN i WAKE UP iS SOME GRiNNiNG FiSH WOMAN LEANiNG OVER ME— HER SCALES ALL SHiNY, AND HER GiLLS...
i MEAN, i HADN'T SEEN MANY PEOPLE MUTATED THAT BAD BEFORE. USUALLY iT'S SOMETHiNG...
LiTTLE.

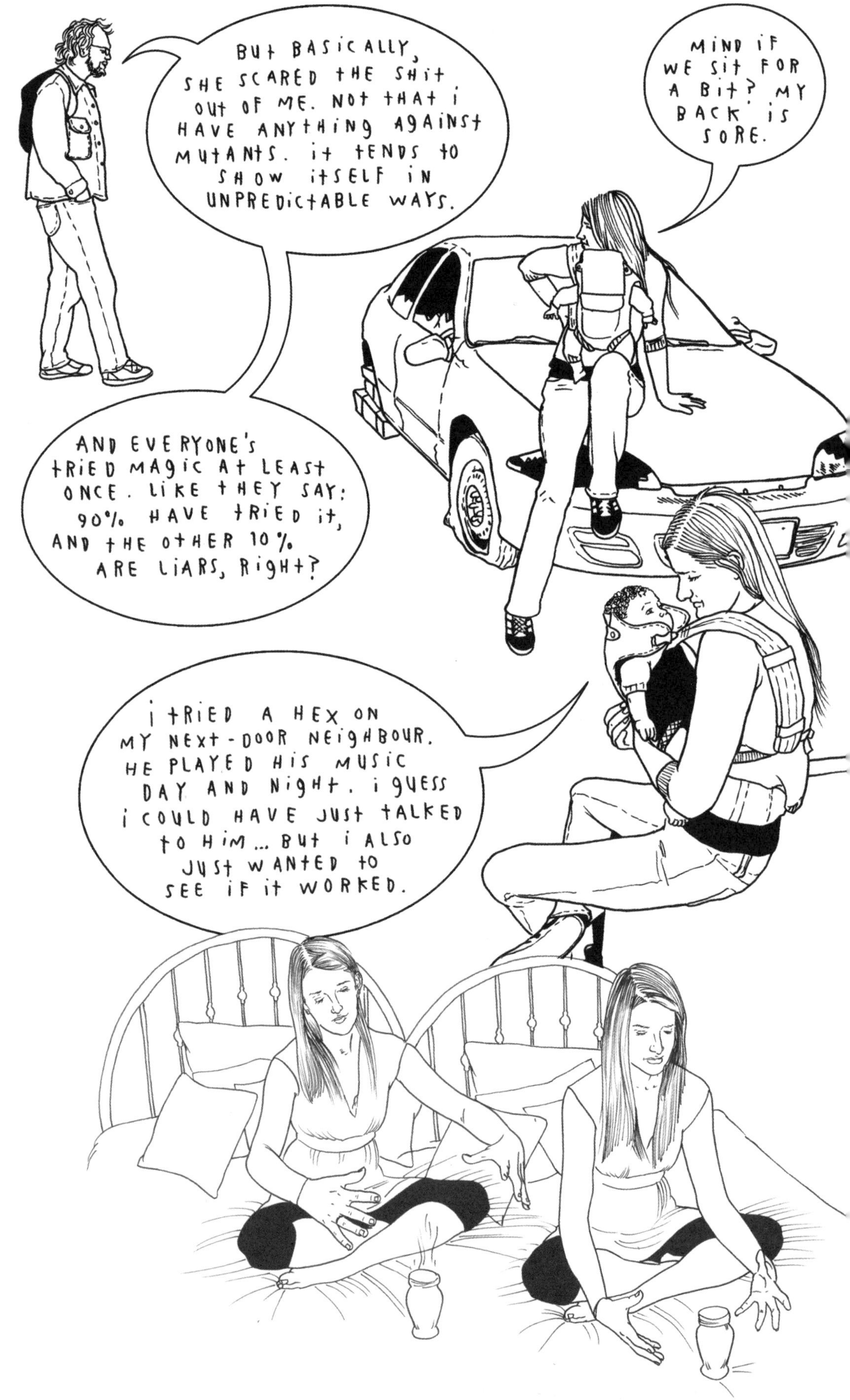
BUT BASICALLY, SHE SCARED THE SHIT OUT OF ME. NOT THAT I HAVE ANYTHING AGAINST MUTANTS. IT TENDS TO SHOW ITSELF IN UNPREDICTABLE WAYS.
MIND IF WE SIT FOR A BIT? MY BACK IS SORE.
AND EVERYONE'S TRIED MAGIC AT LEAST ONCE. LIKE THEY SAY: 90% HAVE TRIED IT, AND THE OTHER 10% ARE LIARS, RIGHT?
I TRIED A HEX ON MY NEXT-DOOR NEIGHBOUR. HE PLAYED HIS MUSIC DAY AND NIGHT. I GUESS I COULD HAVE JUST TALKED TO HIM... BUT I ALSO JUST WANTED TO SEE IF IT WORKED.

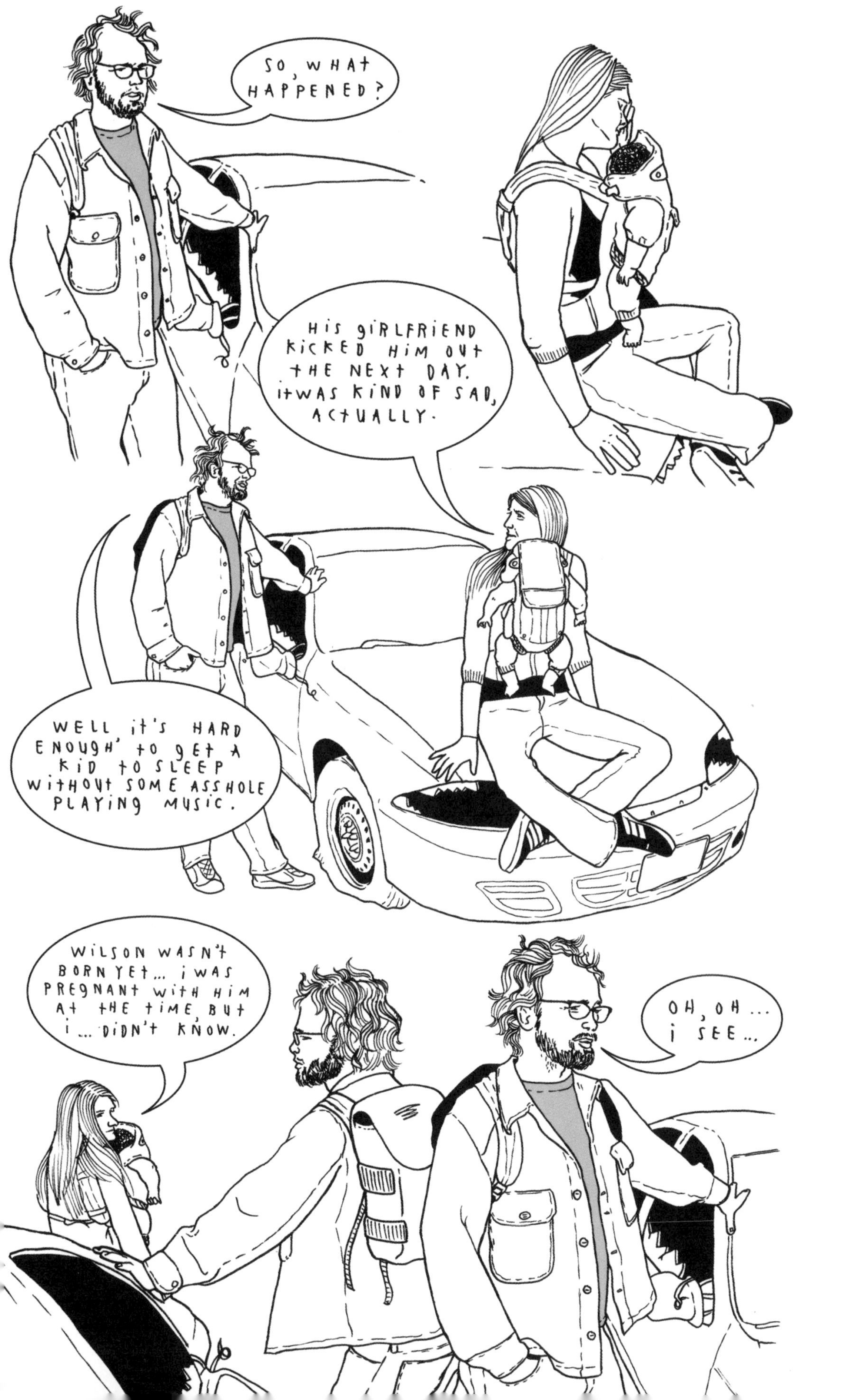
SO, WHAT HAPPENED?
HIS GIRLFRIEND KICKED HIM OUT THE NEXT DAY. IT WAS KIND OF SAD, ACTUALLY.
WELL, IT'S HARD ENOUGH' TO GET A KID TO SLEEP WITHOUT SOME ASSHOLE PLAYING MUSIC.
WILSON WASN'T BORN YET... I WAS PREGNANT WITH HIM AT THE TIME, BUT I... DIDN'T KNOW.
OH, OH... I SEE...

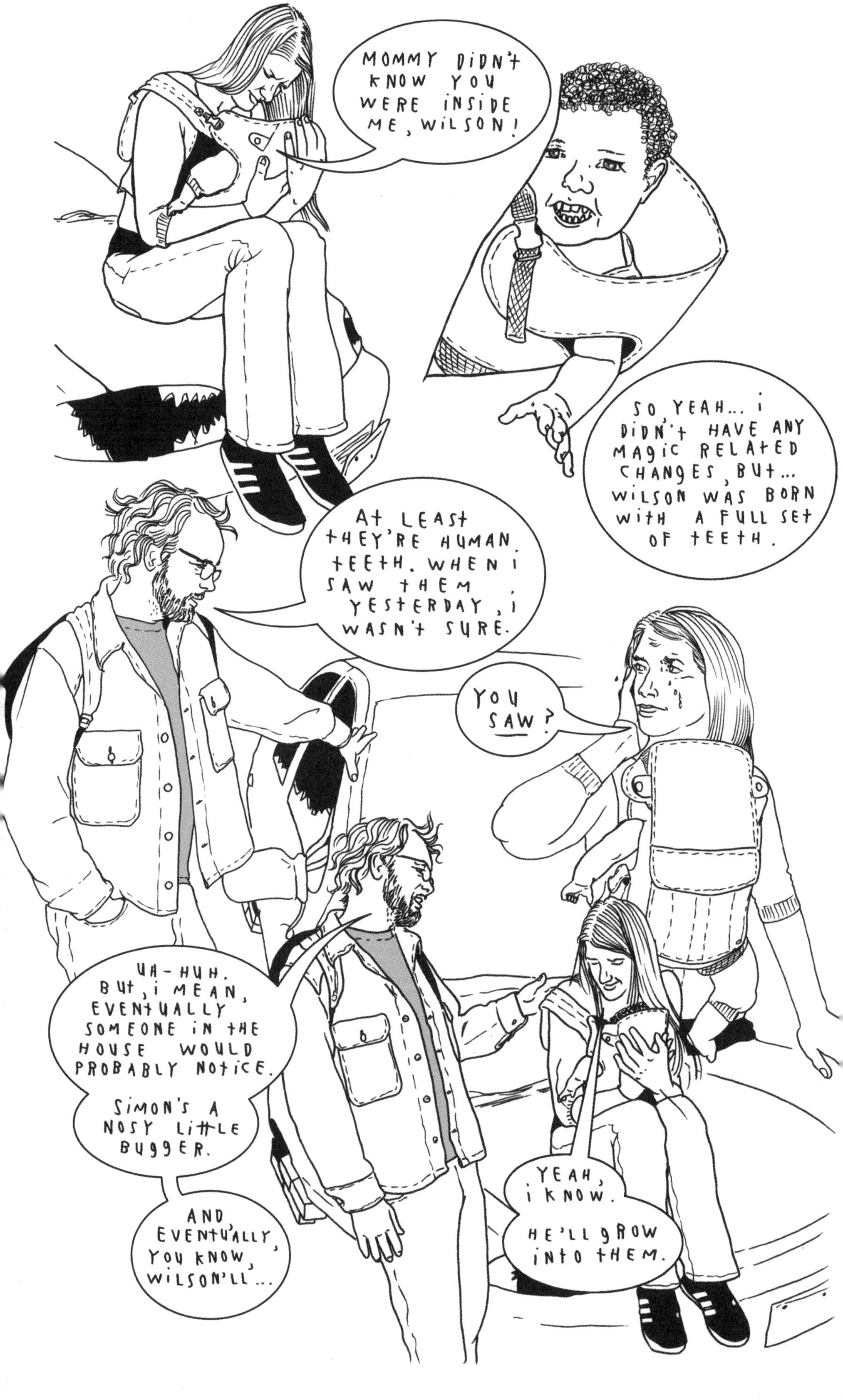
MOMMY DIDN'T KNOW YOU WERE INSIDE ME, WILSON!
SO YEAH... I DIDN'T HAVE ANY MAGIC RELATED CHANGES, BUT... WILSON WAS BORN WITH A FULL SET OF TEETH.
AT LEAST THEY'RE HUMAN TEETH. WHEN I SAW THEM YESTERDAY, I WASN'T SURE.
YOU SAW?
UH-HUH. BUT, I MEAN, EVENTUALLY SOMEONE IN THE HOUSE WOULD PROBABLY NOTICE.
SIMON'S A NOSY LITTLE BUGGER.
AND, EVENTUALLY, YOU KNOW, WILSON'LL...
YEAH, I KNOW.
HE'LL GROW INTO THEM.

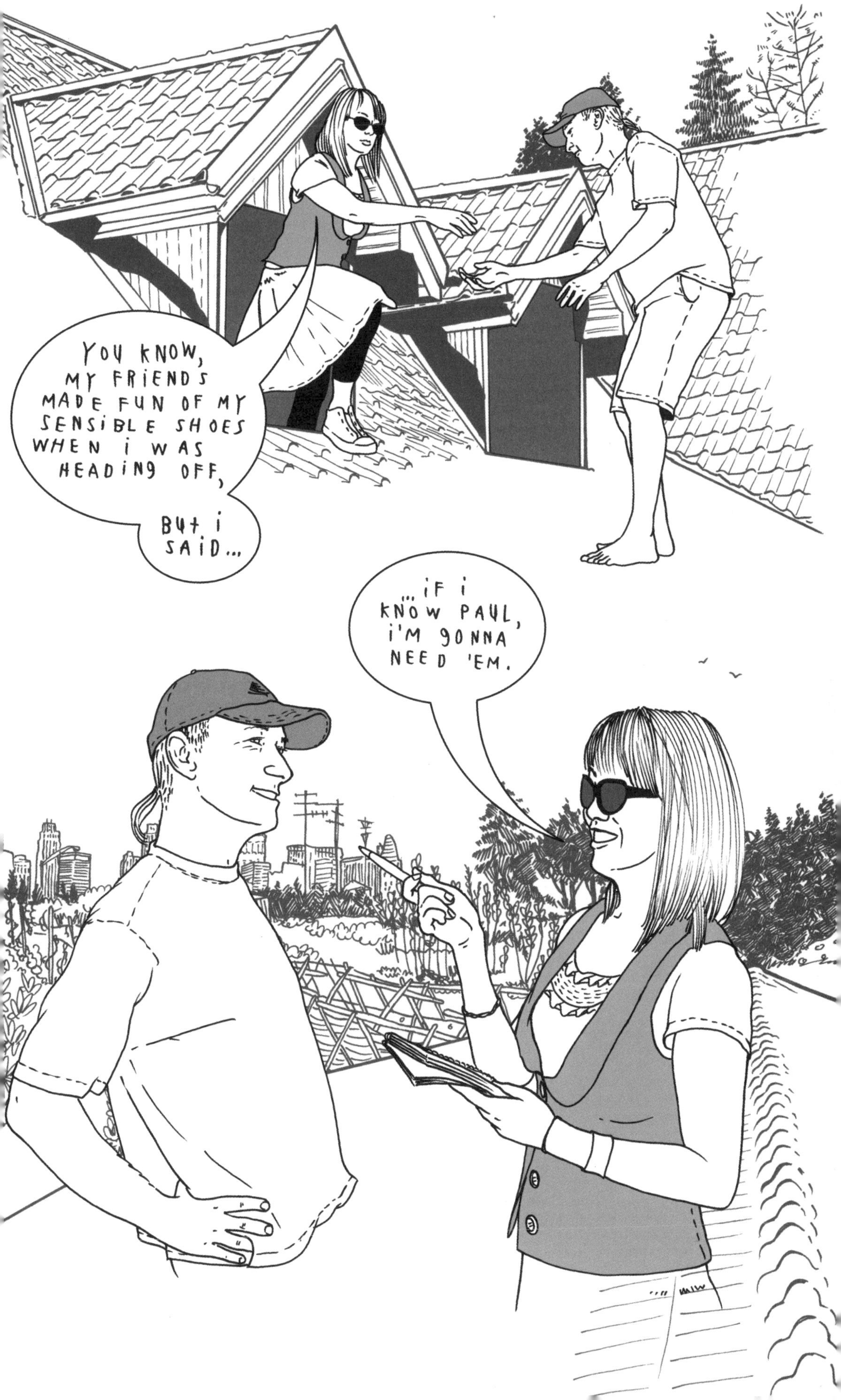
YOU KNOW, MY FRIENDS MADE FUN OF MY SENSIBLE SHOES WHEN I WAS HEADING OFF,
BUT I SAID...
...IF I KNOW PAUL, I'M GONNA NEED 'EM.

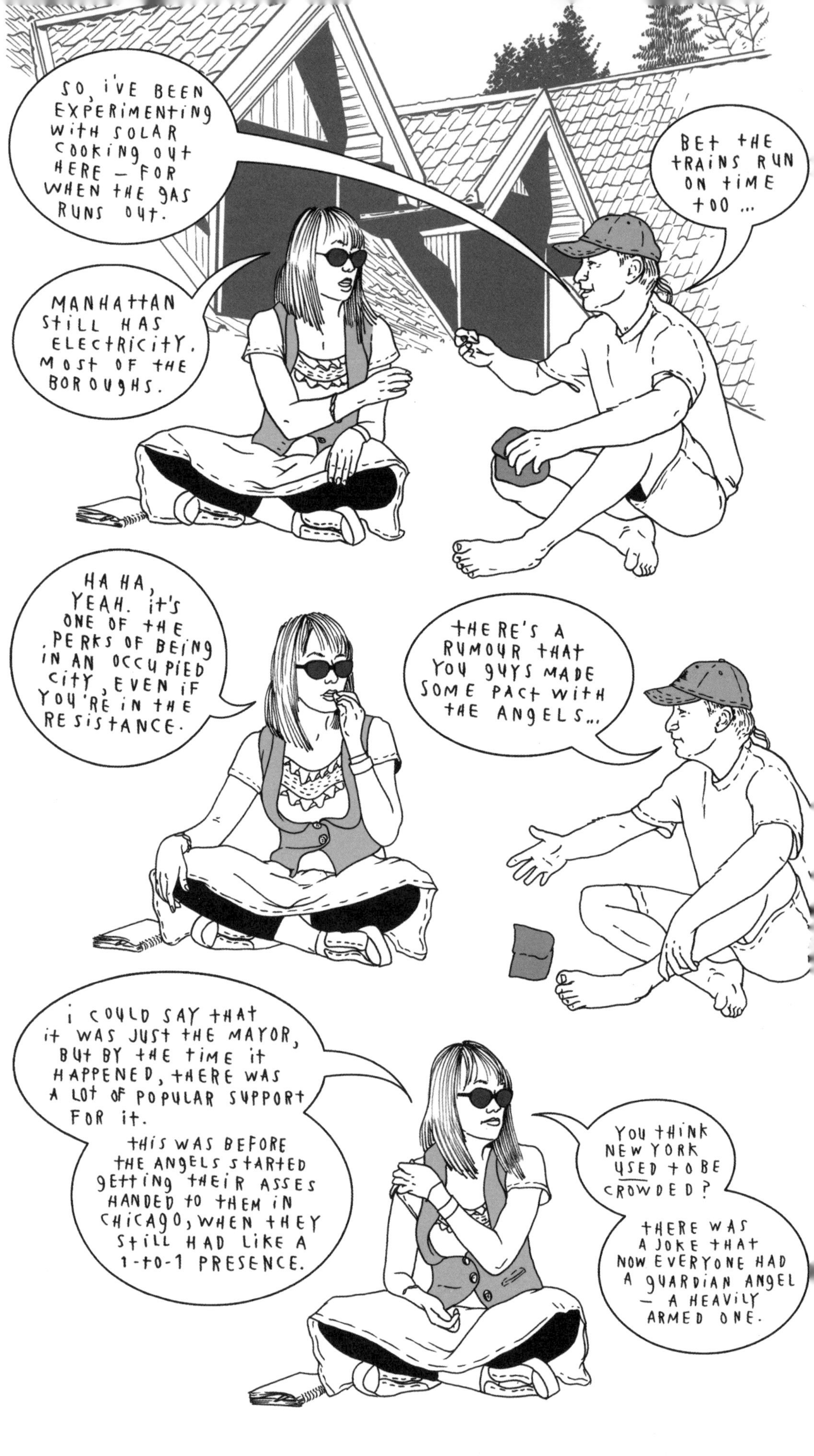
SO, I'VE BEEN EXPERIMENTING WITH SOLAR COOKING OUT HERE — FOR WHEN THE GAS RUNS OUT.
BET THE TRAINS RUN ON TIME TOO...
MANHATTAN STILL HAS ELECTRICITY. MOST OF THE BOROUGHS.
HA HA, YEAH. IT'S ONE OF THE PERKS OF BEING IN AN OCCUPIED CITY, EVEN IF YOU'RE IN THE RESISTANCE.
THERE'S A RUMOUR THAT YOU GUYS MADE SOME PACT WITH THE ANGELS...
I COULD SAY THAT IT WAS JUST THE MAYOR, BUT BY THE TIME IT HAPPENED, THERE WAS A LOT OF POPULAR SUPPORT FOR IT.
THIS WAS BEFORE THE ANGELS STARTED GETTING THEIR ASSES HANDED TO THEM IN CHICAGO, WHEN THEY STILL HAD LIKE A 1-TO-1 PRESENCE.
YOU THINK NEW YORK USED TO BE CROWDED?
THERE WAS A JOKE THAT NOW EVERYONE HAD A GUARDIAN ANGEL — A HEAVILY ARMED ONE.

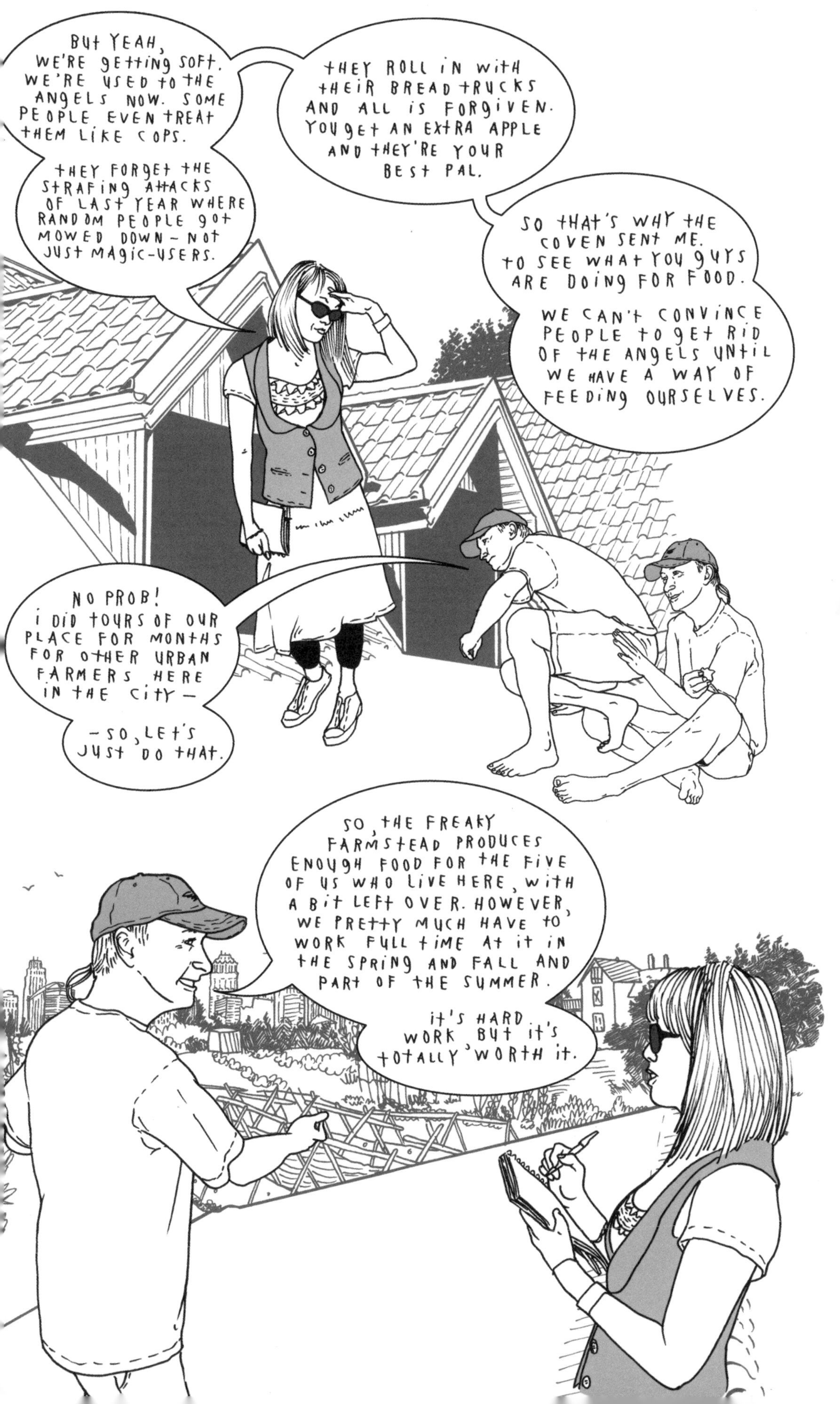
BUT YEAH, WE'RE GETTING SOFT. WE'RE USED TO THE ANGELS NOW. SOME PEOPLE EVEN TREAT THEM LIKE COPS.
THEY ROLL IN WITH THEIR BREAD TRUCKS AND ALL IS FORGIVEN. YOU GET AN EXTRA APPLE AND THEY'RE YOUR BEST PAL.
THEY FORGET THE STRAFING ATTACKS OF LAST YEAR WHERE RANDOM PEOPLE GOT MOWED DOWN – NOT JUST MAGIC-USERS.
SO THAT'S WHY THE COVEN SENT ME. TO SEE WHAT YOU GUYS ARE DOING FOR FOOD.
WE CAN'T CONVINCE PEOPLE TO GET RID OF THE ANGELS UNTIL WE HAVE A WAY OF FEEDING OURSELVES.
NO PROB! I DID TOURS OF OUR PLACE FOR MONTHS FOR OTHER URBAN FARMERS HERE IN THE CITY –
– SO, LET'S JUST DO THAT.
SO, THE FREAKY FARMSTEAD PRODUCES ENOUGH FOOD FOR THE FIVE OF US WHO LIVE HERE, WITH A BIT LEFT OVER. HOWEVER, WE PRETTY MUCH HAVE TO WORK FULL TIME AT IT IN THE SPRING AND FALL AND PART OF THE SUMMER.
IT'S HARD WORK, BUT IT'S TOTALLY WORTH IT.

FROM HERE, YOU CAN SEE THE FIELD... THOSE THINGS ALONG THE SIDE THERE ARE RAIN BARRELS... AND THE BUILDING THERE IS THE CHICKEN COOP.
AS WELL AS THE EGGS AND MEAT, CHICKEN SHIT IS LIKE GOLD FOR MANURE.
gottit.
chicken shit = GOLD!
DON'T WORRY TOO MUCH ABOUT NOTES - I'VE GOT SOME HANDOUTS LEFT OVER.
OF COURSE YOU DO, PAUL.
YOU KNOW, URS, I REMEMBER WHEN MY LITTLE BACKYARD GARDEN COMPOST WAS TOTALLY WEIRD TO YOU, AND NOW YOU'RE ASKING FOR MY RECIPES.
BELIEVE ME, HONEY, WHEN I TELL YOU...
...THAT I SEE THINGS A LITTLE DIFFERENTLY THESE DAYS.

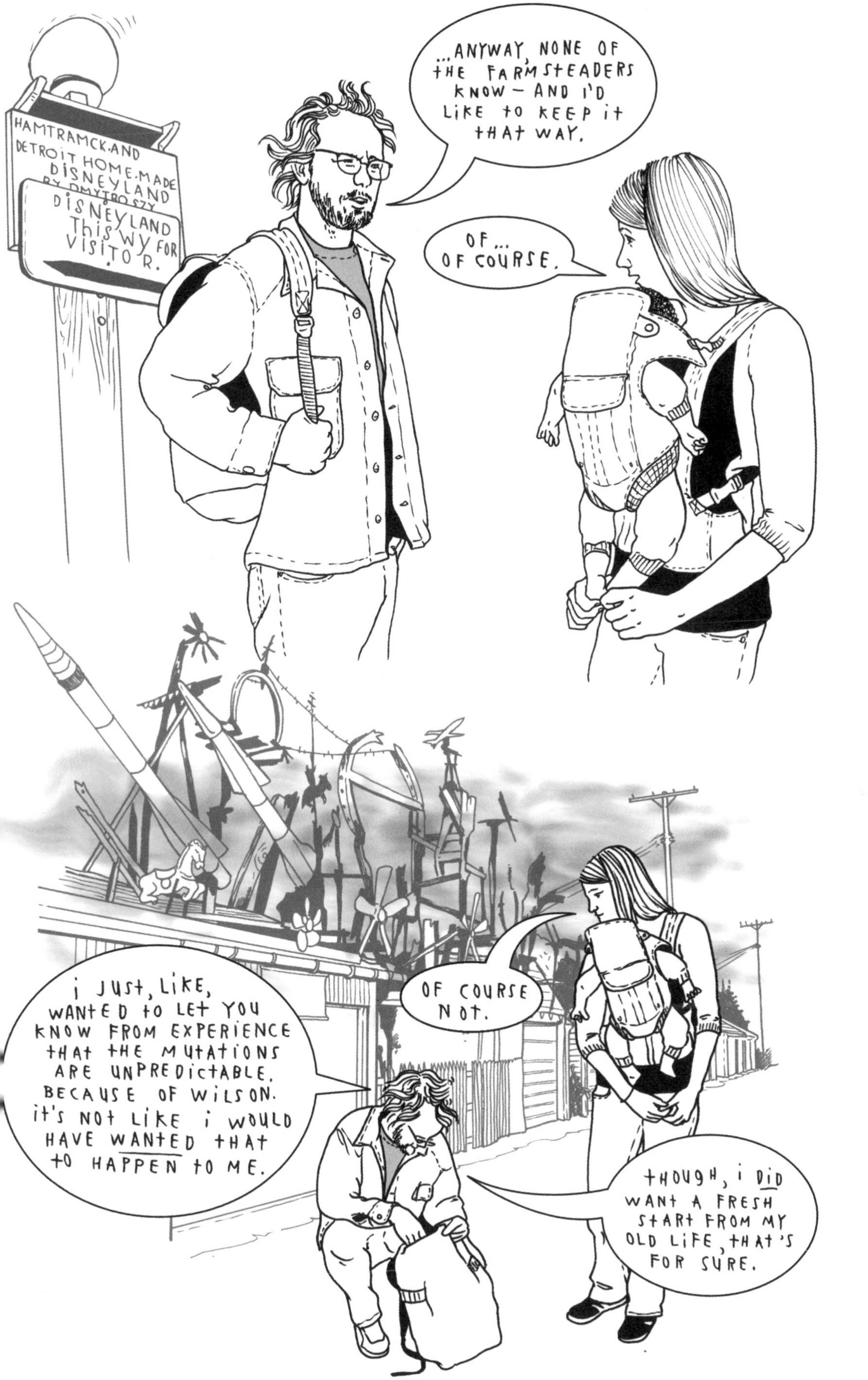
HAMTRAMCK.AND DETROIT HOME.MADE DISNEYLAND
DISNEYLAND This WY FOR VISITO R.
...ANYWAY, NONE OF THE FARMSTEADERS KNOW — AND I'D LIKE TO KEEP IT THAT WAY.
OF... OF COURSE.
I JUST, LIKE, WANTED TO LET YOU KNOW FROM EXPERIENCE THAT THE MUTATIONS ARE UNPREDICTABLE. BECAUSE OF WILSON. IT'S NOT LIKE I WOULD HAVE WANTED THAT TO HAPPEN TO ME.
OF COURSE NOT.
THOUGH, I DID WANT A FRESH START FROM MY OLD LIFE, THAT'S FOR SURE.

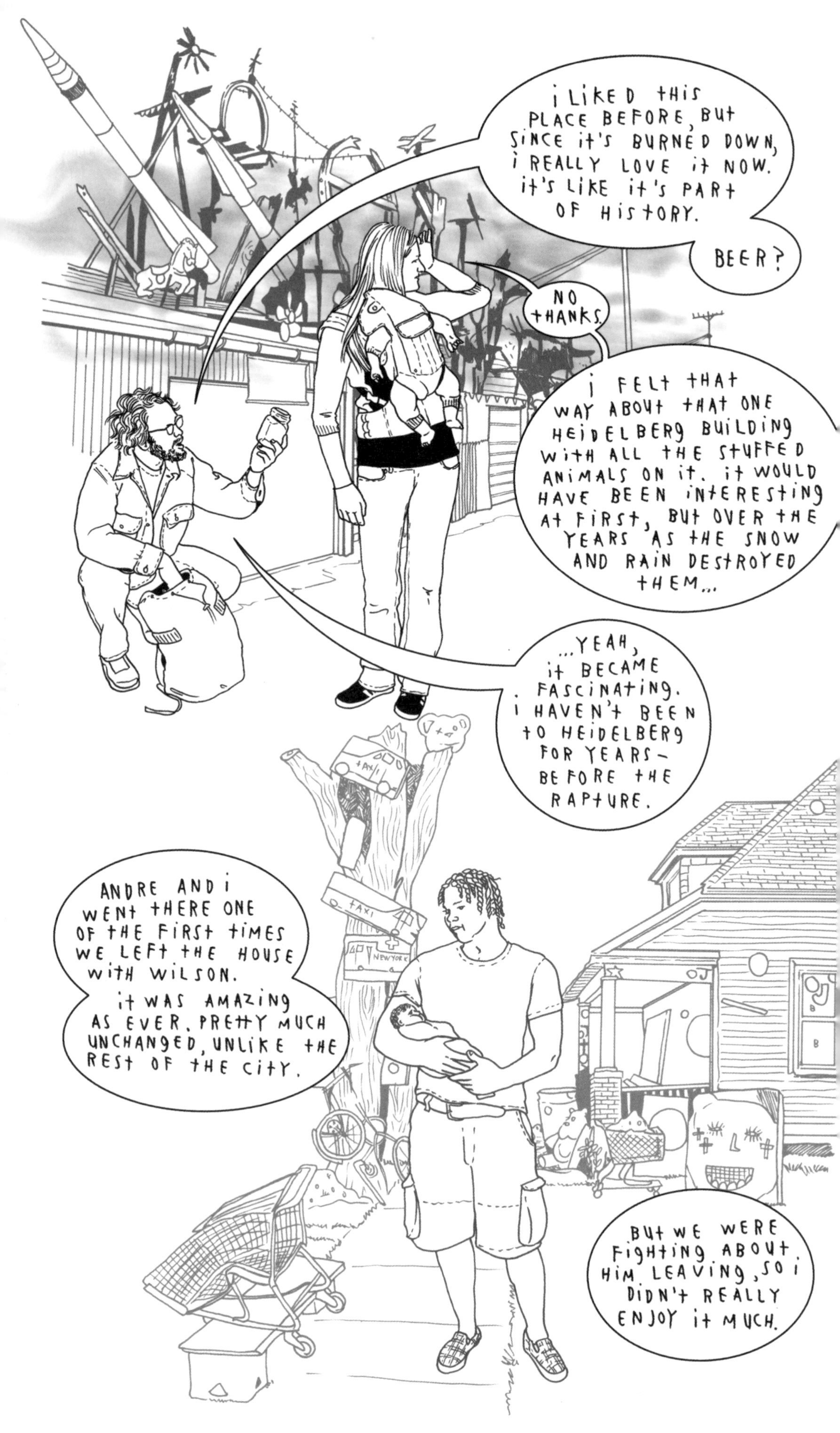
i LIKED this PLACE BEFORE, BUT SINCE it's BURNED DOWN, i REALLY LOVE it NOW. it's LIKE it's PART OF HISTORY.
BEER?
NO thanks.
i FELt that WAY ABOUt that ONE HEIDELBERG BUILDING with ALL tHE StUFFED ANIMALS ON it. it WOULD HAVE BEEN iNtERESTING At FIRSt, BUt OVER tHE YEARS AS tHE SNOW AND RAIN DESTROYED tHEM...
...YEAH, it BECAME FASCiNAtiNG. i HAVEN't BEEN tO HEIDELBERG FOR YEARS– BEFORE tHE RAPtURE.
ANDRE AND i WENt tHERE ONE OF tHE FIRSt tIMES WE LEFt tHE HOUSE with WILSON.
it WAS AMAZING AS EVER. PREttY MUCH UNCHANGED, UNLIKE tHE REST OF tHE CitY.
BUt WE WERE FIGHtING ABOUt HIM LEAVING, SO i DIDN't REALLY ENJOY it MUCH.

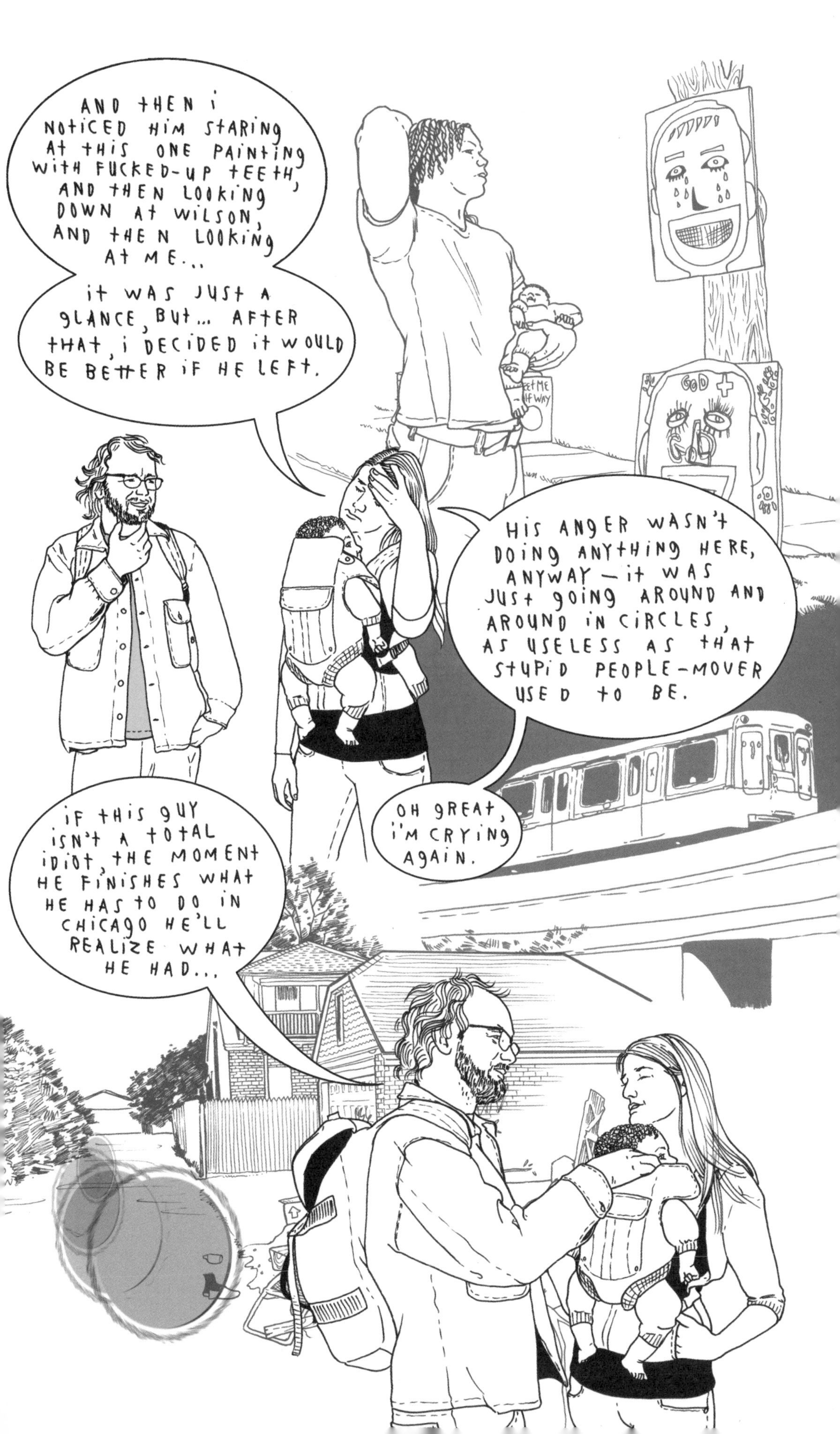
AND THEN I NOTICED HIM STARING AT THIS ONE PAINTING WITH FUCKED-UP TEETH, AND THEN LOOKING DOWN AT WILSON, AND THEN LOOKING AT ME...
IT WAS JUST A GLANCE, BUT... AFTER THAT, I DECIDED IT WOULD BE BETTER IF HE LEFT.
GOD
HIS ANGER WASN'T DOING ANYTHING HERE, ANYWAY — IT WAS JUST GOING AROUND AND AROUND IN CIRCLES, AS USELESS AS THAT STUPID PEOPLE-MOVER USED TO BE.
OH GREAT, I'M CRYING AGAIN.
IF THIS GUY ISN'T A TOTAL IDIOT, THE MOMENT HE FINISHES WHAT HE HAS TO DO IN CHICAGO HE'LL REALIZE WHAT HE HAD...

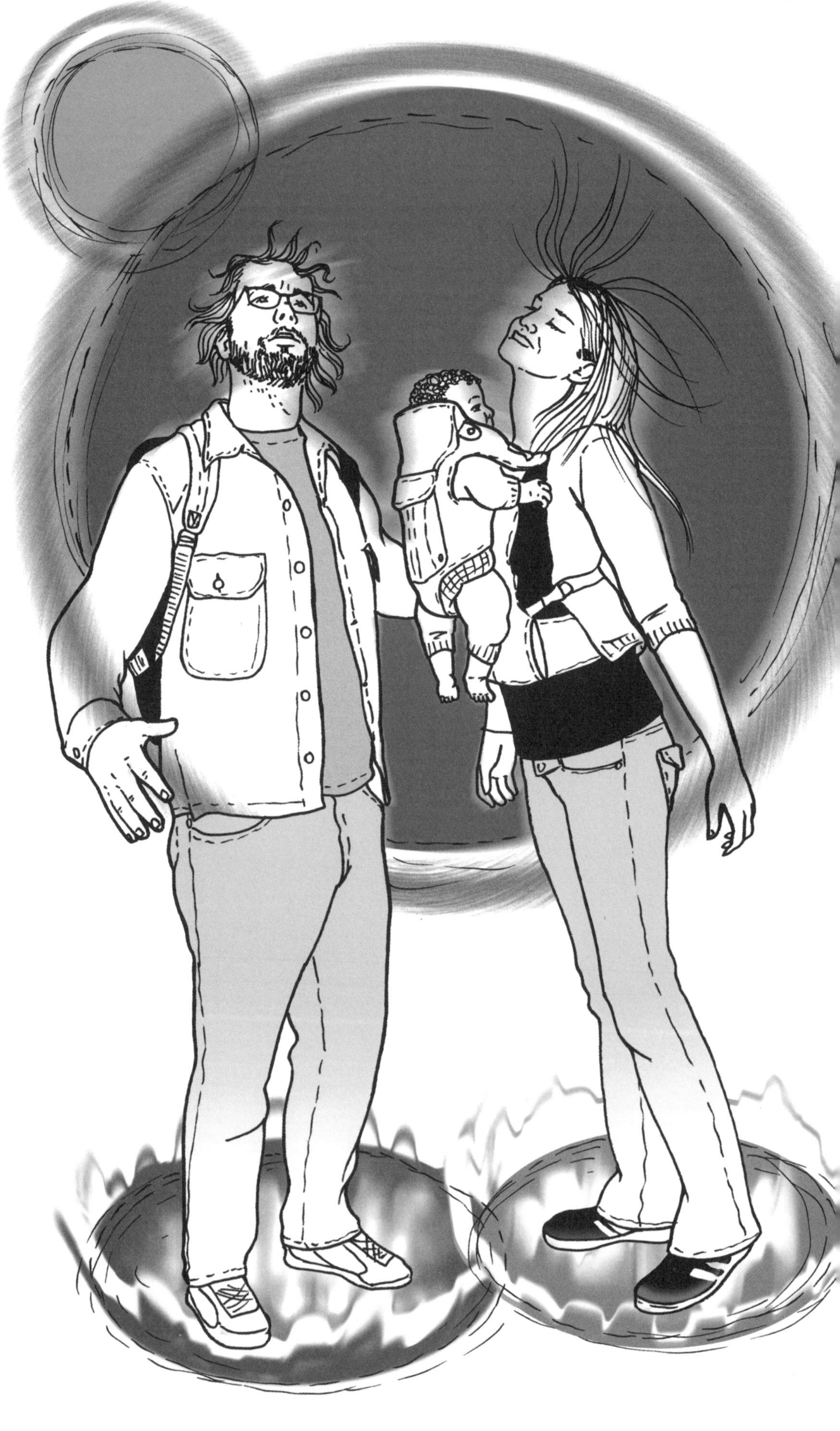

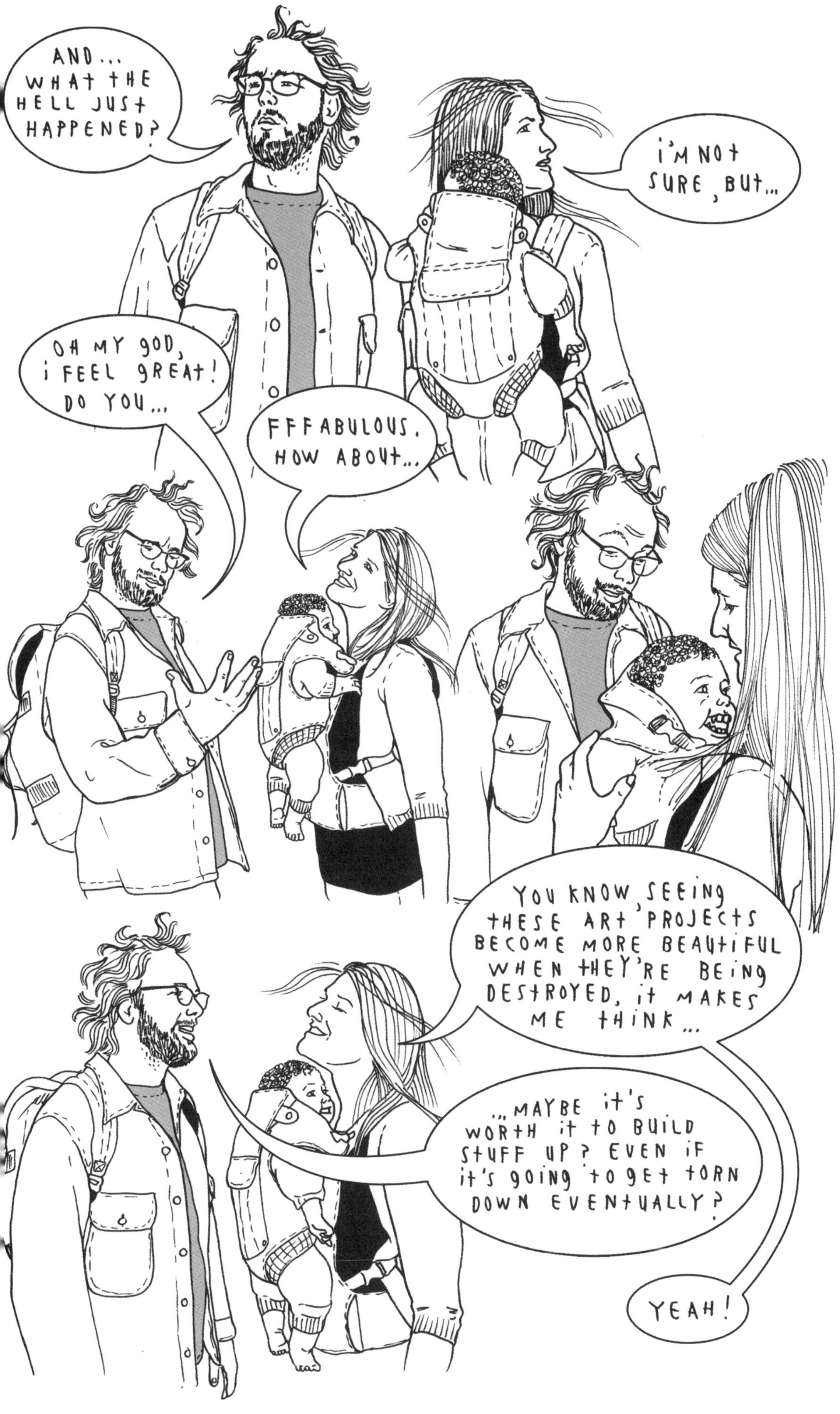
AND... WHAT THE HELL JUST HAPPENED?
I'M NOT SURE, BUT...
OH MY GOD, I FEEL GREAT! DO YOU...
FFFABULOUS. HOW ABOUT...
YOU KNOW, SEEING THESE ART PROJECTS BECOME MORE BEAUTIFUL WHEN THEY'RE BEING DESTROYED, IT MAKES ME THINK...
...MAYBE IT'S WORTH IT TO BUILD STUFF UP? EVEN IF IT'S GOING TO GET TORN DOWN EVENTUALLY?
YEAH!

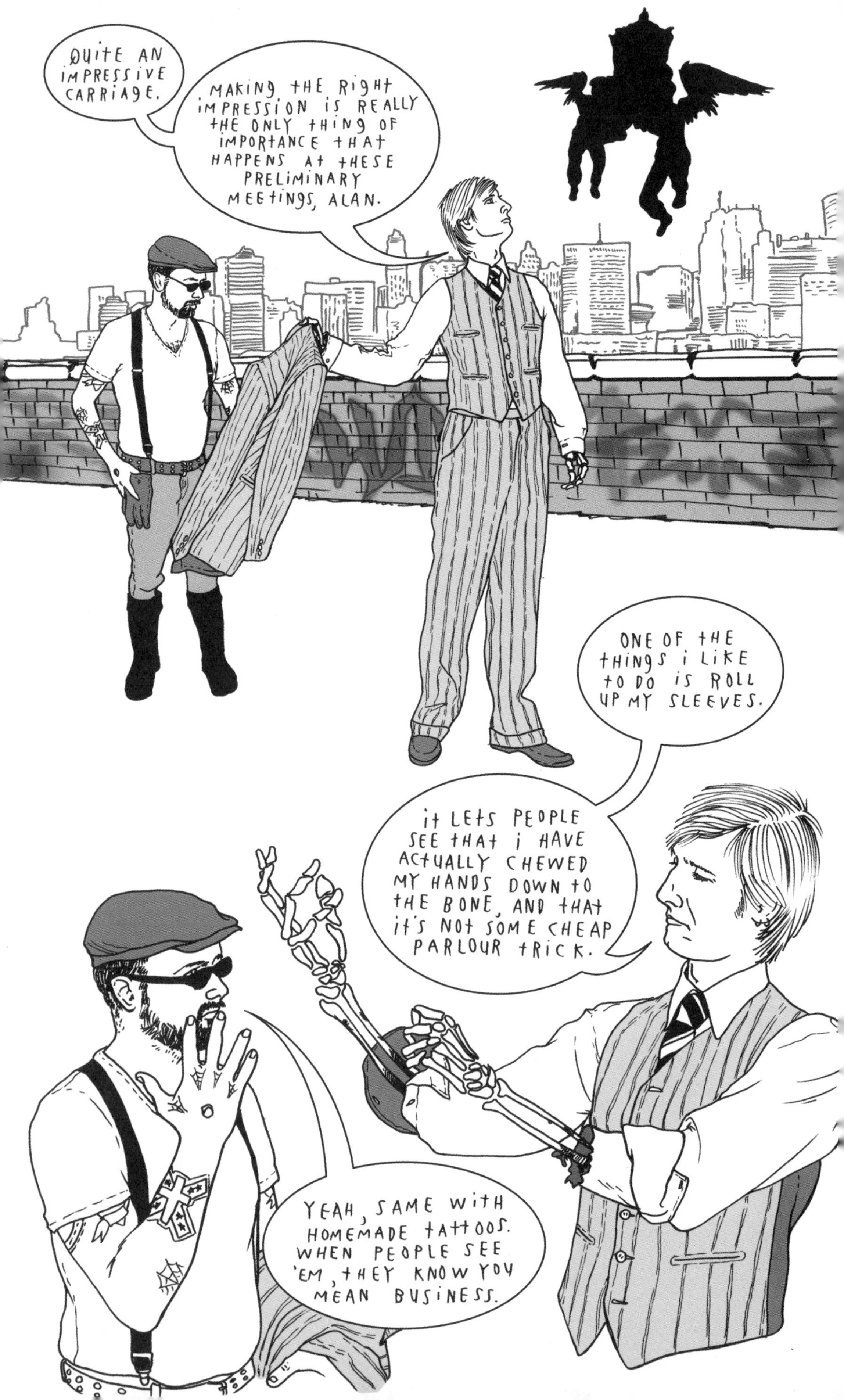
QUITE AN IMPRESSIVE CARRIAGE.
MAKING THE RIGHT IMPRESSION IS REALLY THE ONLY THING OF IMPORTANCE THAT HAPPENS AT THESE PRELIMINARY MEETINGS, ALAN.
ONE OF THE THINGS I LIKE TO DO IS ROLL UP MY SLEEVES.
IT LETS PEOPLE SEE THAT I HAVE ACTUALLY CHEWED MY HANDS DOWN TO THE BONE, AND THAT IT'S NOT SOME CHEAP PARLOUR TRICK.
YEAH, SAME WITH HOMEMADE TATTOOS. WHEN PEOPLE SEE 'EM, THEY KNOW YOU MEAN BUSINESS.

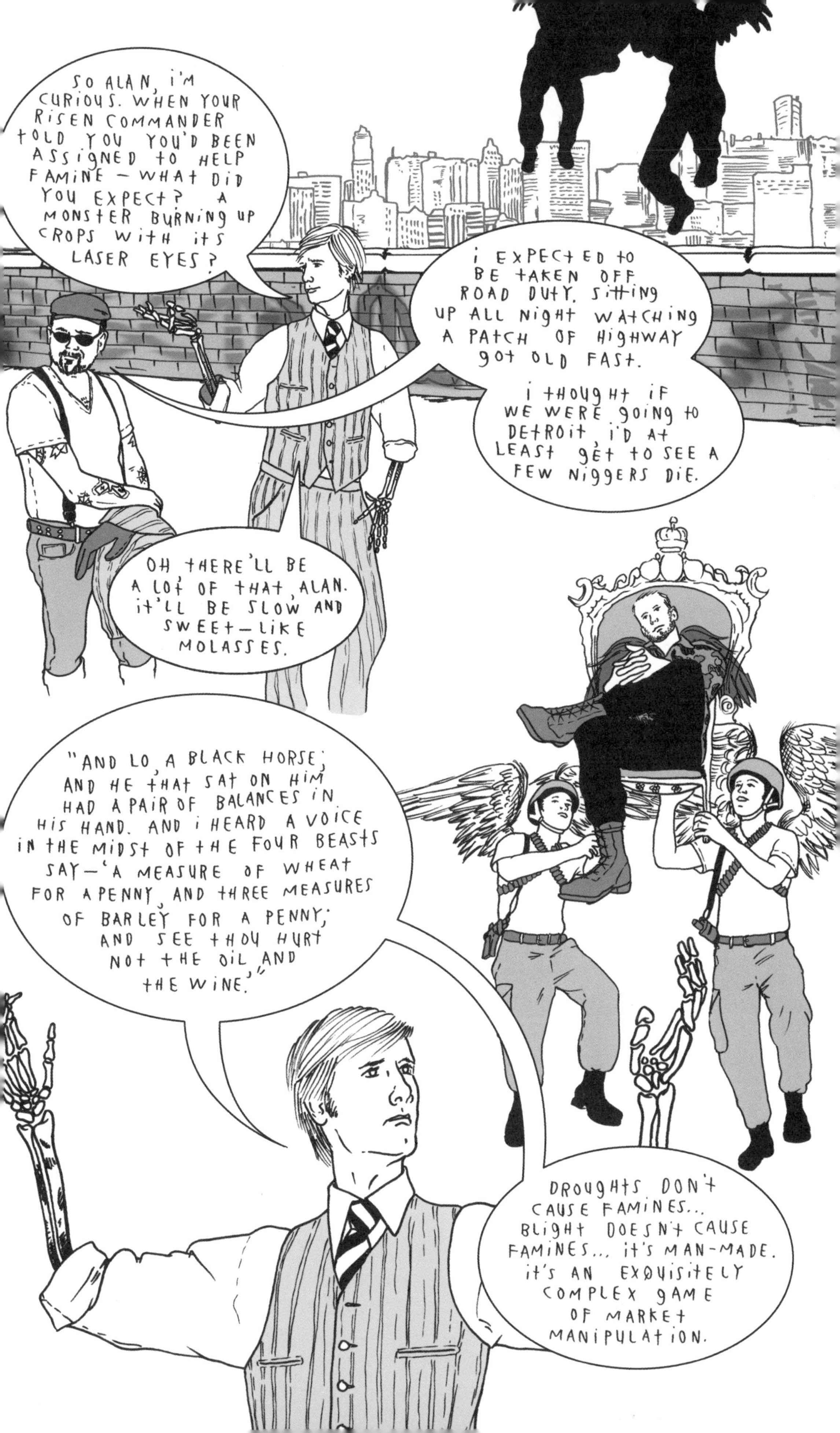
SO ALAN, I'M CURIOUS. WHEN YOUR RISEN COMMANDER TOLD YOU YOU'D BEEN ASSIGNED TO HELP FAMINE – WHAT DID YOU EXPECT? A MONSTER BURNING UP CROPS WITH ITS LASER EYES?
I EXPECTED TO BE TAKEN OFF ROAD DUTY. SITTING UP ALL NIGHT WATCHING A PATCH OF HIGHWAY GOT OLD FAST.
I THOUGHT IF WE WERE GOING TO DETROIT, I'D AT LEAST GET TO SEE A FEW NIGGERS DIE.
OH THERE'LL BE A LOT OF THAT, ALAN. IT'LL BE SLOW AND SWEET–LIKE MOLASSES.
"AND LO, A BLACK HORSE; AND HE THAT SAT ON HIM HAD A PAIR OF BALANCES IN HIS HAND. AND I HEARD A VOICE IN THE MIDST OF THE FOUR BEASTS SAY–'A MEASURE OF WHEAT FOR A PENNY, AND THREE MEASURES OF BARLEY FOR A PENNY; AND SEE THOU HURT NOT THE OIL AND THE WINE.'"
DROUGHTS DON'T CAUSE FAMINES... BLIGHT DOESN'T CAUSE FAMINES... IT'S MAN-MADE. IT'S AN EXQUISITELY COMPLEX GAME OF MARKET MANIPULATION.

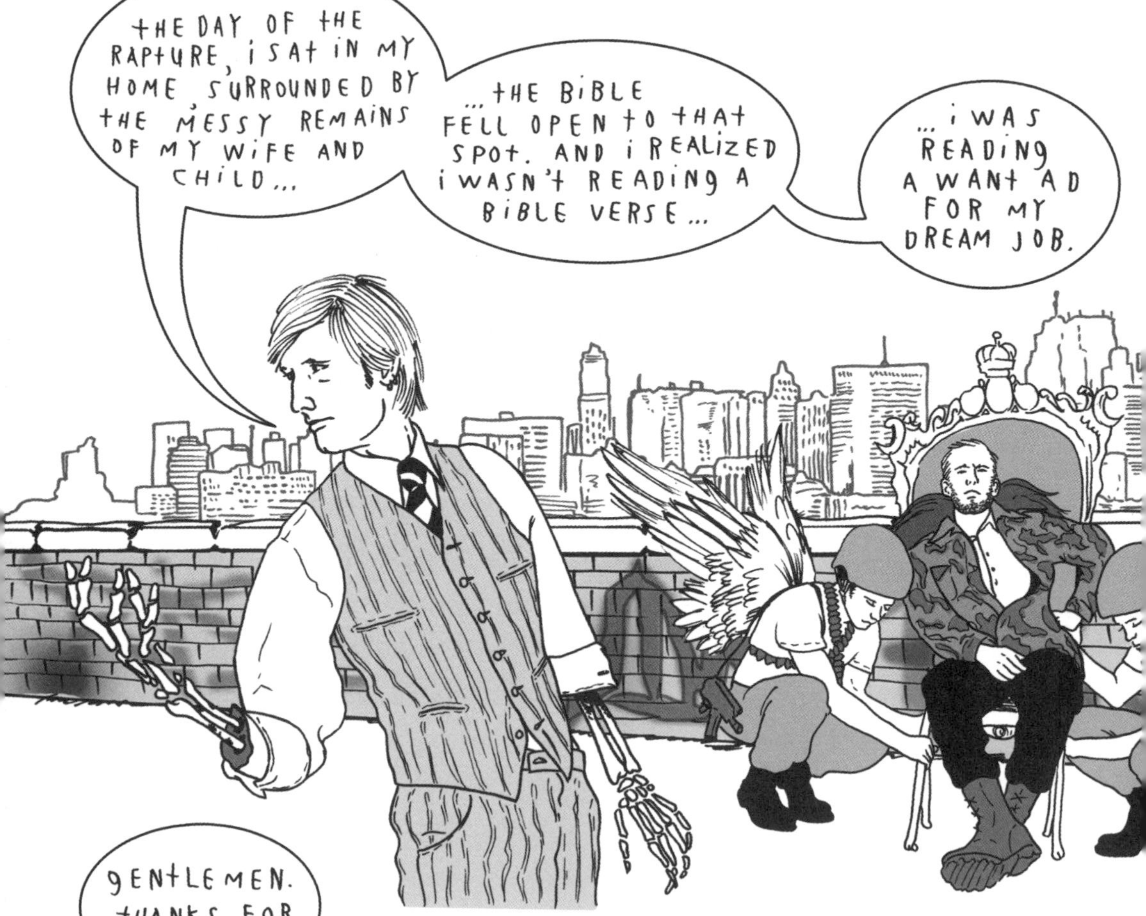
THE DAY OF THE RAPTURE, I SAT IN MY HOME, SURROUNDED BY THE MESSY REMAINS OF MY WIFE AND CHILD...
...THE BIBLE FELL OPEN TO THAT SPOT. AND I REALIZED I WASN'T READING A BIBLE VERSE...
...I WAS READING A WANT AD FOR MY DREAM JOB.

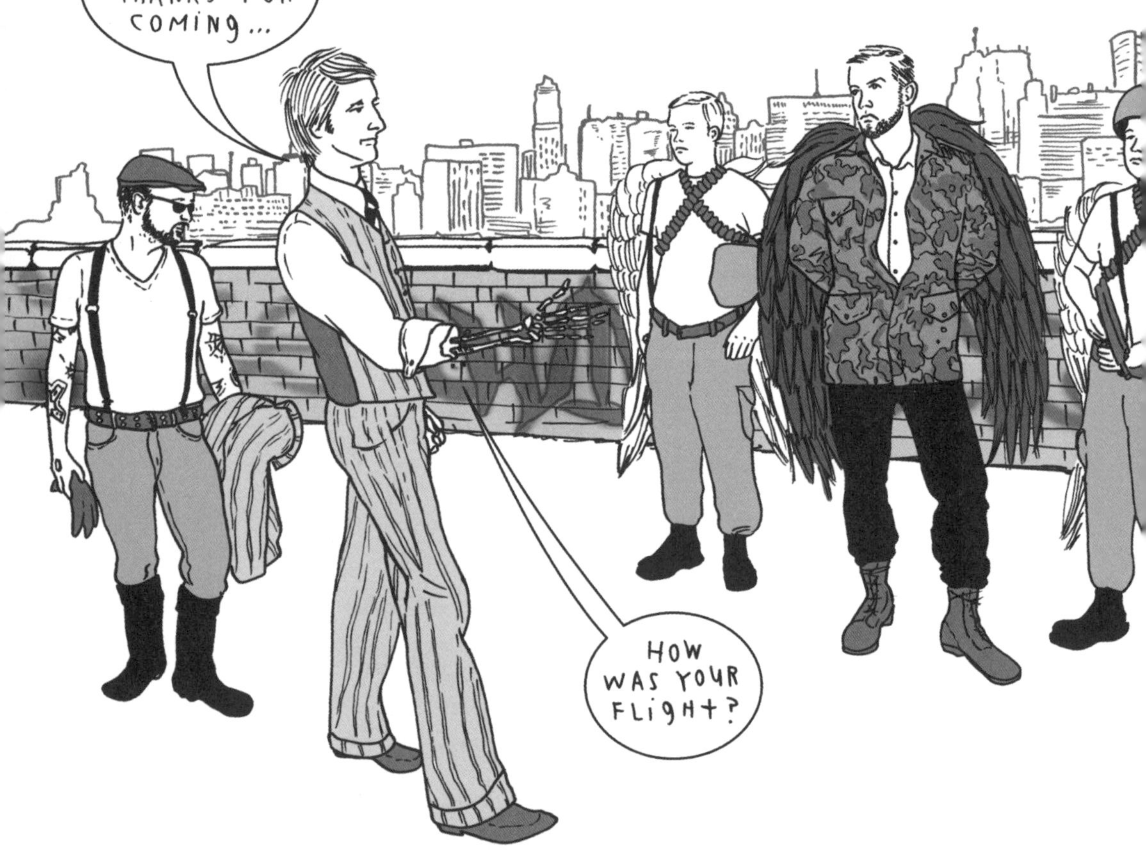
GENTLEMEN. THANKS FOR COMING...
HOW WAS YOUR FLIGHT?

FOUR

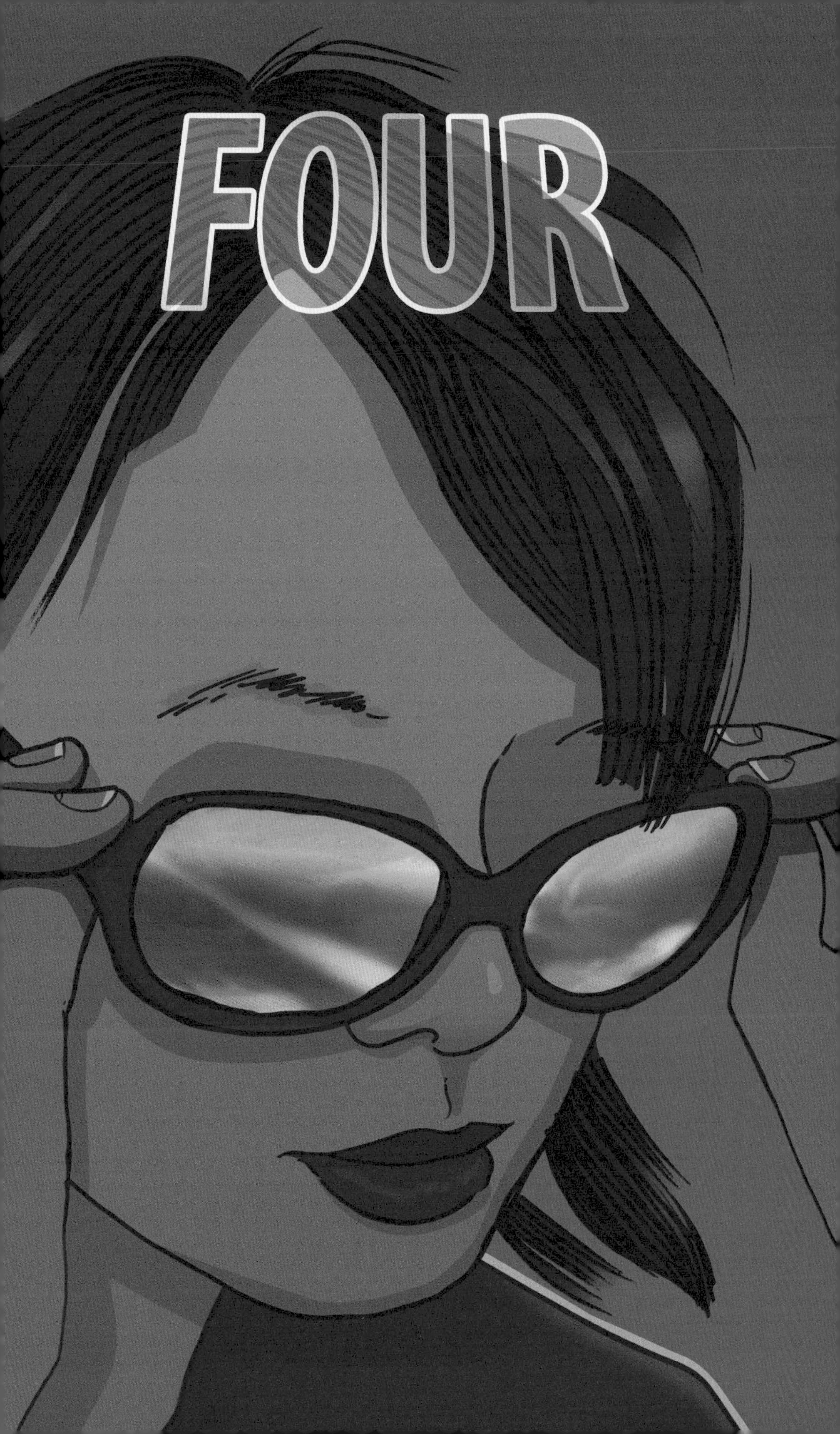

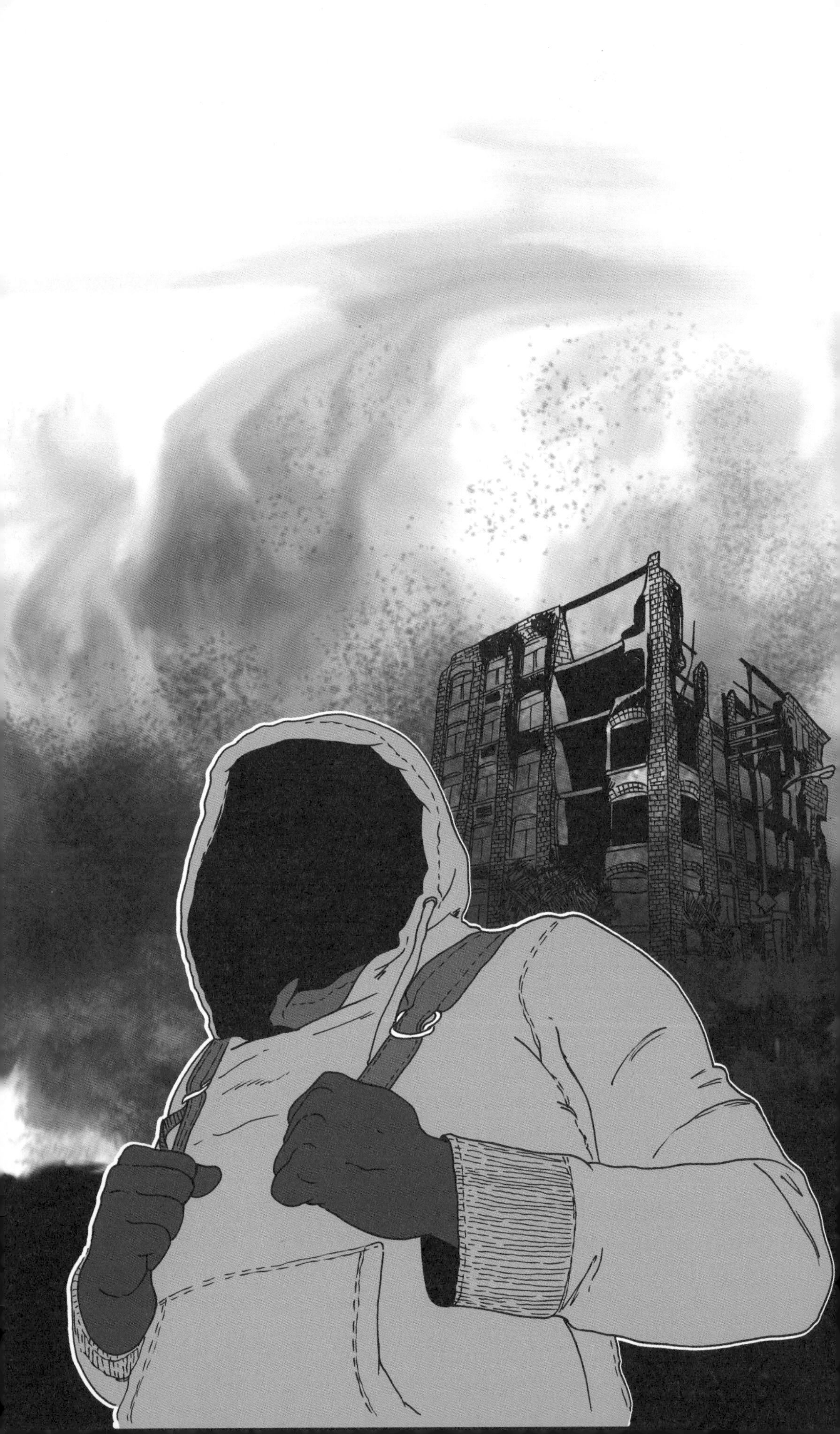

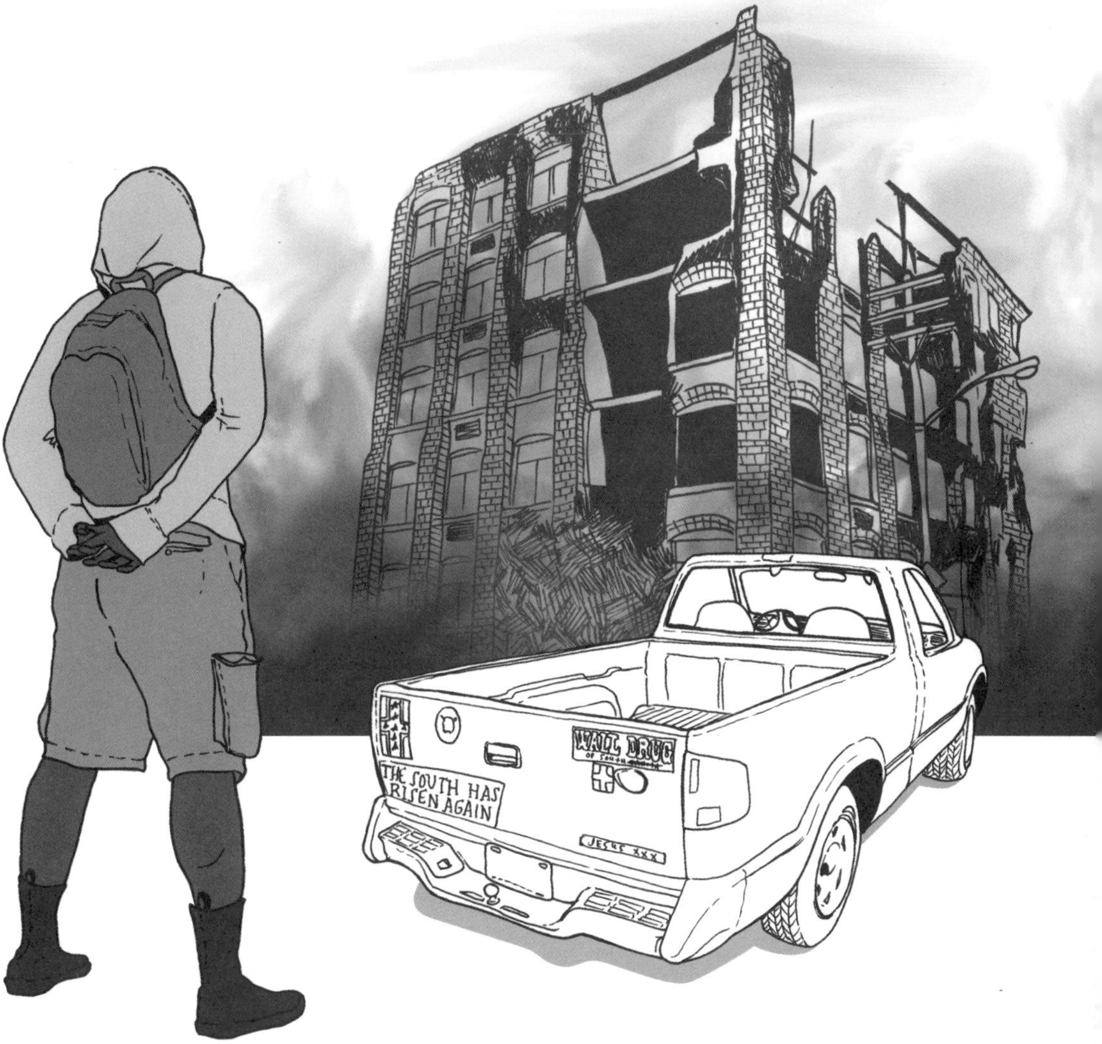
WALL DRUG
THE SOUTH HAS RISEN AGAIN
JESUS XXX

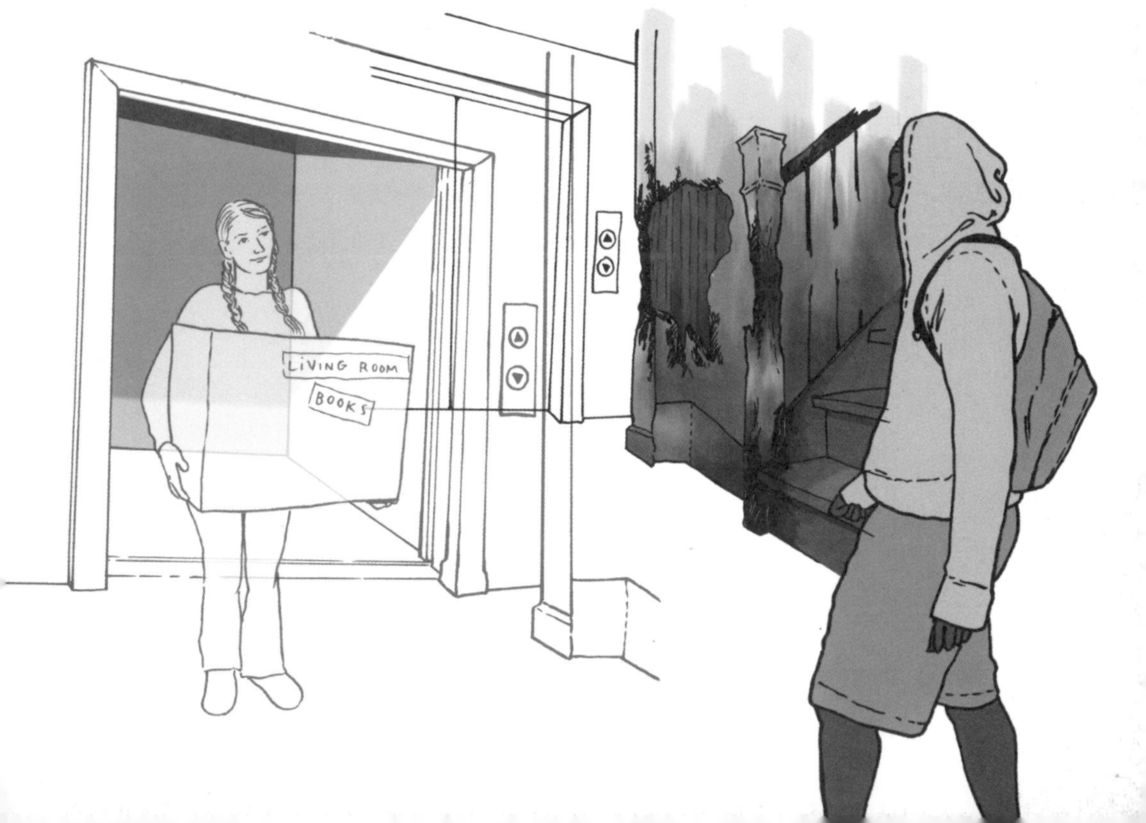
LIVING ROOM
BOOKS

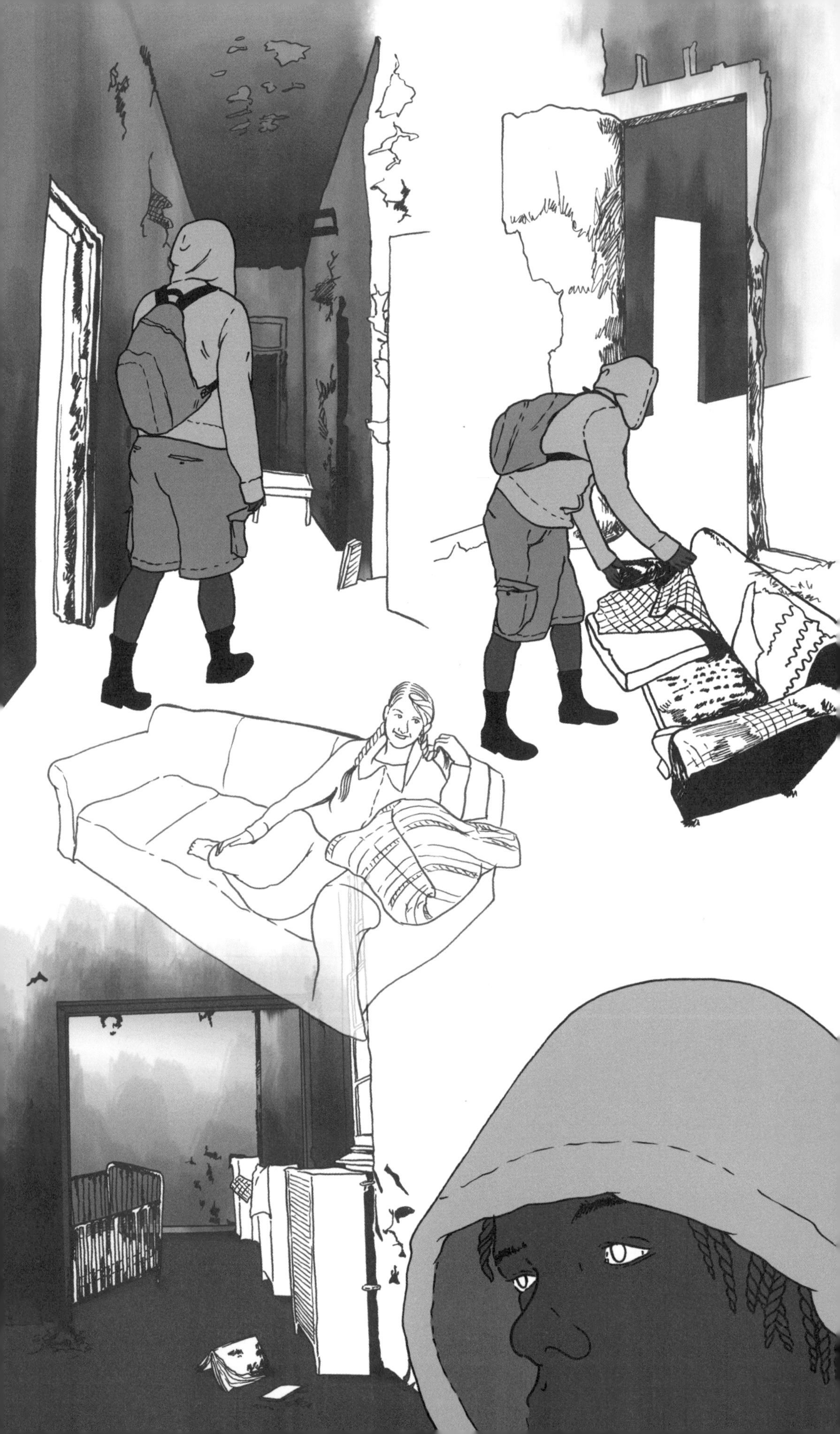

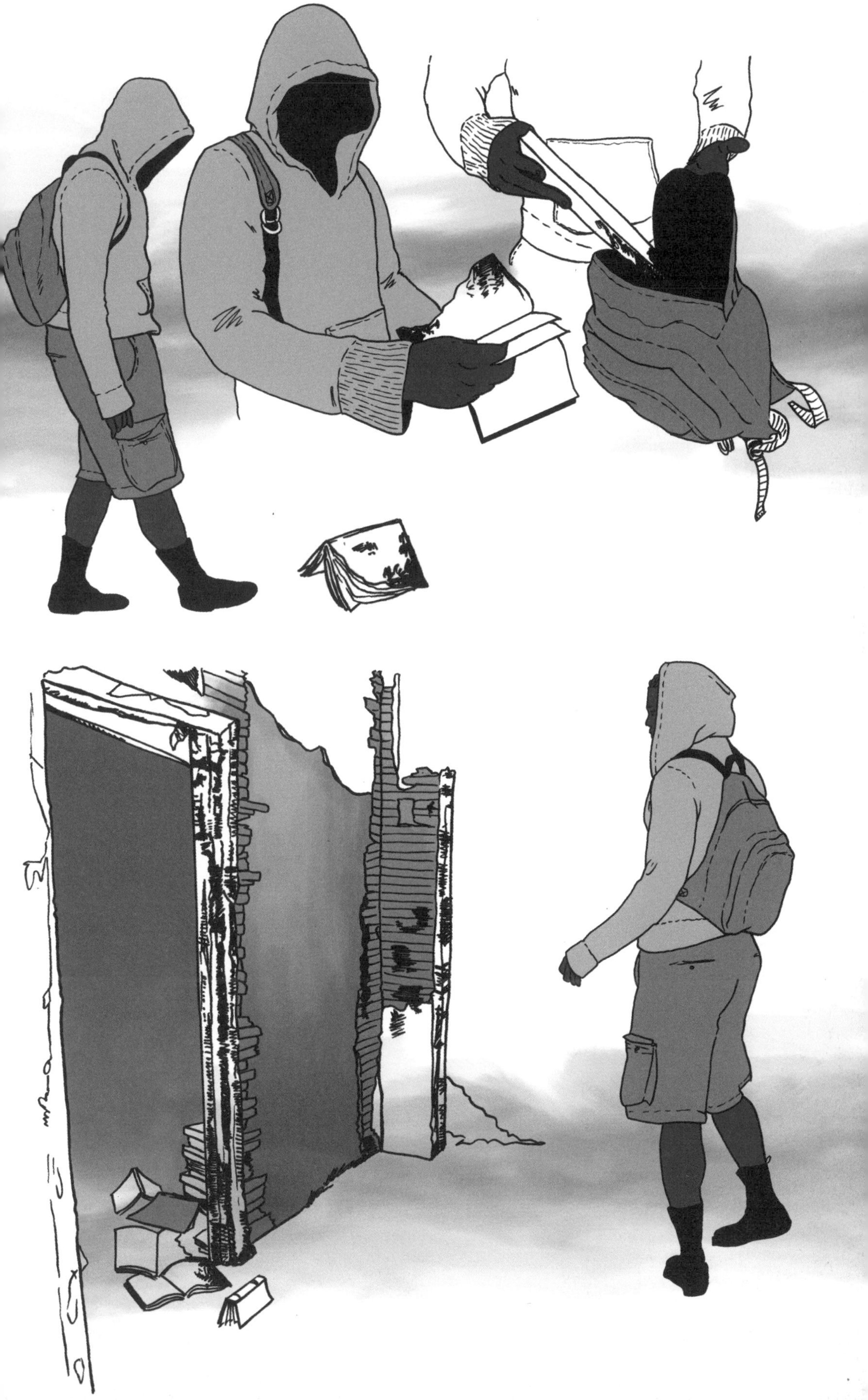

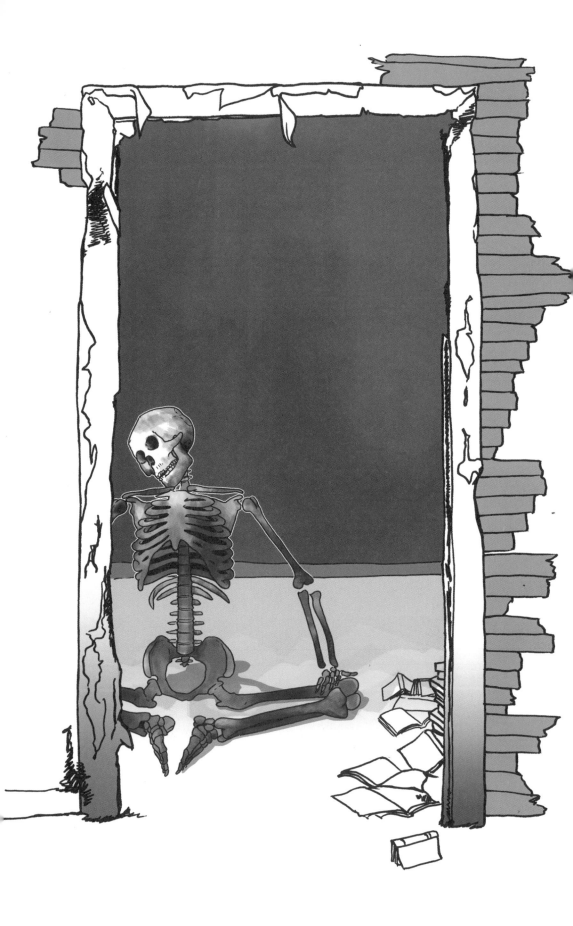

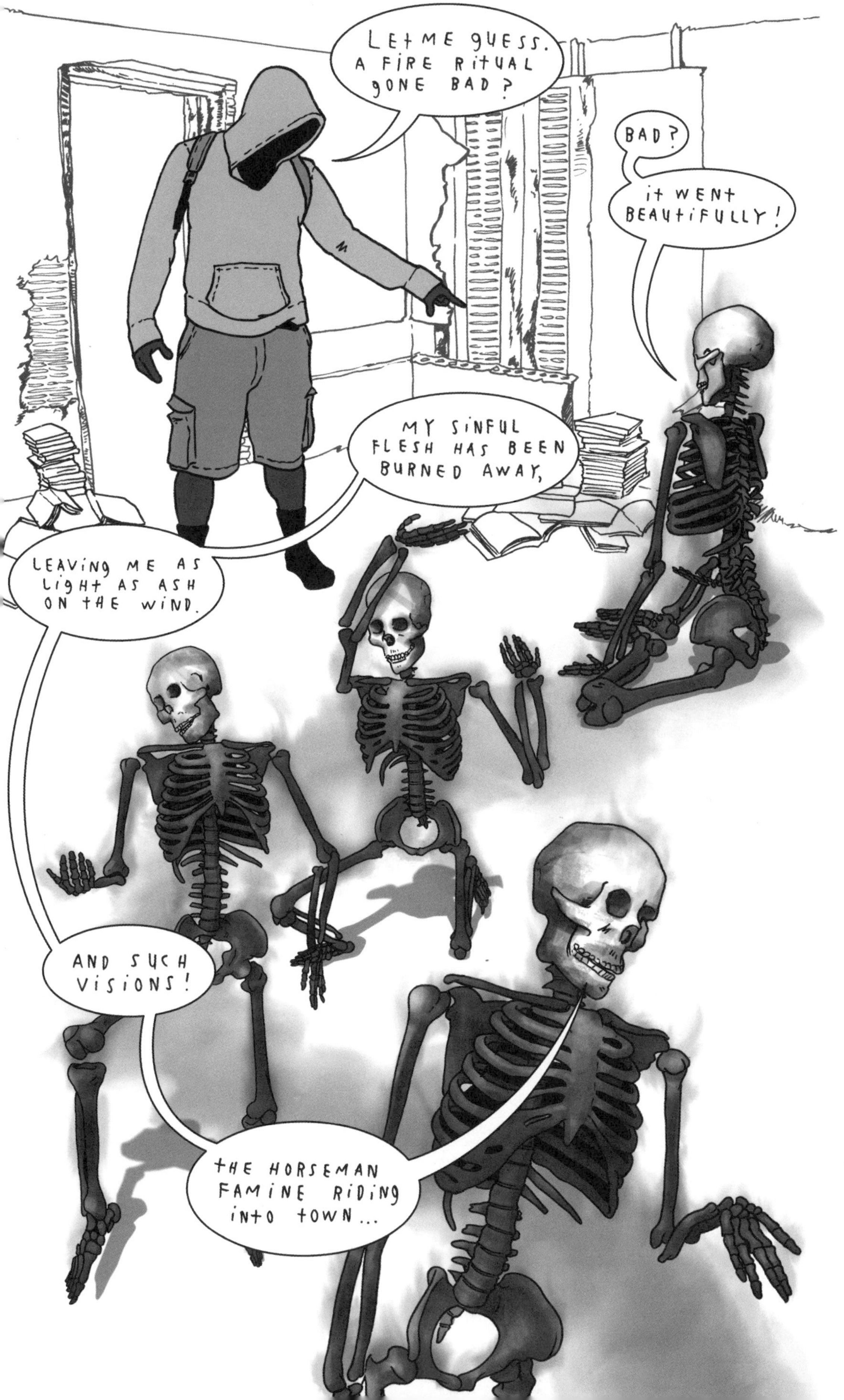
LET ME GUESS. A FIRE RITUAL GONE BAD?
BAD?
IT WENT BEAUTIFULLY!
MY SINFUL FLESH HAS BEEN BURNED AWAY,
LEAVING ME AS LIGHT AS ASH ON THE WIND.
AND SUCH VISIONS!
THE HORSEMAN FAMINE RIDING INTO TOWN...

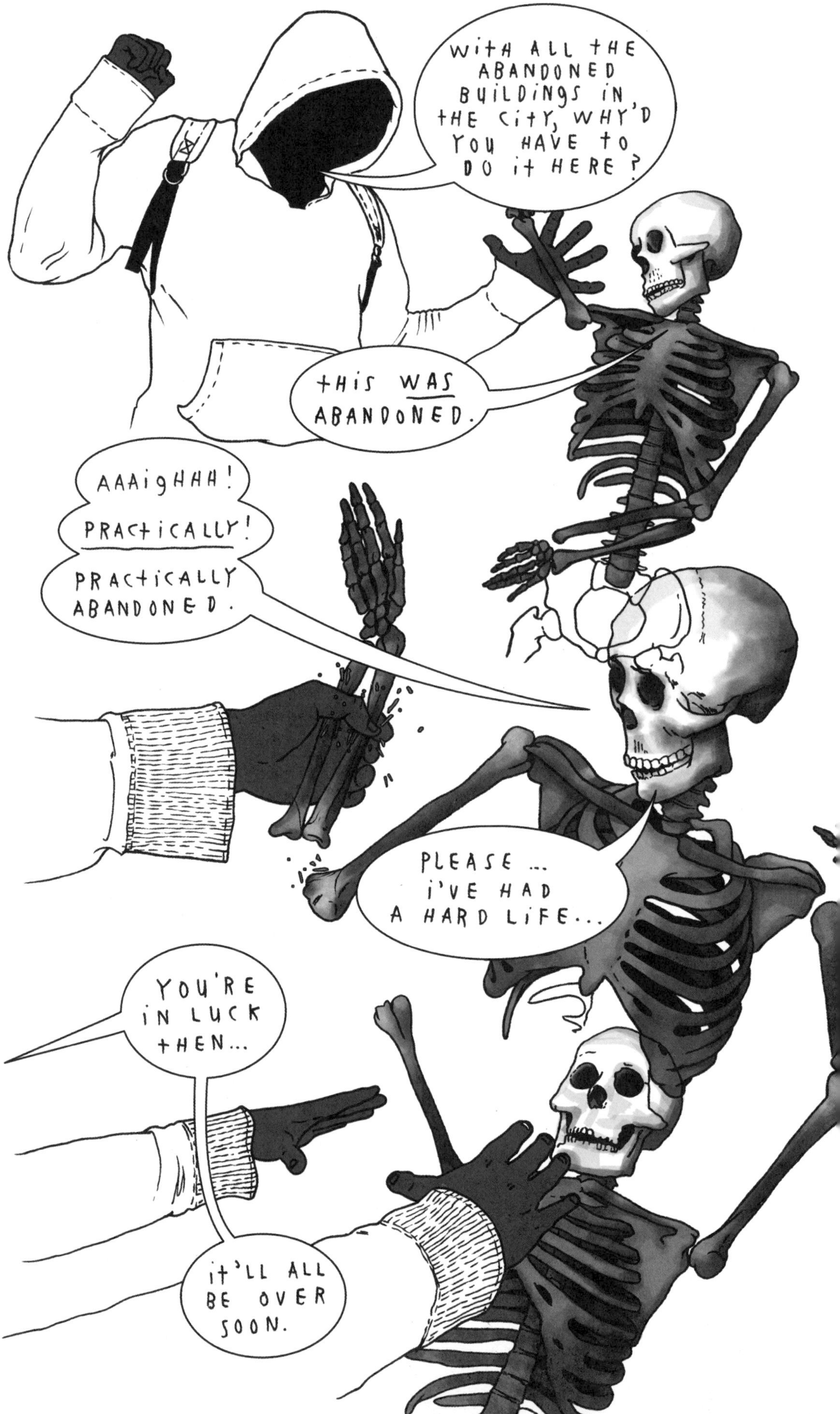
WITH ALL THE ABANDONED BUILDINGS IN THE CITY, WHY'D YOU HAVE TO DO IT HERE?
THIS WAS ABANDONED.
AAAIGHHH!
PRACTICALLY!
PRACTICALLY ABANDONED.
PLEASE ... I'VE HAD A HARD LIFE...
YOU'RE IN LUCK THEN...
IT'LL ALL BE OVER SOON.

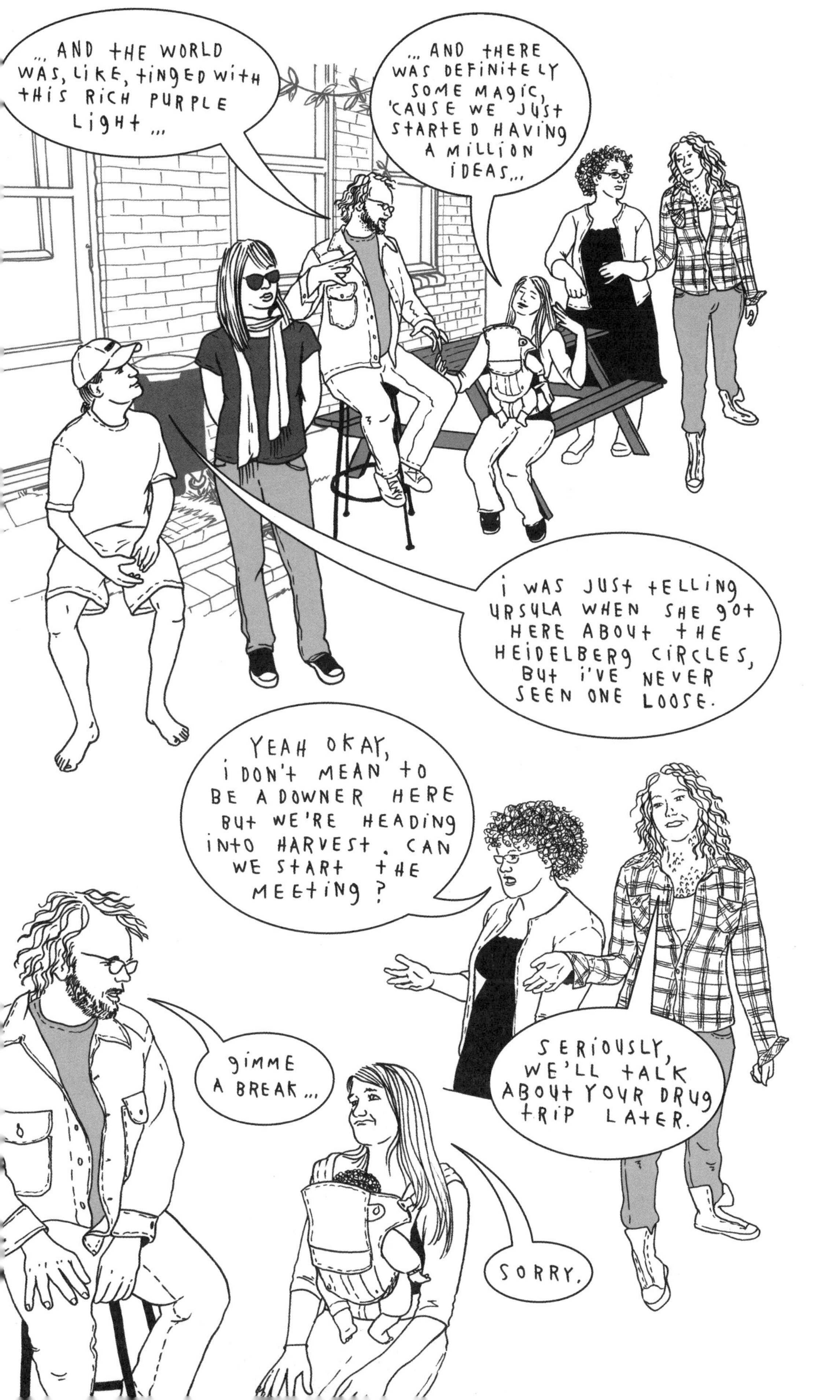
... AND THE WORLD WAS, LIKE, TINGED WITH THIS RICH PURPLE LIGHT ...
... AND THERE WAS DEFINITELY SOME MAGIC, 'CAUSE WE JUST STARTED HAVING A MILLION IDEAS...
I WAS JUST TELLING URSULA WHEN SHE GOT HERE ABOUT THE HEIDELBERG CIRCLES, BUT I'VE NEVER SEEN ONE LOOSE.
YEAH OKAY, I DON'T MEAN TO BE A DOWNER HERE BUT WE'RE HEADING INTO HARVEST. CAN WE START THE MEETING?
GIMME A BREAK...
SERIOUSLY, WE'LL TALK ABOUT YOUR DRUG TRIP LATER.
SORRY.

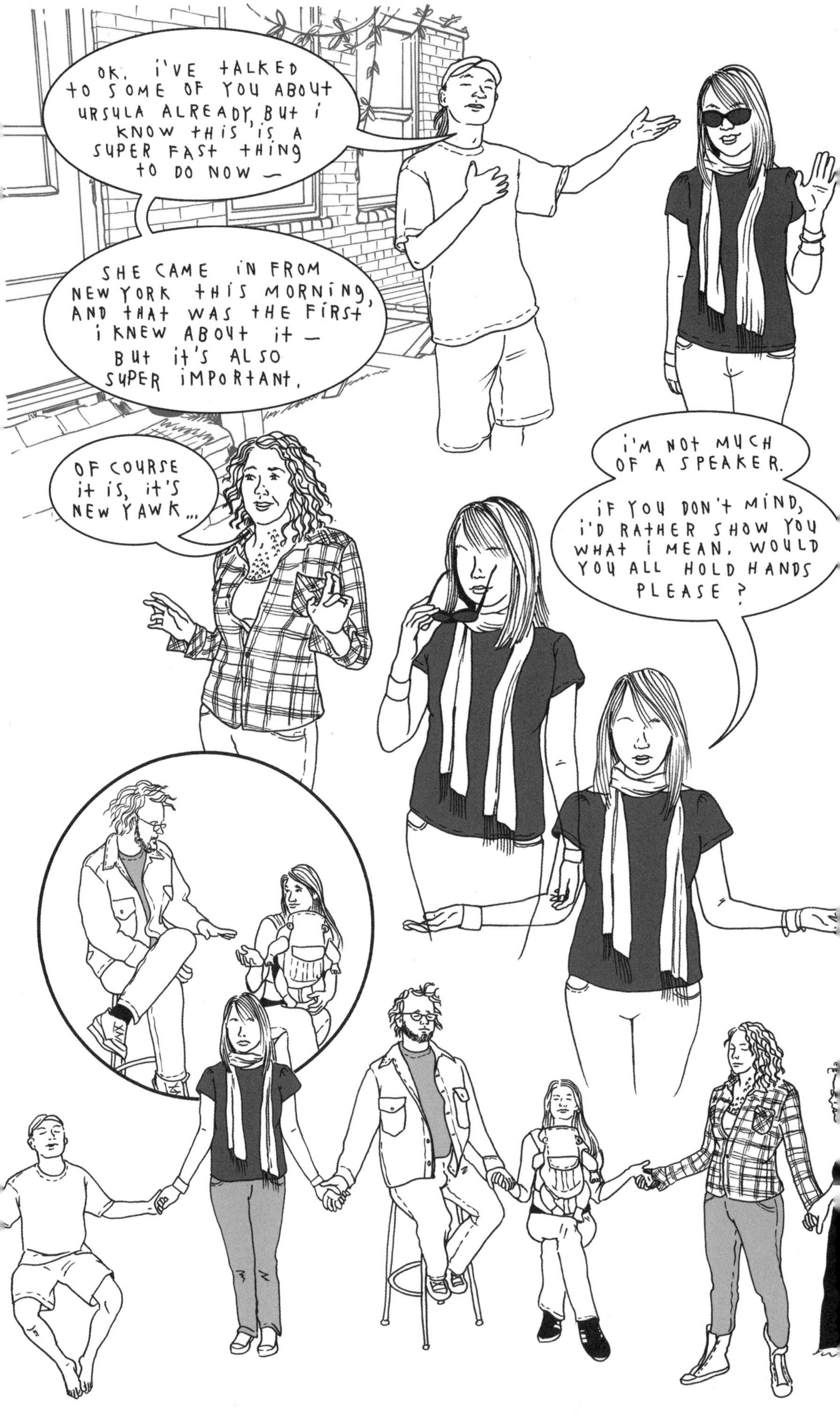
OK. I'VE TALKED TO SOME OF YOU ABOUT URSULA ALREADY, BUT I KNOW THIS IS A SUPER FAST THING TO DO NOW —
SHE CAME IN FROM NEW YORK THIS MORNING, AND THAT WAS THE FIRST I KNEW ABOUT IT — BUT IT'S ALSO SUPER IMPORTANT.
OF COURSE IT IS, IT'S NEW YAWK...
I'M NOT MUCH OF A SPEAKER.
IF YOU DON'T MIND, I'D RATHER SHOW YOU WHAT I MEAN. WOULD YOU ALL HOLD HANDS PLEASE?

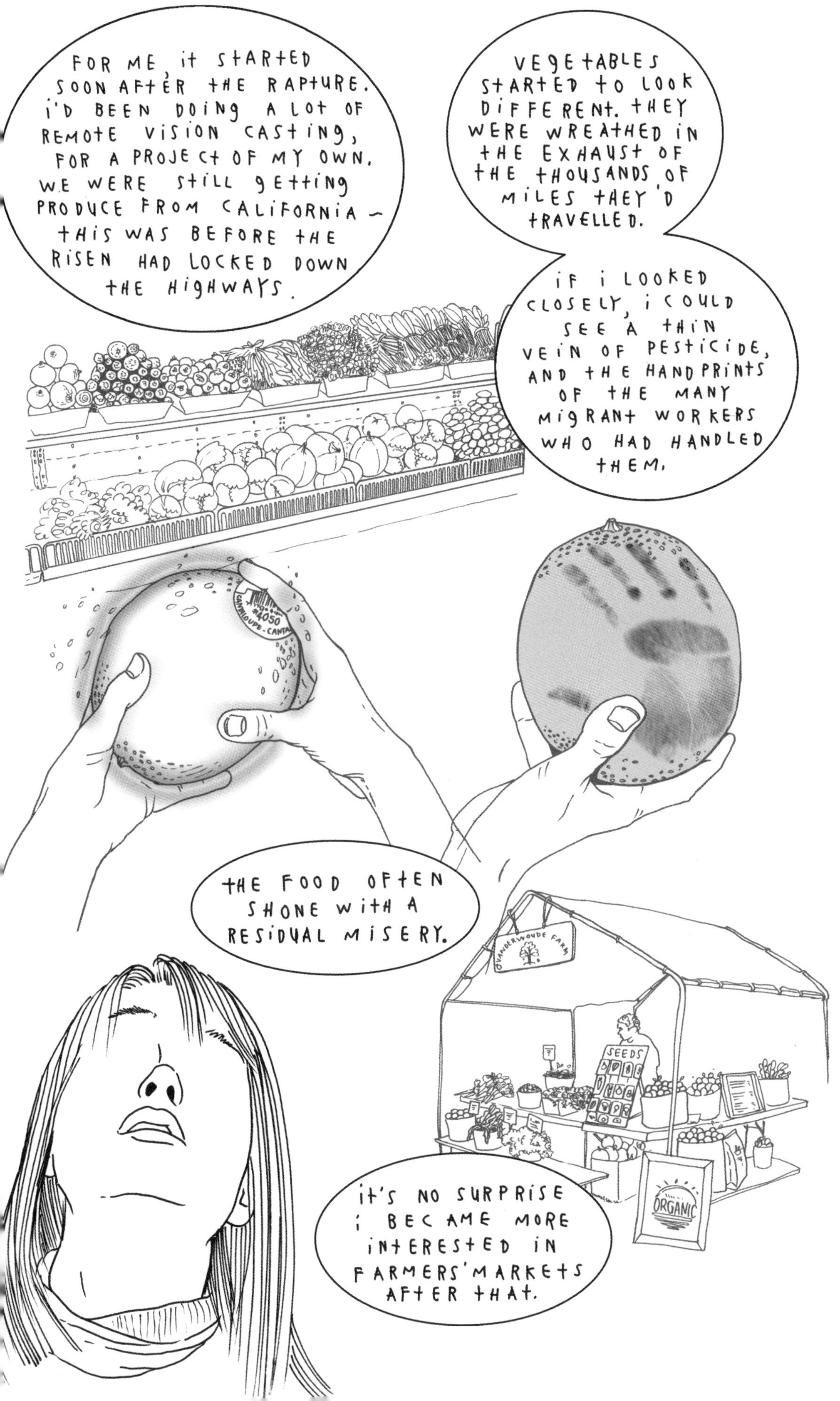
FOR ME, IT STARTED SOON AFTER THE RAPTURE. I'D BEEN DOING A LOT OF REMOTE VISION CASTING, FOR A PROJECT OF MY OWN. WE WERE STILL GETTING PRODUCE FROM CALIFORNIA — THIS WAS BEFORE THE RISEN HAD LOCKED DOWN THE HIGHWAYS.
VEGETABLES STARTED TO LOOK DIFFERENT. THEY WERE WREATHED IN THE EXHAUST OF THE THOUSANDS OF MILES THEY'D TRAVELLED.
IF I LOOKED CLOSELY, I COULD SEE A THIN VEIN OF PESTICIDE, AND THE HANDPRINTS OF THE MANY MIGRANT WORKERS WHO HAD HANDLED THEM.
#4050
CANTALOUPE-CANTA
THE FOOD OFTEN SHONE WITH A RESIDUAL MISERY.
VANDERWOUDE FARM
SEEDS
ORGANIC
IT'S NO SURPRISE I BECAME MORE INTERESTED IN FARMERS' MARKETS AFTER THAT.

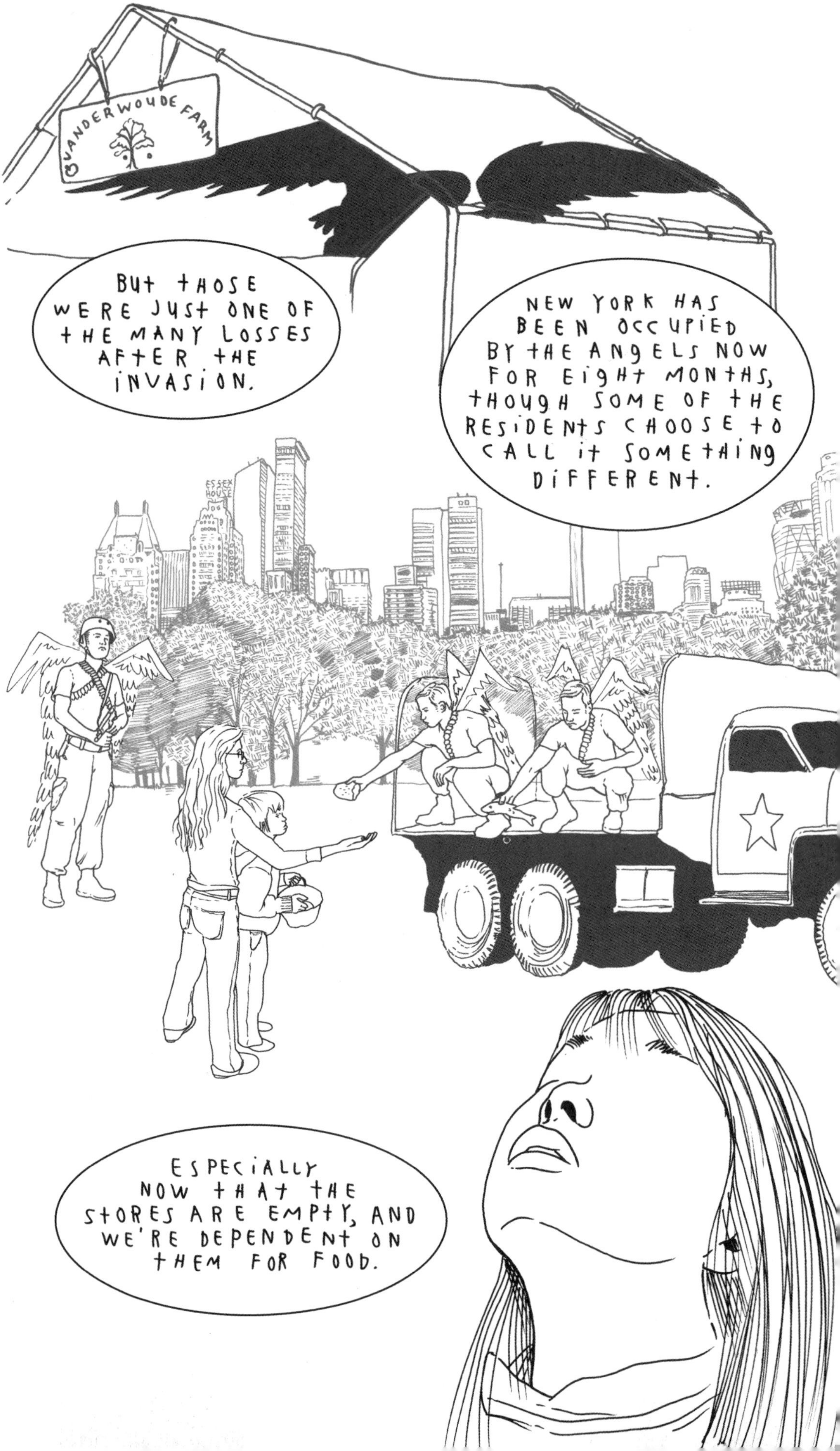
VANDERWOUDE FARM
BUT THOSE WERE JUST ONE OF THE MANY LOSSES AFTER THE INVASION.
NEW YORK HAS BEEN OCCUPIED BY THE ANGELS NOW FOR EIGHT MONTHS, THOUGH SOME OF THE RESIDENTS CHOOSE TO CALL IT SOMETHING DIFFERENT.
ESSEX HOUSE
ESPECIALLY NOW THAT THE STORES ARE EMPTY, AND WE'RE DEPENDENT ON THEM FOR FOOD.

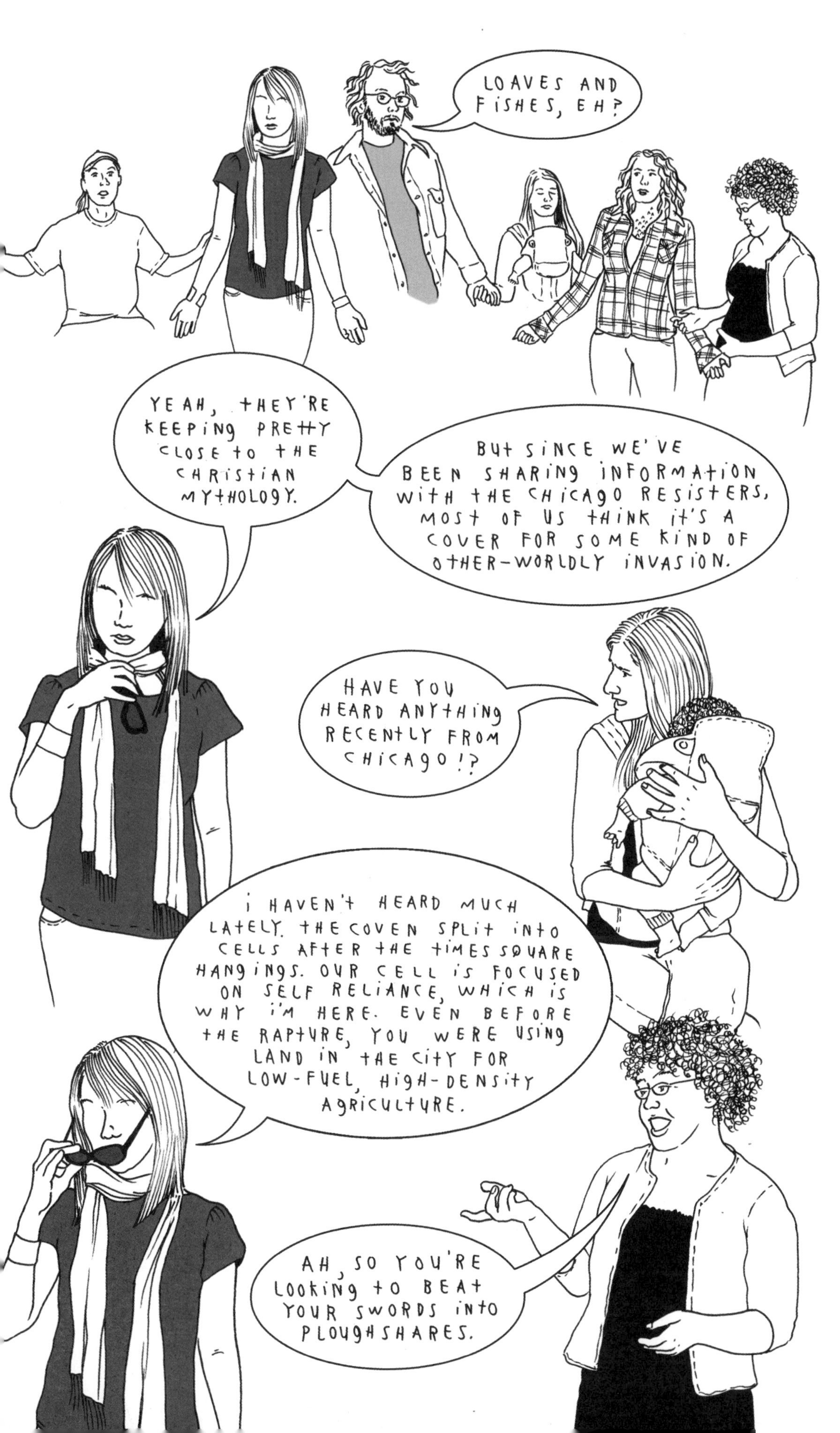
LOAVES AND FISHES, EH?
YEAH, THEY'RE KEEPING PRETTY CLOSE TO THE CHRISTIAN MYTHOLOGY.
BUT SINCE WE'VE BEEN SHARING INFORMATION WITH THE CHICAGO RESISTERS, MOST OF US THINK IT'S A COVER FOR SOME KIND OF OTHER-WORLDLY INVASION.
HAVE YOU HEARD ANYTHING RECENTLY FROM CHICAGO!?
I HAVEN'T HEARD MUCH LATELY. THE COVEN SPLIT INTO CELLS AFTER THE TIMES SQUARE HANGINGS. OUR CELL IS FOCUSED ON SELF RELIANCE, WHICH IS WHY I'M HERE. EVEN BEFORE THE RAPTURE, YOU WERE USING LAND IN THE CITY FOR LOW-FUEL, HIGH-DENSITY AGRICULTURE.
AH, SO YOU'RE LOOKING TO BEAT YOUR SWORDS INTO PLOUGHSHARES.

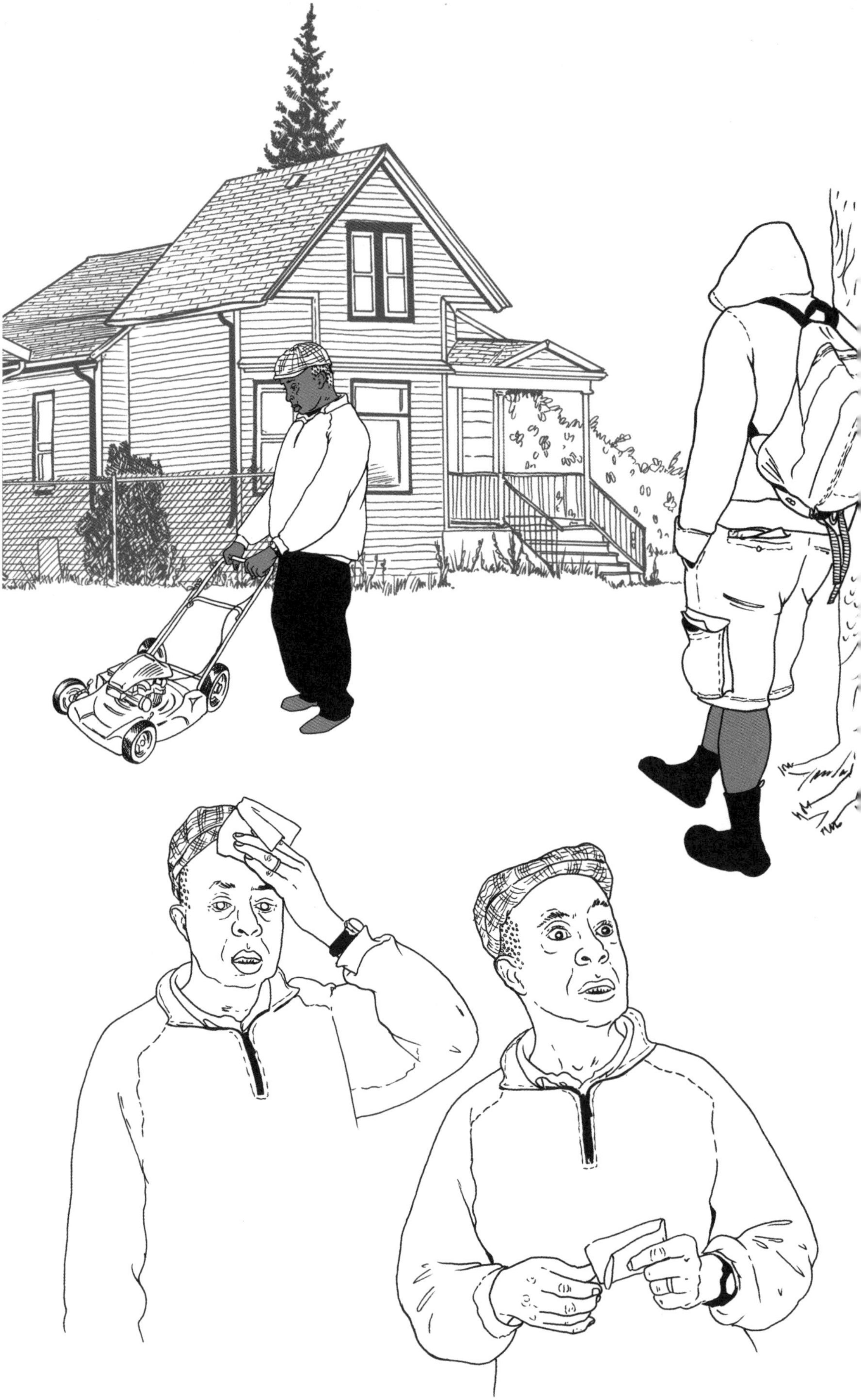

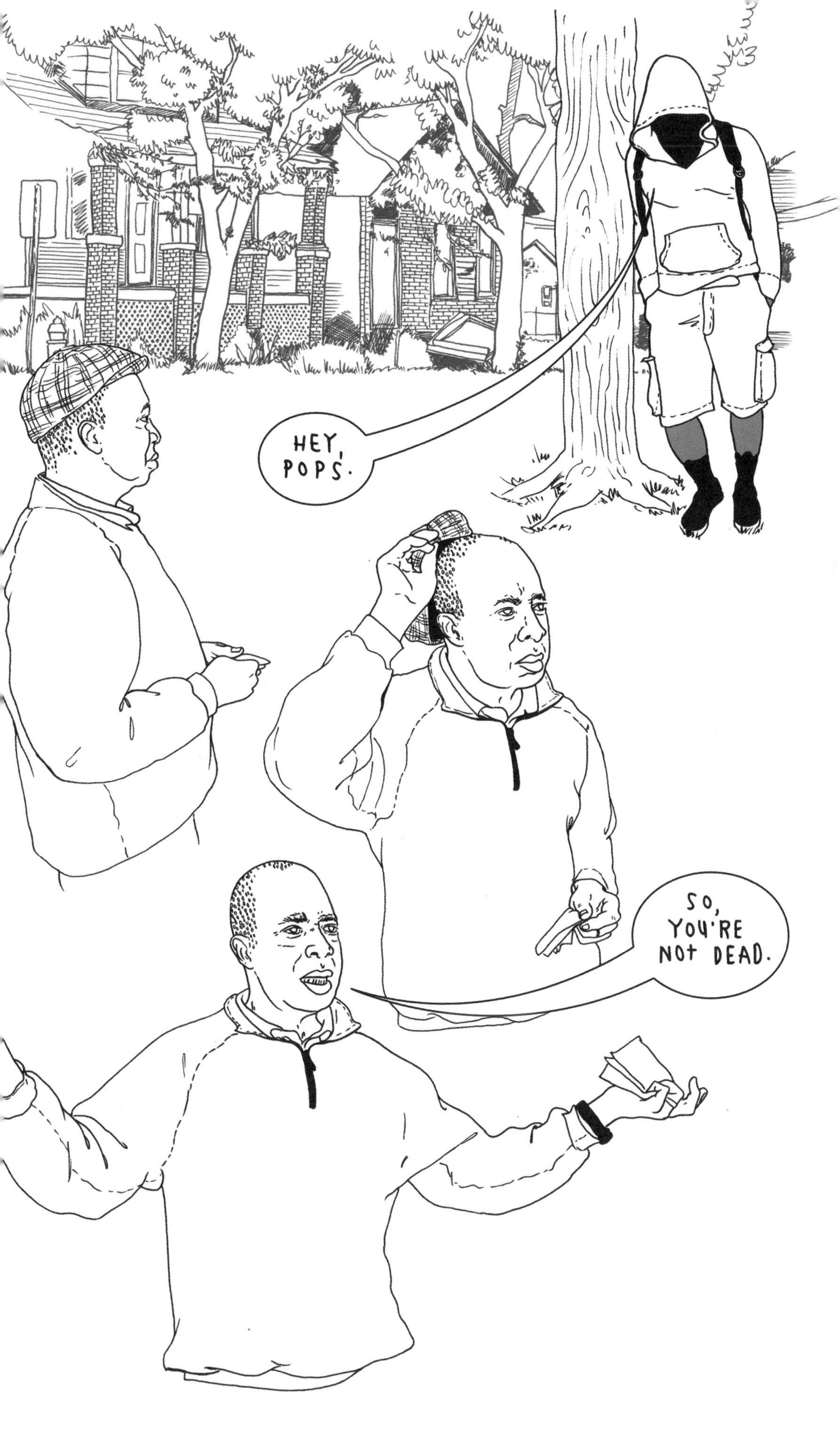
HEY, POPS!
SO, YOU'RE NOT DEAD.

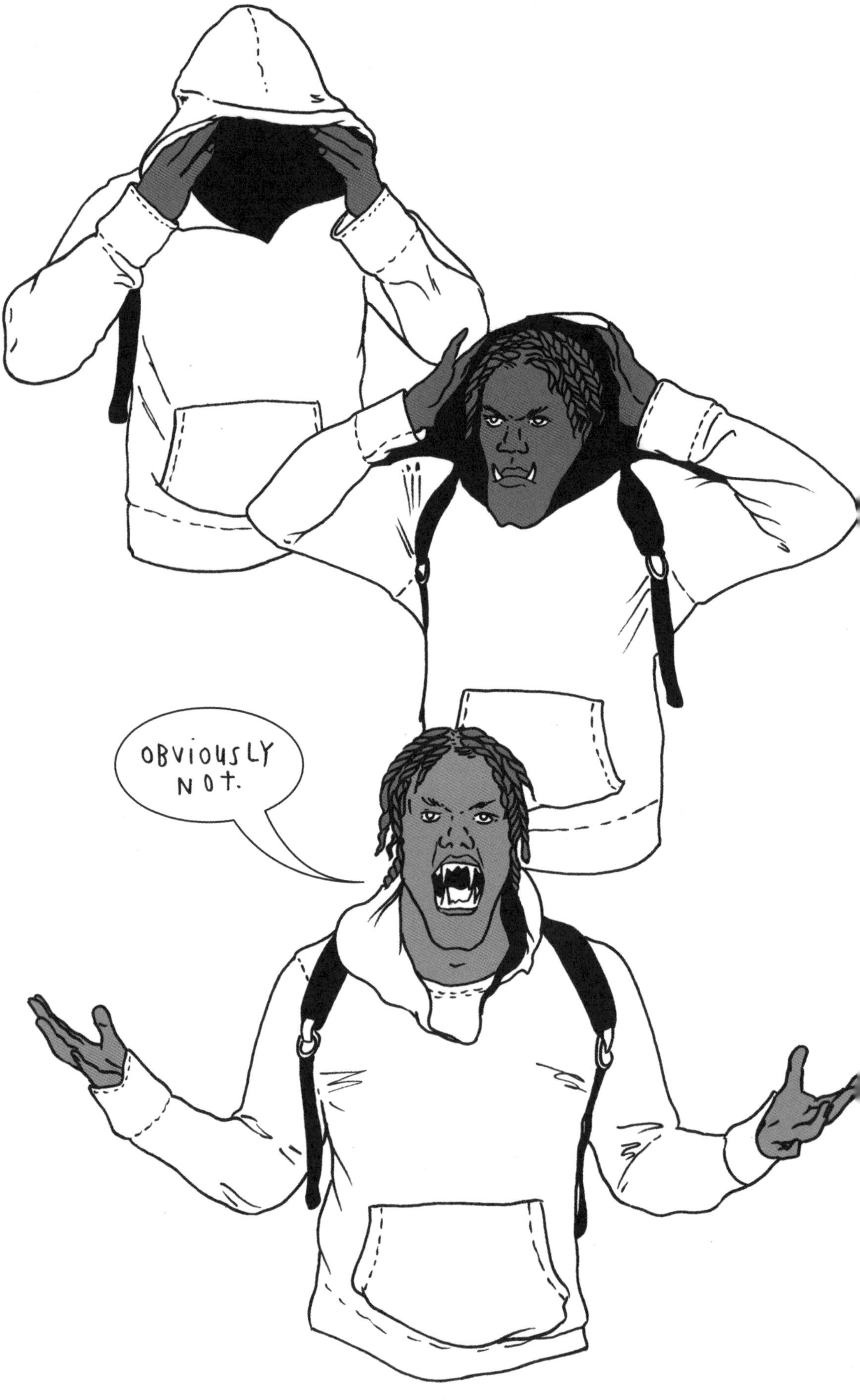
OBVIOUSLY NOT.

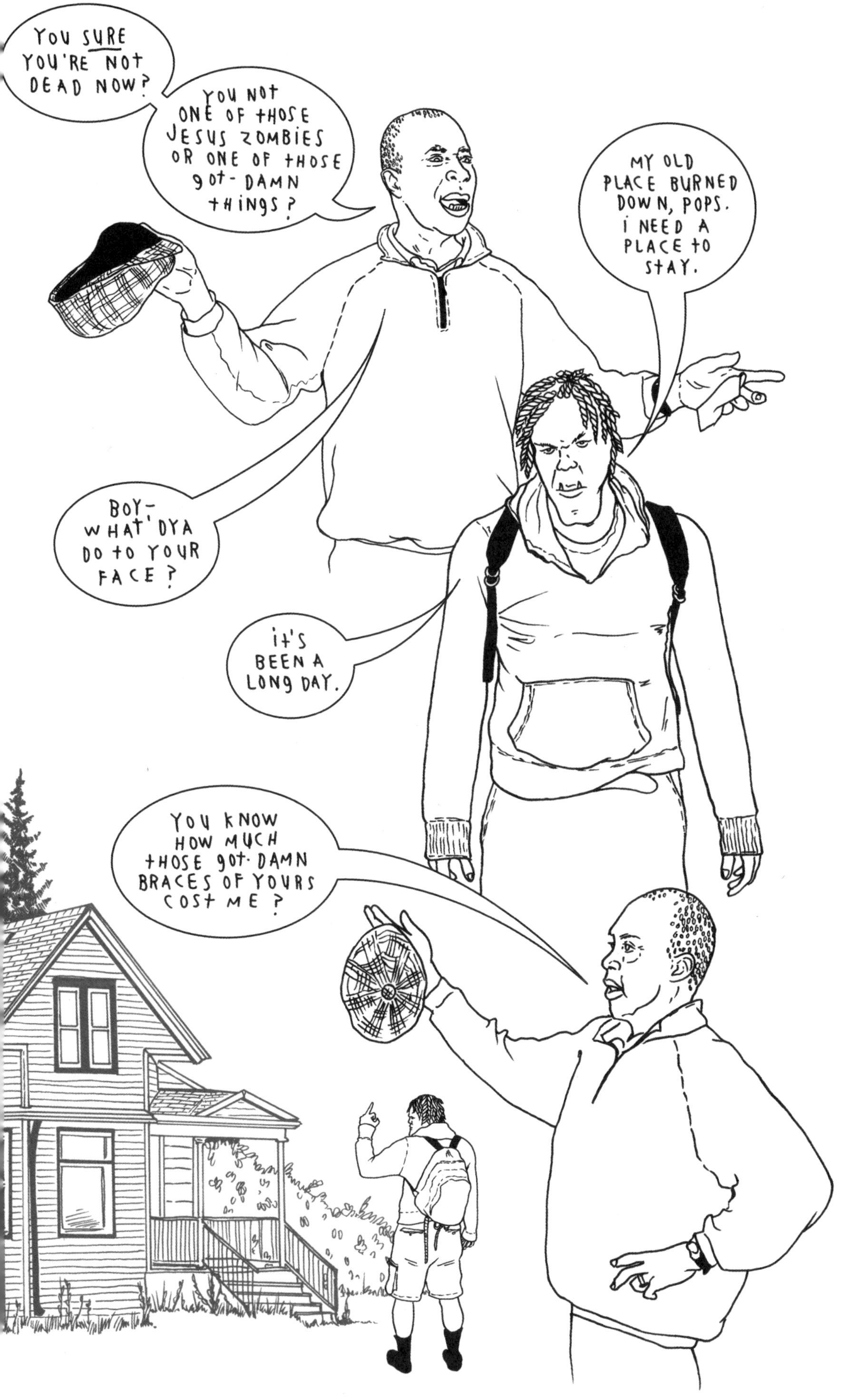
YOU SURE YOU'RE NOT DEAD NOW?
YOU NOT ONE OF THOSE JESUS ZOMBIES OR ONE OF THOSE GOT-DAMN THINGS?
MY OLD PLACE BURNED DOWN, POPS. I NEED A PLACE TO STAY.
BOY- WHAT'DYA DO TO YOUR FACE?
IT'S BEEN A LONG DAY.
YOU KNOW HOW MUCH THOSE GOT-DAMN BRACES OF YOURS COST ME?

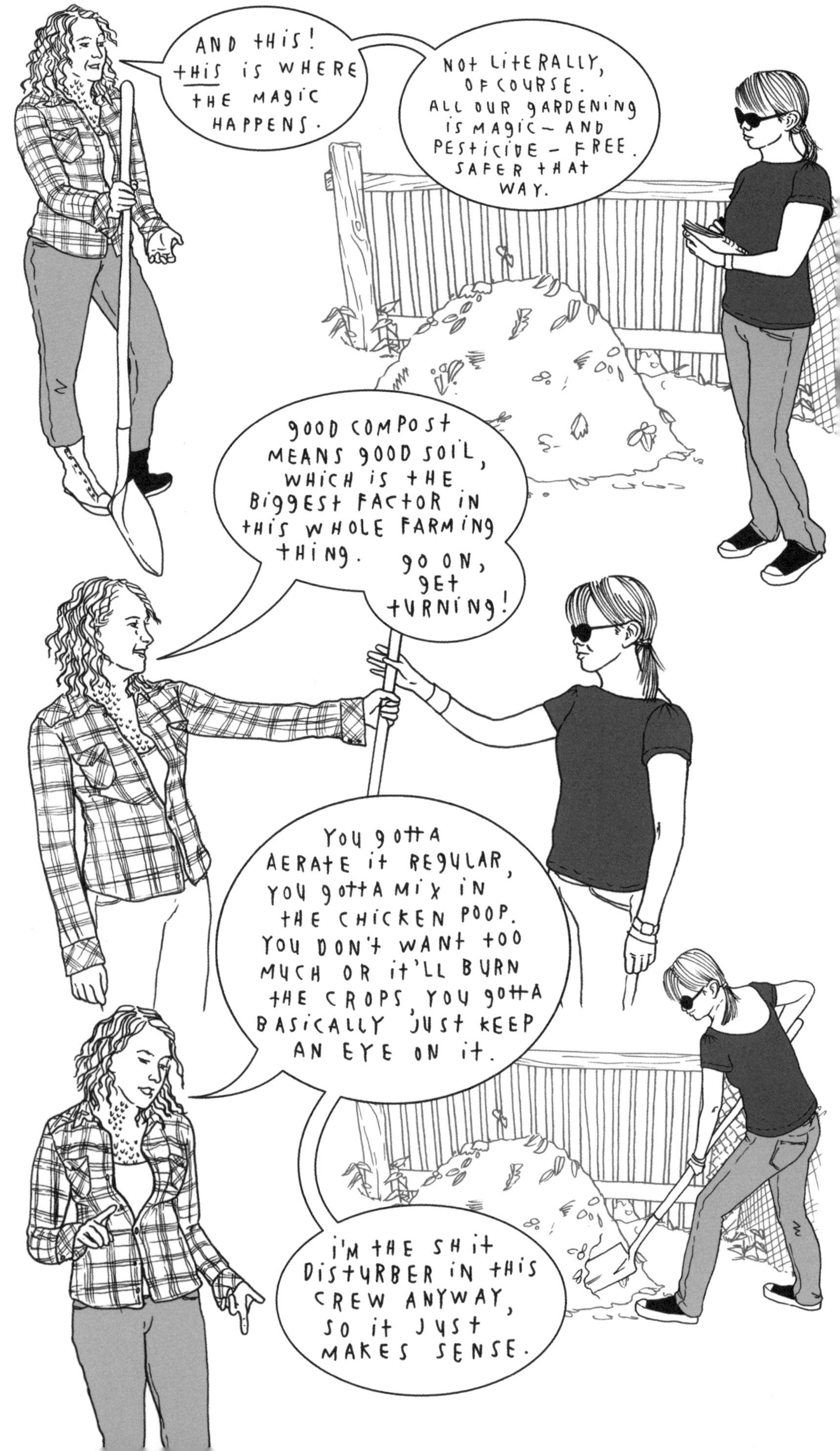
AND THIS! THIS IS WHERE THE MAGIC HAPPENS.
NOT LITERALLY, OF COURSE. ALL OUR GARDENING IS MAGIC— AND PESTICIDE— FREE. SAFER THAT WAY.
GOOD COMPOST MEANS GOOD SOIL, WHICH IS THE BIGGEST FACTOR IN THIS WHOLE FARMING THING.
GO ON, GET TURNING!
YOU GOTTA AERATE IT REGULAR, YOU GOTTA MIX IN THE CHICKEN POOP. YOU DON'T WANT TOO MUCH OR IT'LL BURN THE CROPS, YOU GOTTA BASICALLY JUST KEEP AN EYE ON IT.
I'M THE SHIT DISTURBER IN THIS CREW ANYWAY, SO IT JUST MAKES SENSE.

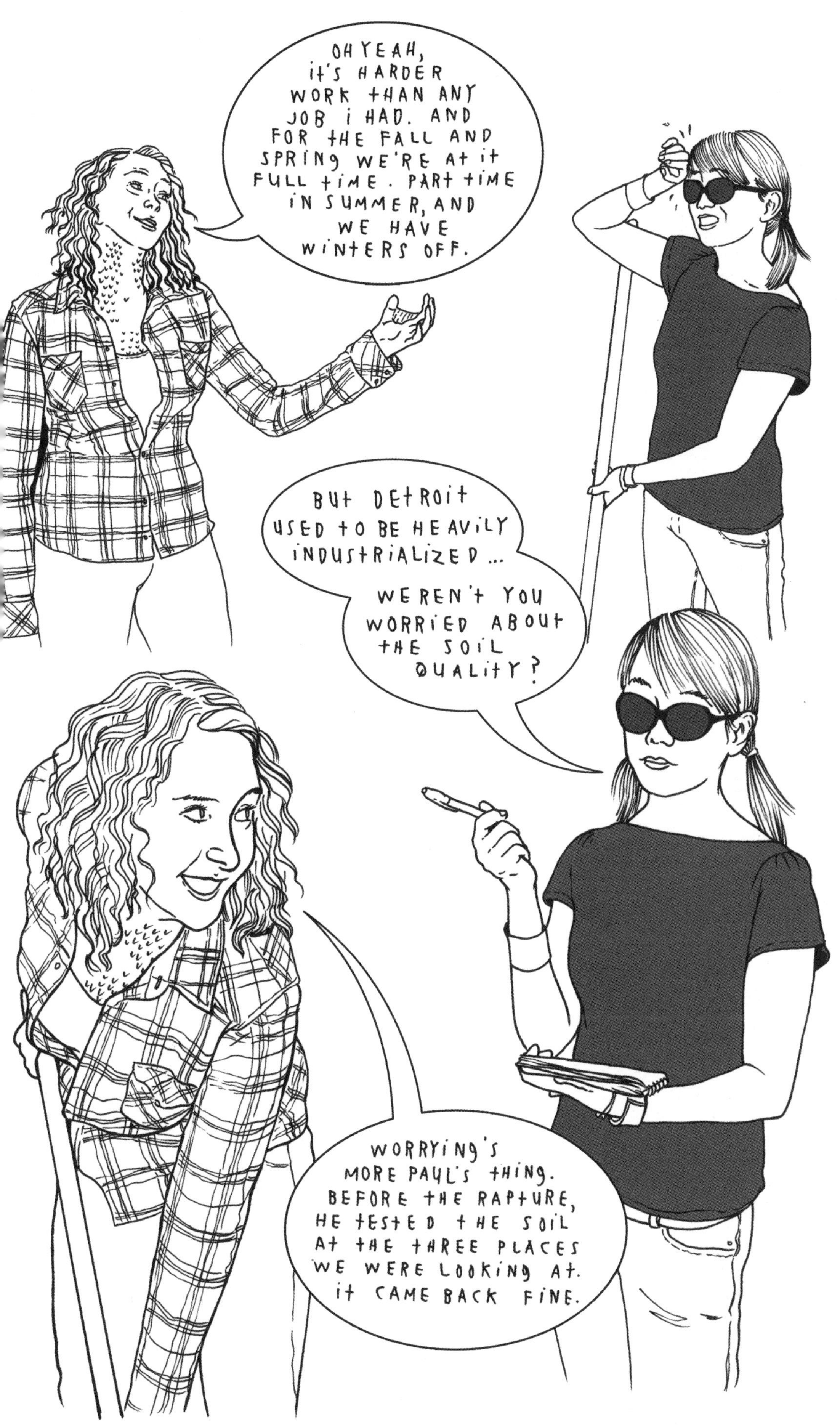
OH YEAH, it's HARDER WORK than ANY JOB i HAD. AND FOR the FALL AND SPRING WE'RE At it FULL time. PARt time iN SUMMER, AND WE HAVE WiNtERS OFF.
BUt DEtROit USED tO BE HEAViLY iNDUStRiALiZED...
WEREN't YOU WORRiED ABOUt the SOiL QUALitY?
WORRYiNG'S MORE PAUL'S tHiNG. BEFORE tHE RAPtURE, HE tEStED tHE SOiL At tHE tHREE PLACES WE WERE LOOKiNG At. it CAME BACK FiNE.

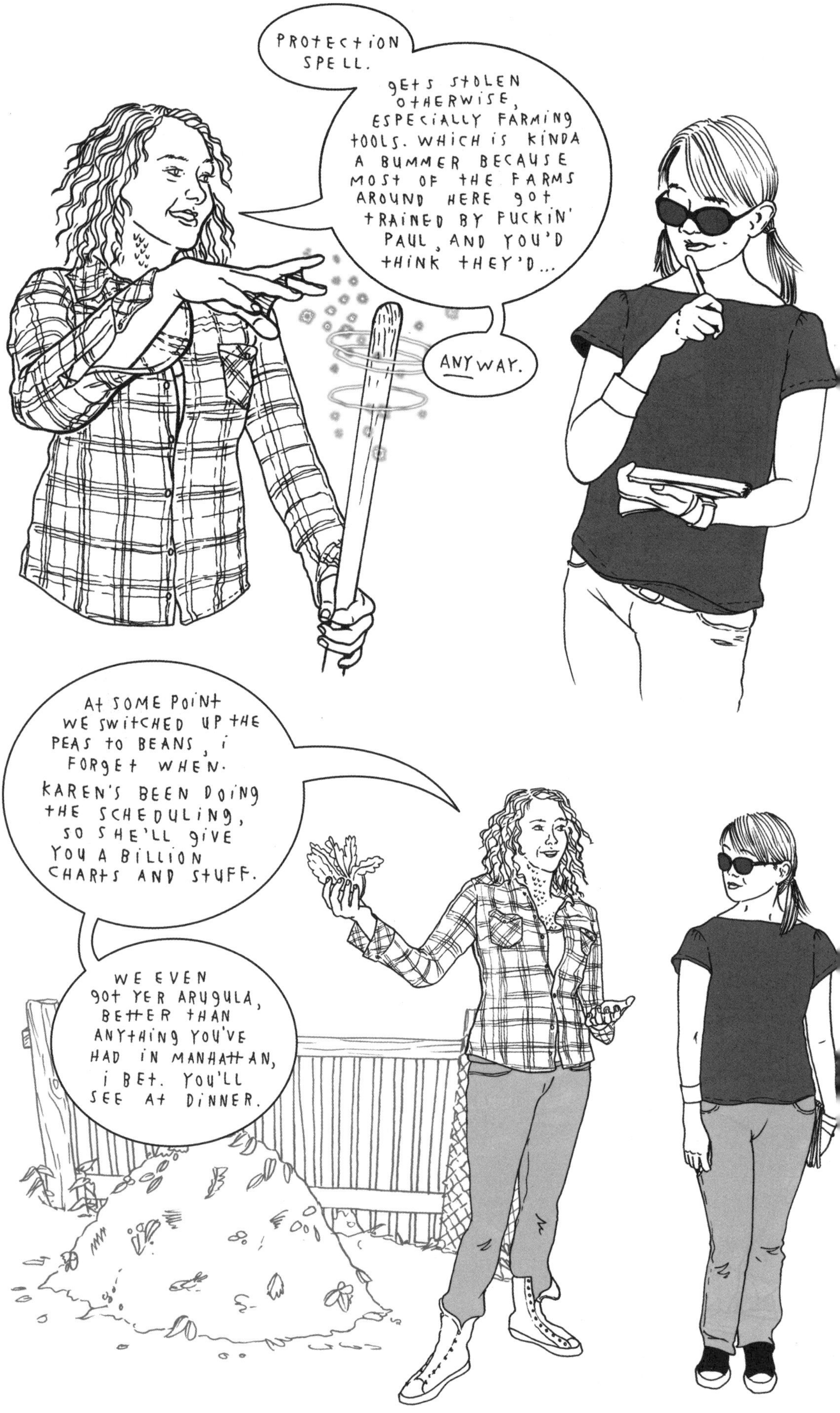
PROTECTION SPELL.
GETS STOLEN OTHERWISE, ESPECIALLY FARMING TOOLS. WHICH IS KINDA A BUMMER BECAUSE MOST OF THE FARMS AROUND HERE GOT TRAINED BY FUCKIN' PAUL, AND YOU'D THINK THEY'D...
ANYWAY.
AT SOME POINT WE SWITCHED UP THE PEAS TO BEANS, I FORGET WHEN.
KAREN'S BEEN DOING THE SCHEDULING, SO SHE'LL GIVE YOU A BILLION CHARTS AND STUFF.
WE EVEN GOT YER ARUGULA, BETTER THAN ANYTHING YOU'VE HAD IN MANHATTAN, I BET. YOU'LL SEE AT DINNER.

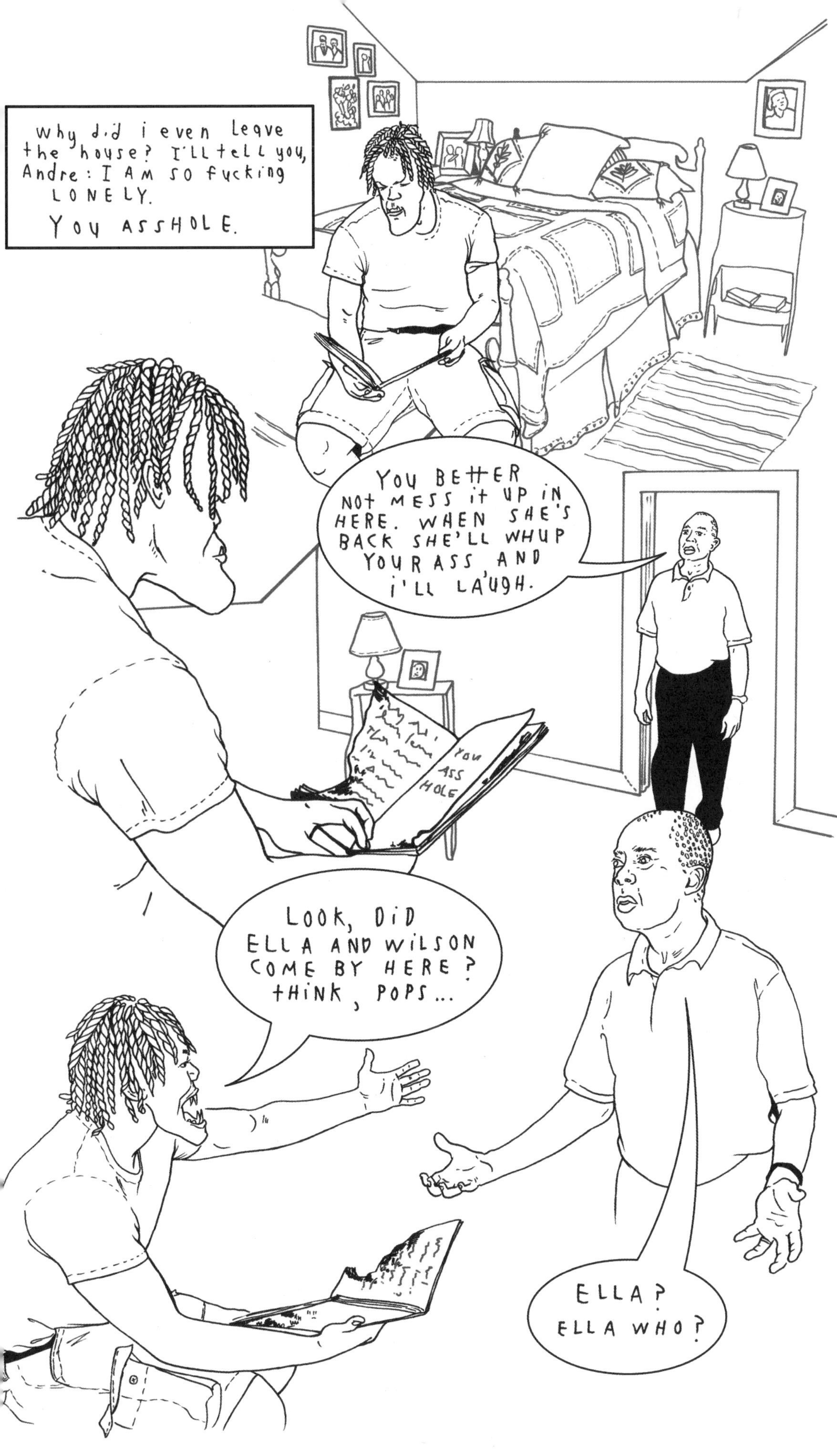
why did i even leave the house? I'll tell you, Andre: I AM so fucking LONELY.
YOU ASSHOLE.
YOU ASS HOLE
YOU BETTER NOT MESS IT UP IN HERE. WHEN SHE'S BACK SHE'LL WHUP YOUR ASS AND I'LL LAUGH.
LOOK, DID ELLA AND WILSON COME BY HERE? THINK, POPS...
ELLA? ELLA WHO?

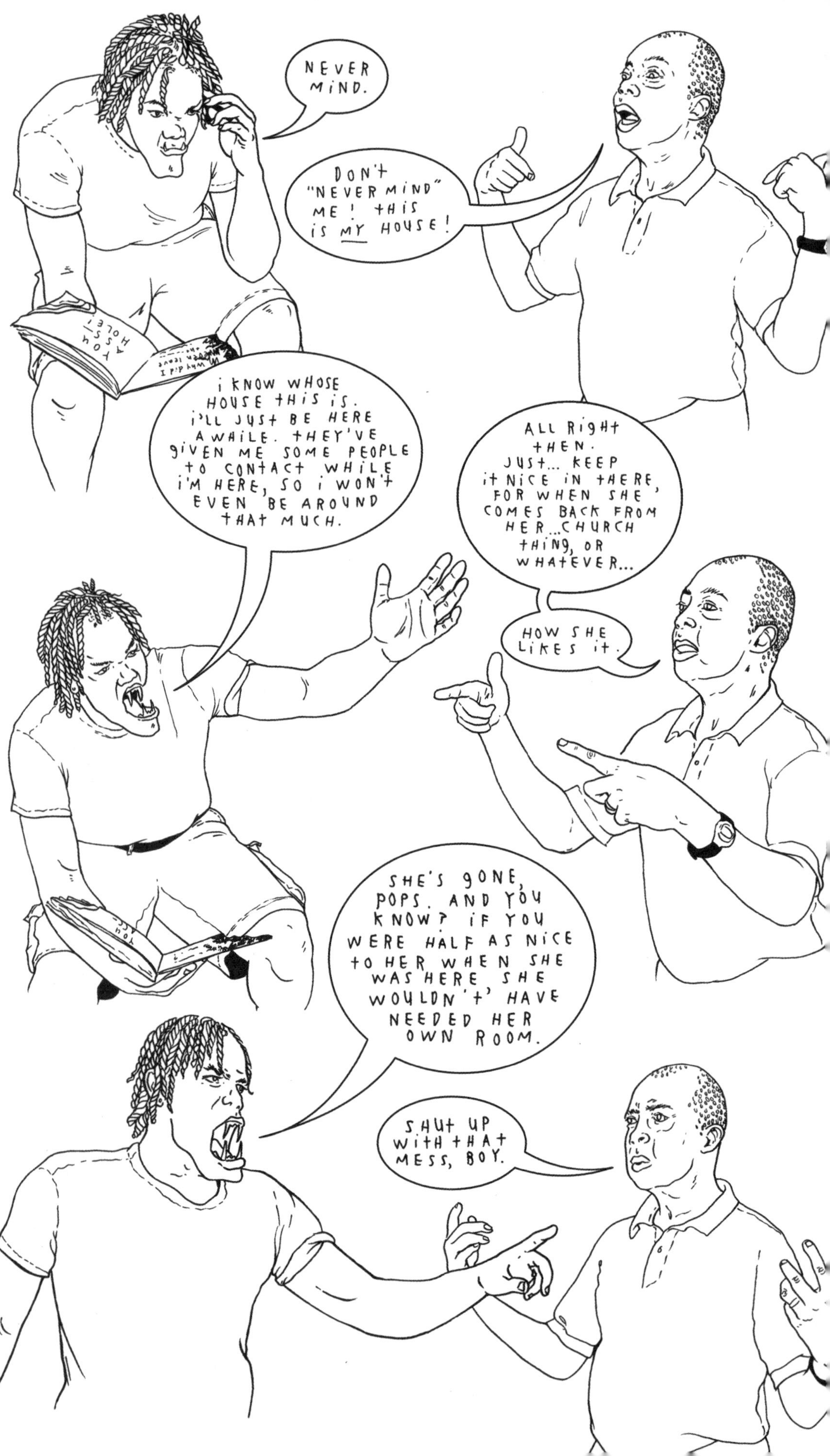
NEVER MIND.
DON'T "NEVER MIND" ME! THIS IS MY HOUSE!
I KNOW WHOSE HOUSE THIS IS. I'LL JUST BE HERE AWHILE. THEY'VE GIVEN ME SOME PEOPLE TO CONTACT WHILE I'M HERE, SO I WON'T EVEN BE AROUND THAT MUCH.
ALL RIGHT THEN. JUST... KEEP IT NICE IN THERE, FOR WHEN SHE COMES BACK FROM HER...CHURCH THING, OR WHATEVER...
HOW SHE LIKES IT.
SHE'S GONE, POPS. AND YOU KNOW? IF YOU WERE HALF AS NICE TO HER WHEN SHE WAS HERE, SHE WOULDN'T HAVE NEEDED HER OWN ROOM.
SHUT UP WITH THAT MESS, BOY.

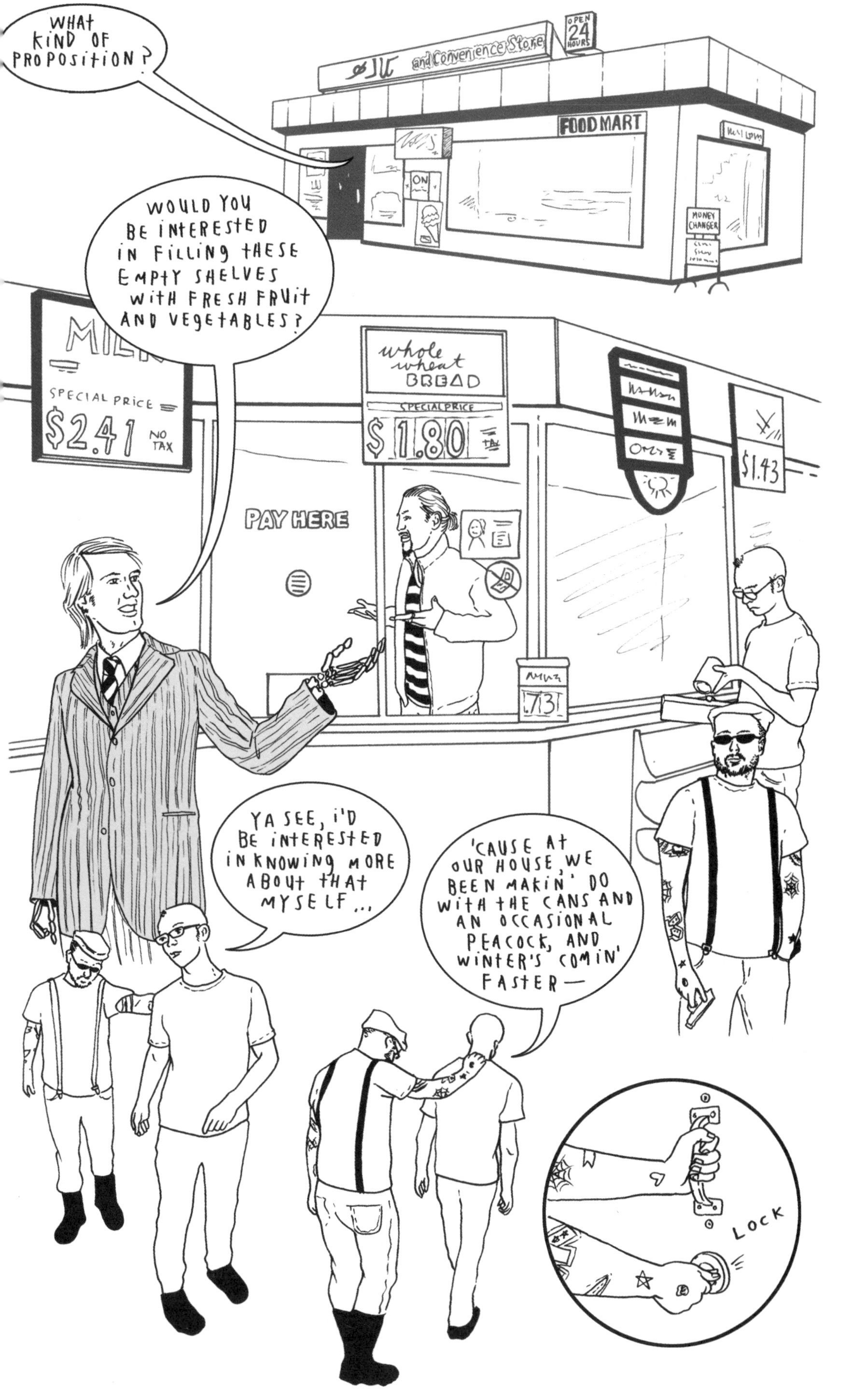

WHAT KIND OF PROPOSITION?
and Convenience Store
OPEN 24 HOURS
FOOD MART
MONEY CHANGER
WOULD YOU BE INTERESTED IN FILLING THESE EMPTY SHELVES WITH FRESH FRUIT AND VEGETABLES?
SPECIAL PRICE $2.41 NO TAX
whole wheat BREAD
SPECIAL PRICE $1.80
$1.43
PAY HERE
.73
YA SEE, I'D BE INTERESTED IN KNOWING MORE ABOUT THAT MYSELF...
'CAUSE AT OUR HOUSE, WE BEEN MAKIN' DO WITH THE CANS AND AN OCCASIONAL PEACOCK, AND WINTER'S COMIN' FASTER—
LOCK

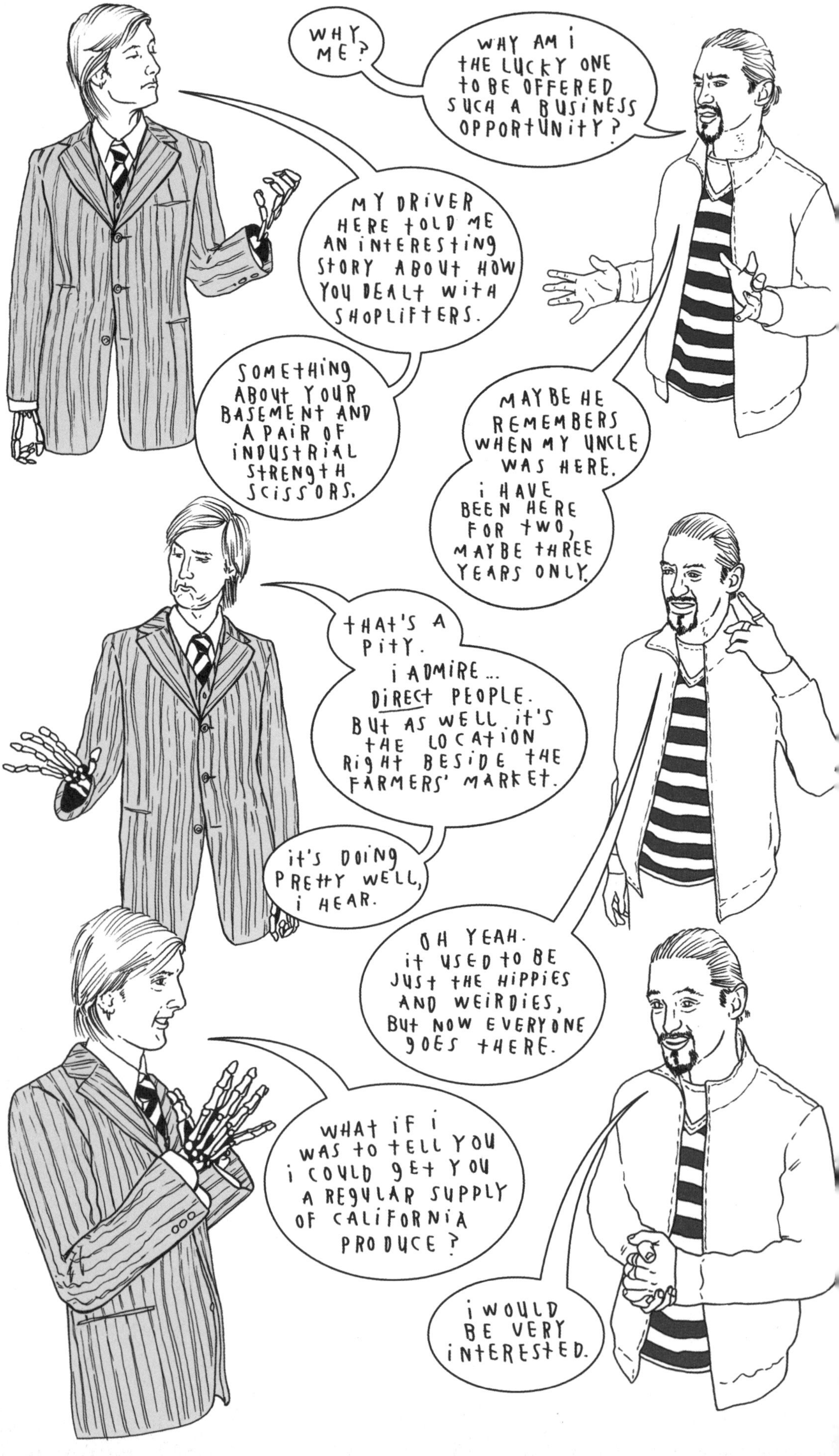
WHY ME?
WHY AM i THE LUCKY ONE TO BE OFFERED SUCH A BUSINESS OPPORTUNITY?
MY DRIVER HERE TOLD ME AN INTERESTING STORY ABOUT HOW YOU DEALT WITH SHOPLIFTERS.
SOMETHING ABOUT YOUR BASEMENT AND A PAIR OF INDUSTRIAL STRENGTH SCISSORS.
MAYBE HE REMEMBERS WHEN MY UNCLE WAS HERE.
i HAVE BEEN HERE FOR TWO, MAYBE THREE YEARS ONLY.
THAT'S A PITY.
i ADMIRE... DIRECT PEOPLE.
BUT AS WELL IT'S THE LOCATION RIGHT BESIDE THE FARMERS' MARKET.
iT'S DOING PRETTY WELL, i HEAR.
OH YEAH. iT USED TO BE JUST THE HIPPIES AND WEIRDIES, BUT NOW EVERYONE GOES THERE.
WHAT iF i WAS TO TELL YOU i COULD GET YOU A REGULAR SUPPLY OF CALIFORNIA PRODUCE?
i WOULD BE VERY INTERESTED.

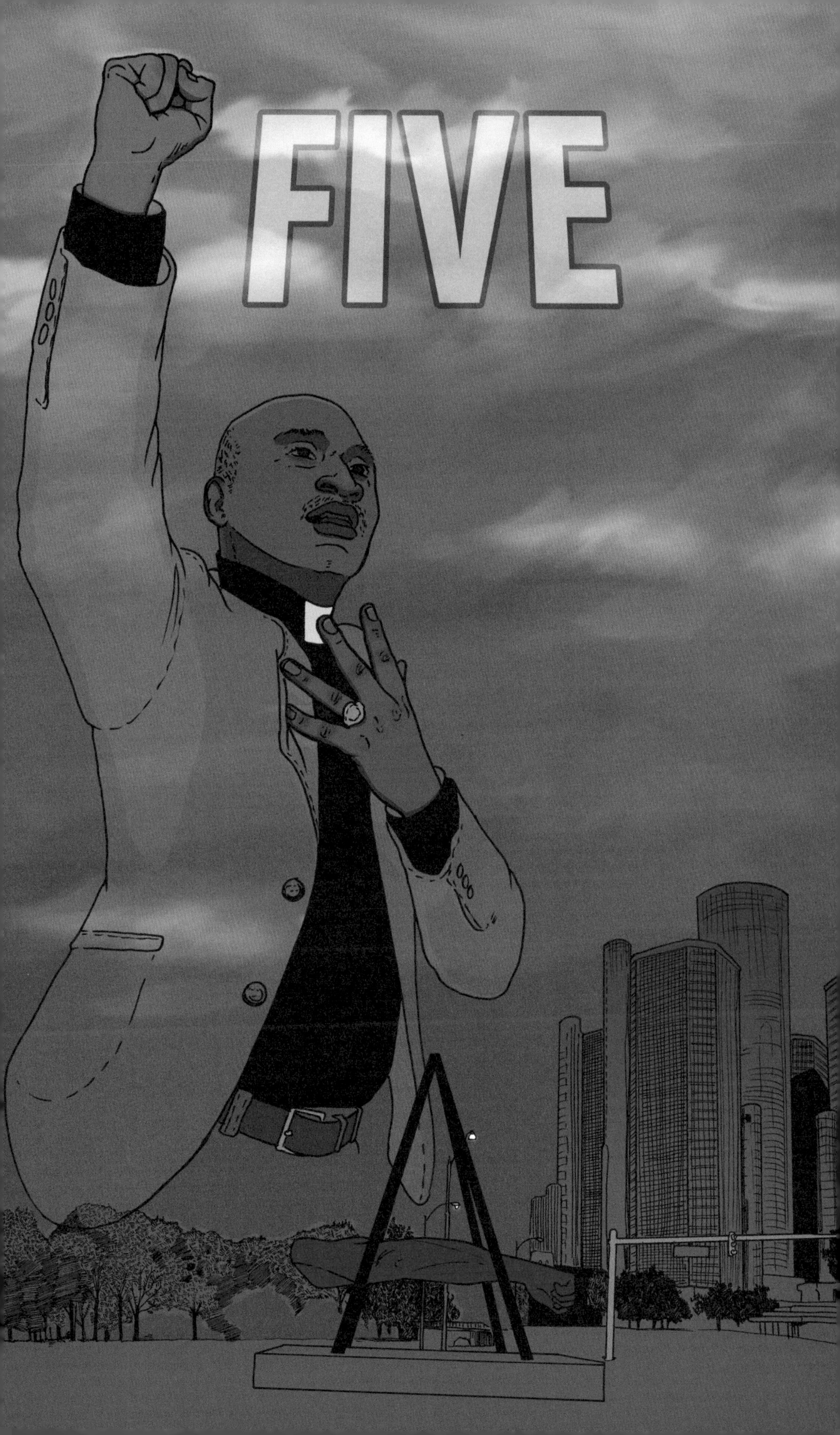
FIVE

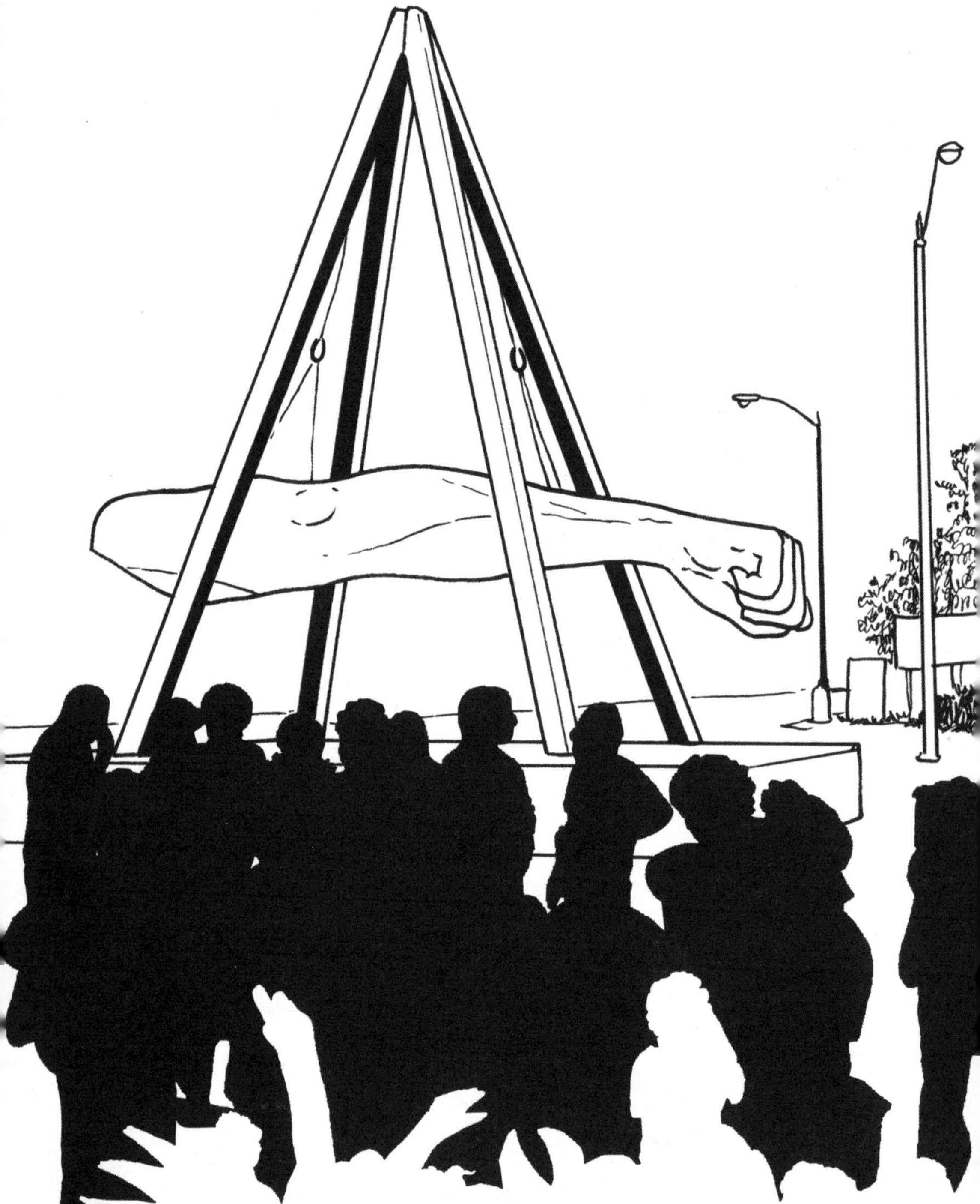

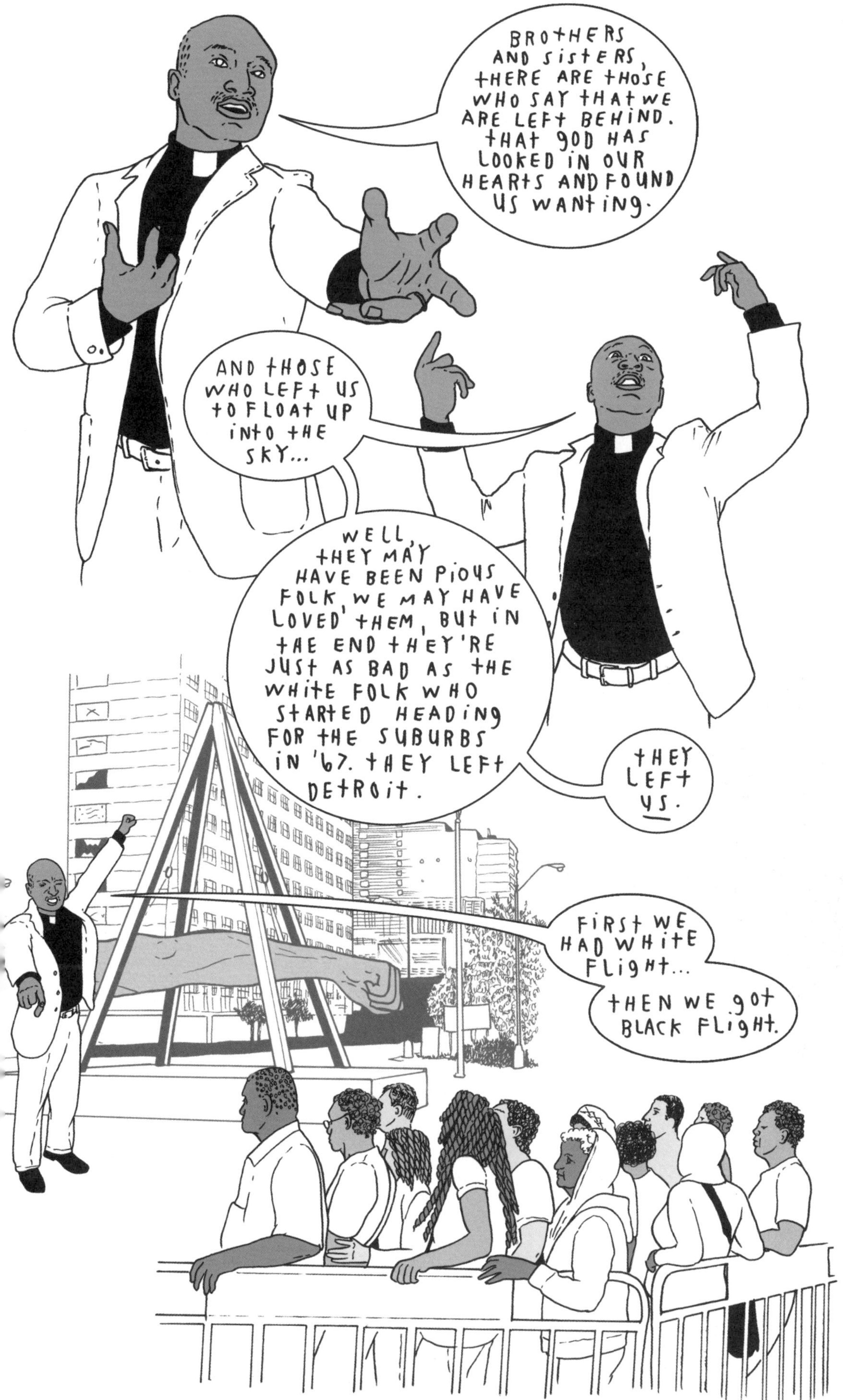
BROTHERS AND SISTERS, THERE ARE THOSE WHO SAY THAT WE ARE LEFT BEHIND. THAT GOD HAS LOOKED IN OUR HEARTS AND FOUND US WANTING.
AND THOSE WHO LEFT US TO FLOAT UP INTO THE SKY...
WELL, THEY MAY HAVE BEEN PIOUS FOLK, WE MAY HAVE LOVED THEM, BUT IN THE END THEY'RE JUST AS BAD AS THE WHITE FOLK WHO STARTED HEADING FOR THE SUBURBS IN '67. THEY LEFT DETROIT.
THEY LEFT US.
FIRST WE HAD WHITE FLIGHT...
THEN WE GOT BLACK FLIGHT.

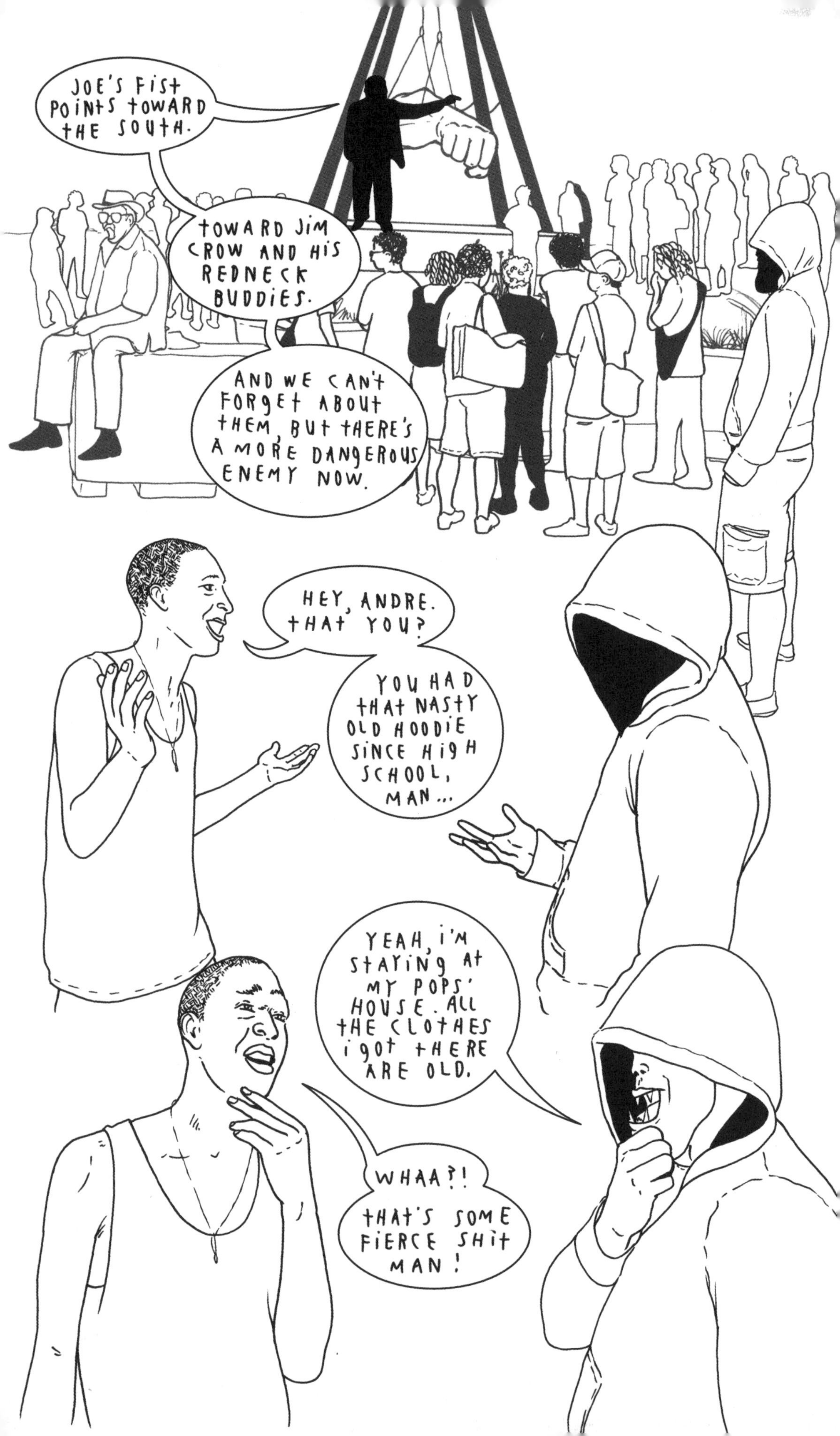
JOE'S FIST POINTS TOWARD THE SOUTH.
TOWARD JIM CROW AND HIS REDNECK BUDDIES.
AND WE CAN'T FORGET ABOUT THEM, BUT THERE'S A MORE DANGEROUS ENEMY NOW.
HEY, ANDRE. THAT YOU?
YOU HAD THAT NASTY OLD HOODIE SINCE HIGH SCHOOL, MAN...
YEAH, I'M STAYING AT MY POPS' HOUSE. ALL THE CLOTHES I GOT THERE ARE OLD.
WHAA?!
THAT'S SOME FIERCE SHIT MAN!

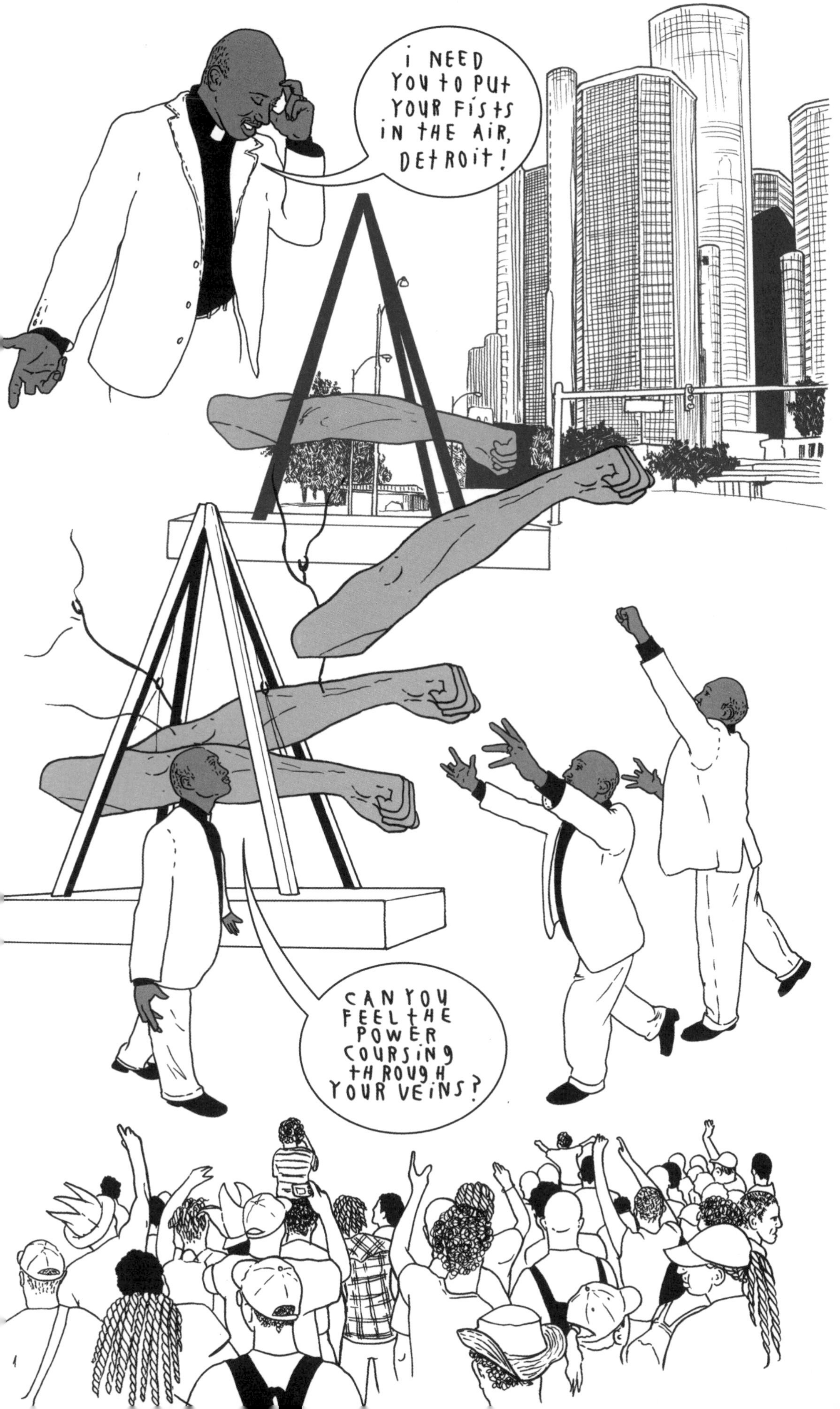
I NEED YOU TO PUT YOUR FISTS IN THE AIR, DETROIT!
CAN YOU FEEL THE POWER COURSING THROUGH YOUR VEINS?

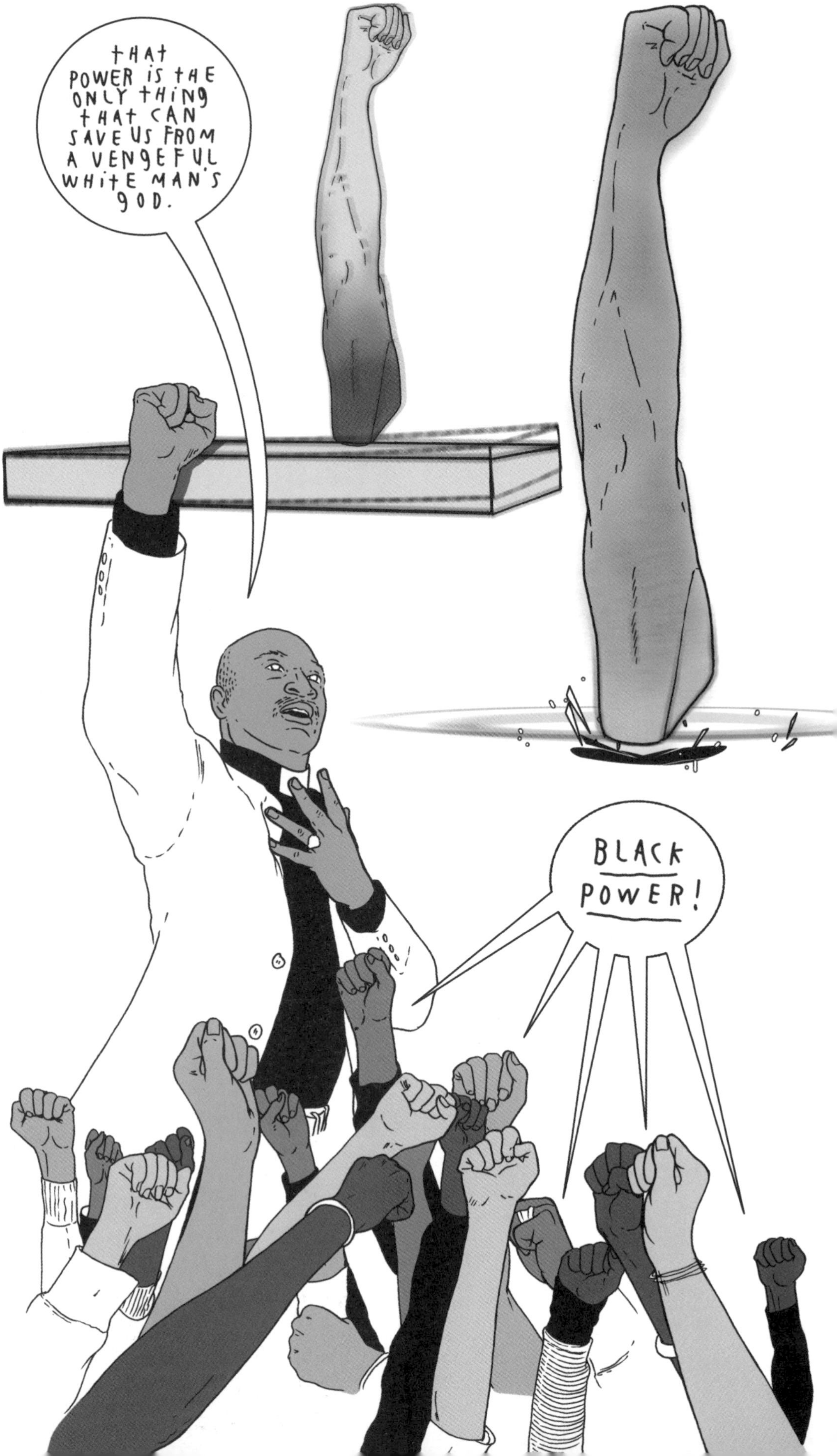
THAT POWER IS THE ONLY THING THAT CAN SAVE US FROM A VENGEFUL WHITE MAN'S GOD.
BLACK POWER!

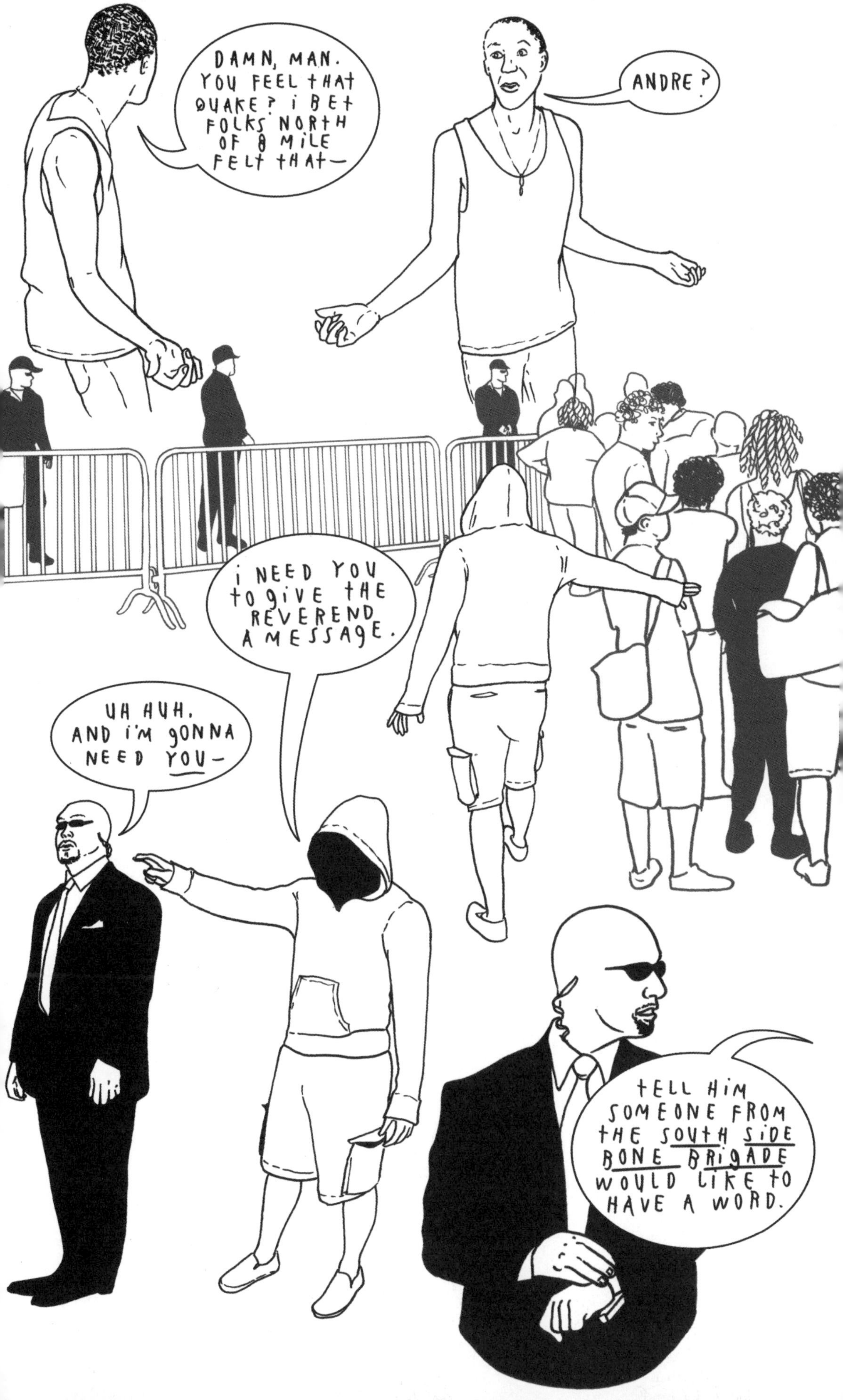
DAMN, MAN. YOU FEEL THAT QUAKE? I BET FOLKS NORTH OF 8 MILE FELT THAT—
ANDRE?
I NEED YOU TO GIVE THE REVEREND A MESSAGE.
UH HUH. AND I'M GONNA NEED YOU—
TELL HIM SOMEONE FROM THE SOUTH SIDE BONE BRIGADE WOULD LIKE TO HAVE A WORD.

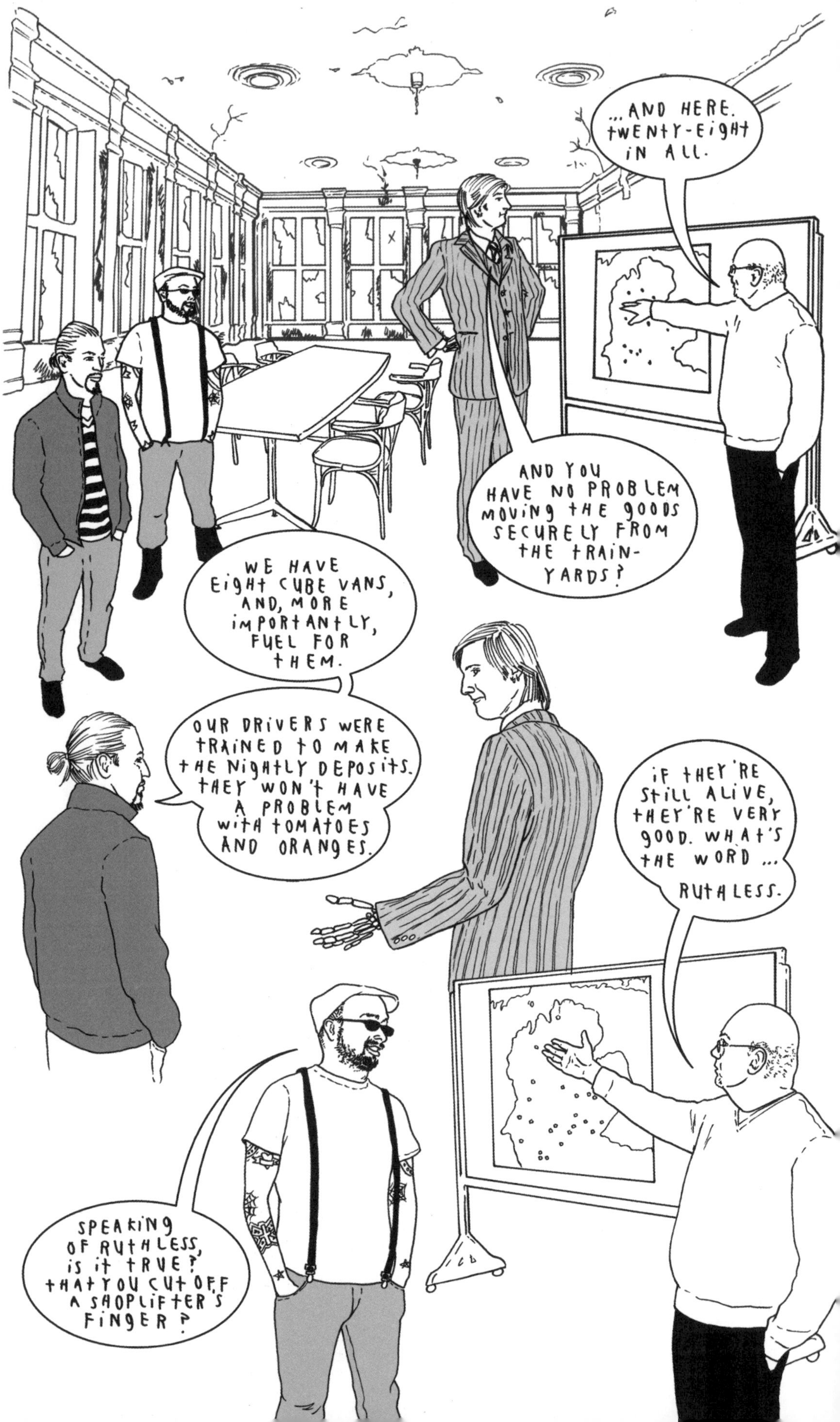
...AND HERE. TWENTY-EIGHT IN ALL.
AND YOU HAVE NO PROBLEM MOVING THE GOODS SECURELY FROM THE TRAIN-YARDS?
WE HAVE EIGHT CUBE VANS, AND, MORE IMPORTANTLY, FUEL FOR THEM.
OUR DRIVERS WERE TRAINED TO MAKE THE NIGHTLY DEPOSITS. THEY WON'T HAVE A PROBLEM WITH TOMATOES AND ORANGES.
IF THEY'RE STILL ALIVE, THEY'RE VERY GOOD. WHAT'S THE WORD ... RUTHLESS.
SPEAKING OF RUTHLESS, IS IT TRUE? THAT YOU CUT OFF A SHOPLIFTER'S FINGER?

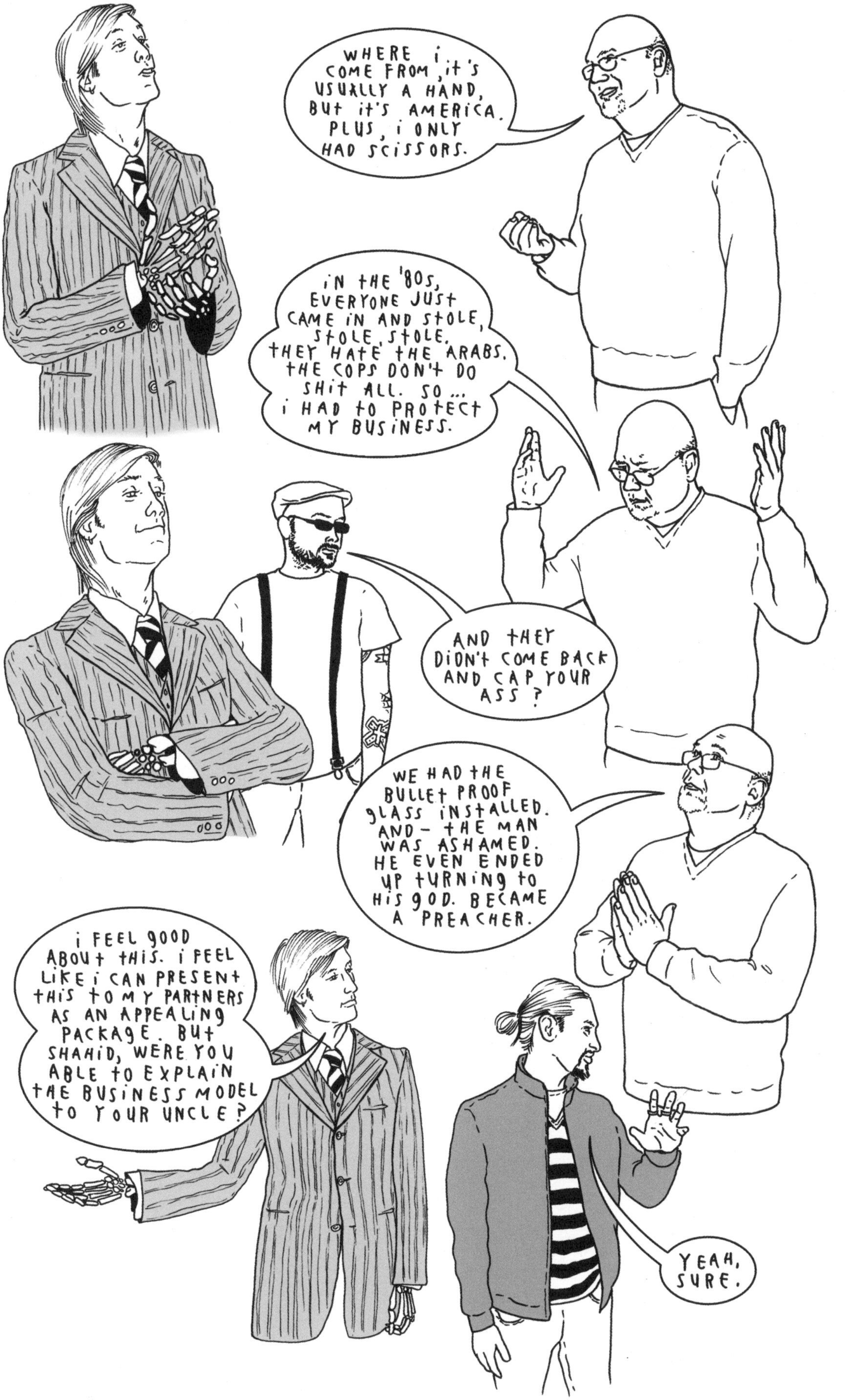
WHERE i COME FROM, it'S USUALLY A HAND, But it'S AMERICA. PLUS, i ONLY HAD SCISSORS.
iN tHE '80S, EVERYONE JUSt CAME iN AND StOLE, StOLE, StOLE. tHEY HAtE tHE ARABS. tHE COPS DON't DO SHit ALL. SO... i HAD tO PROtECt MY BUSiNESS.
AND tHEY DiDN't COME BACK AND CAP YOUR ASS ?
WE HAD tHE BULLEt PROOF gLASS iNStALLED. AND - tHE MAN WAS ASHAMED. HE EVEN ENDED UP tURNiNg tO HiS gOD. BECAME A PREACHER.
i FEEL gOOD ABOUt tHiS. i FEEL LiKE i CAN PRESENt tHiS tO MY PARtNERS AS AN APPEALiNg PACKAgE. But SHAHiD, WERE YOU ABLE tO EXPLAiN tHE BUSiNESS MODEL tO YOUR UNCLE?
YEAH, SURE.

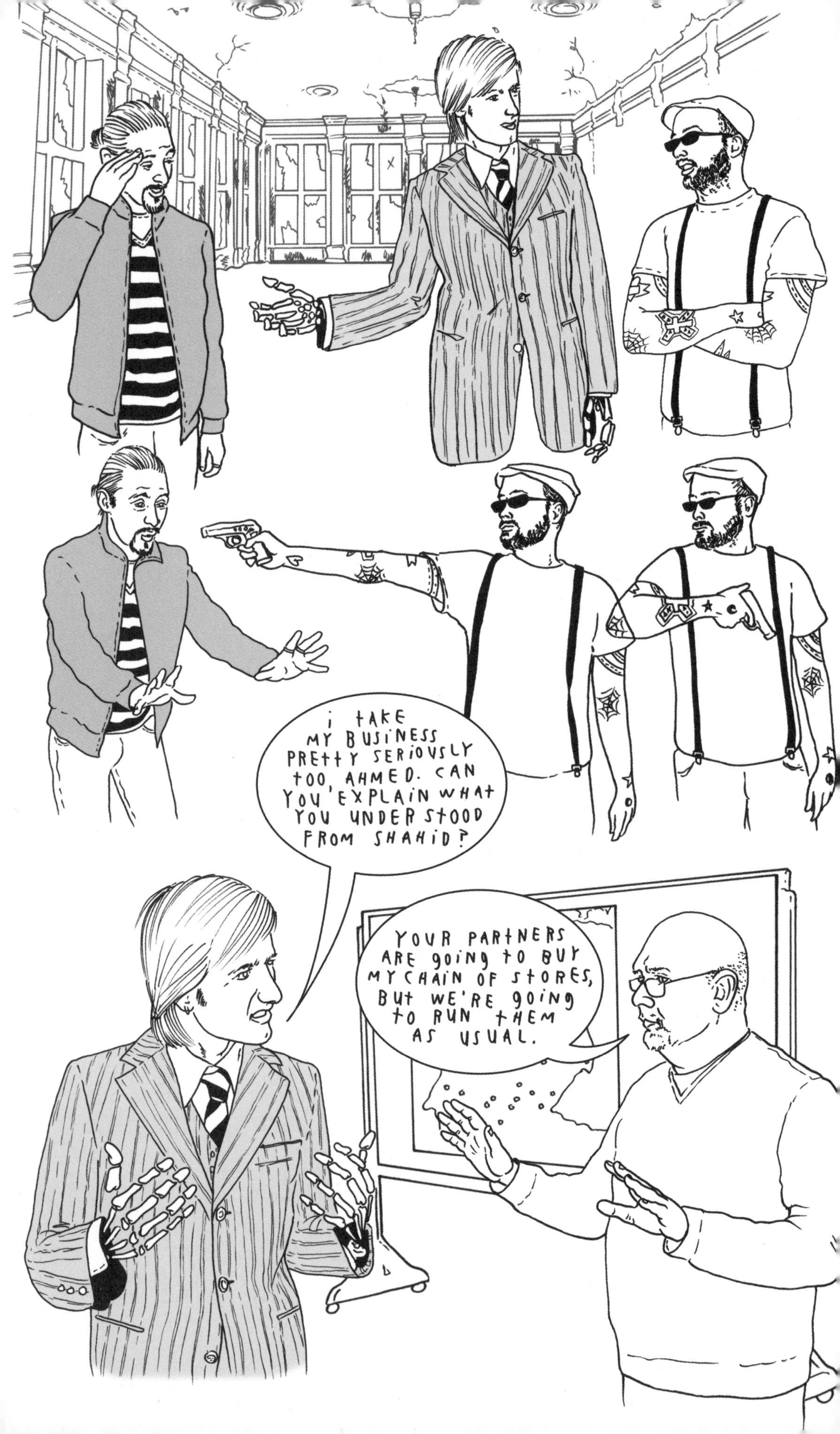
I TAKE MY BUSINESS PRETTY SERIOUSLY TOO, AHMED. CAN YOU EXPLAIN WHAT YOU UNDERSTOOD FROM SHAHID?
YOUR PARTNERS ARE GOING TO BUY MY CHAIN OF STORES, BUT WE'RE GOING TO RUN THEM AS USUAL.

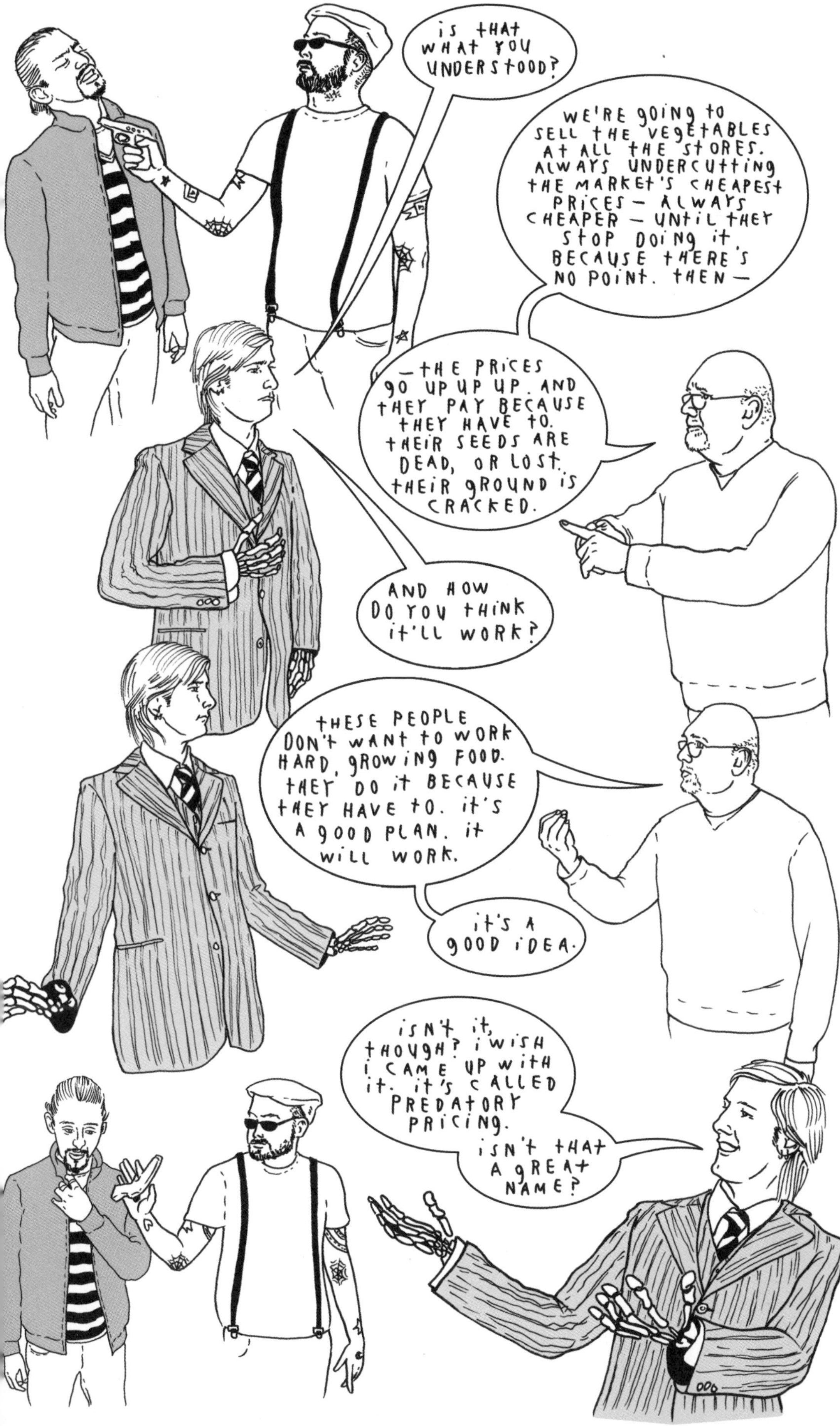
IS THAT WHAT YOU UNDERSTOOD?
WE'RE GOING TO SELL THE VEGETABLES AT ALL THE STORES. ALWAYS UNDERCUTTING THE MARKET'S CHEAPEST PRICES — ALWAYS CHEAPER — UNTIL THEY STOP DOING IT, BECAUSE THERE'S NO POINT. THEN —
— THE PRICES GO UP UP UP. AND THEY PAY BECAUSE THEY HAVE TO. THEIR SEEDS ARE DEAD, OR LOST. THEIR GROUND IS CRACKED.
AND HOW DO YOU THINK IT'LL WORK?
THESE PEOPLE DON'T WANT TO WORK HARD, GROWING FOOD. THEY DO IT BECAUSE THEY HAVE TO. IT'S A GOOD PLAN. IT WILL WORK.
IT'S A GOOD IDEA.
ISN'T IT, THOUGH? I WISH I CAME UP WITH IT. IT'S CALLED PREDATORY PRICING.
ISN'T THAT A GREAT NAME?

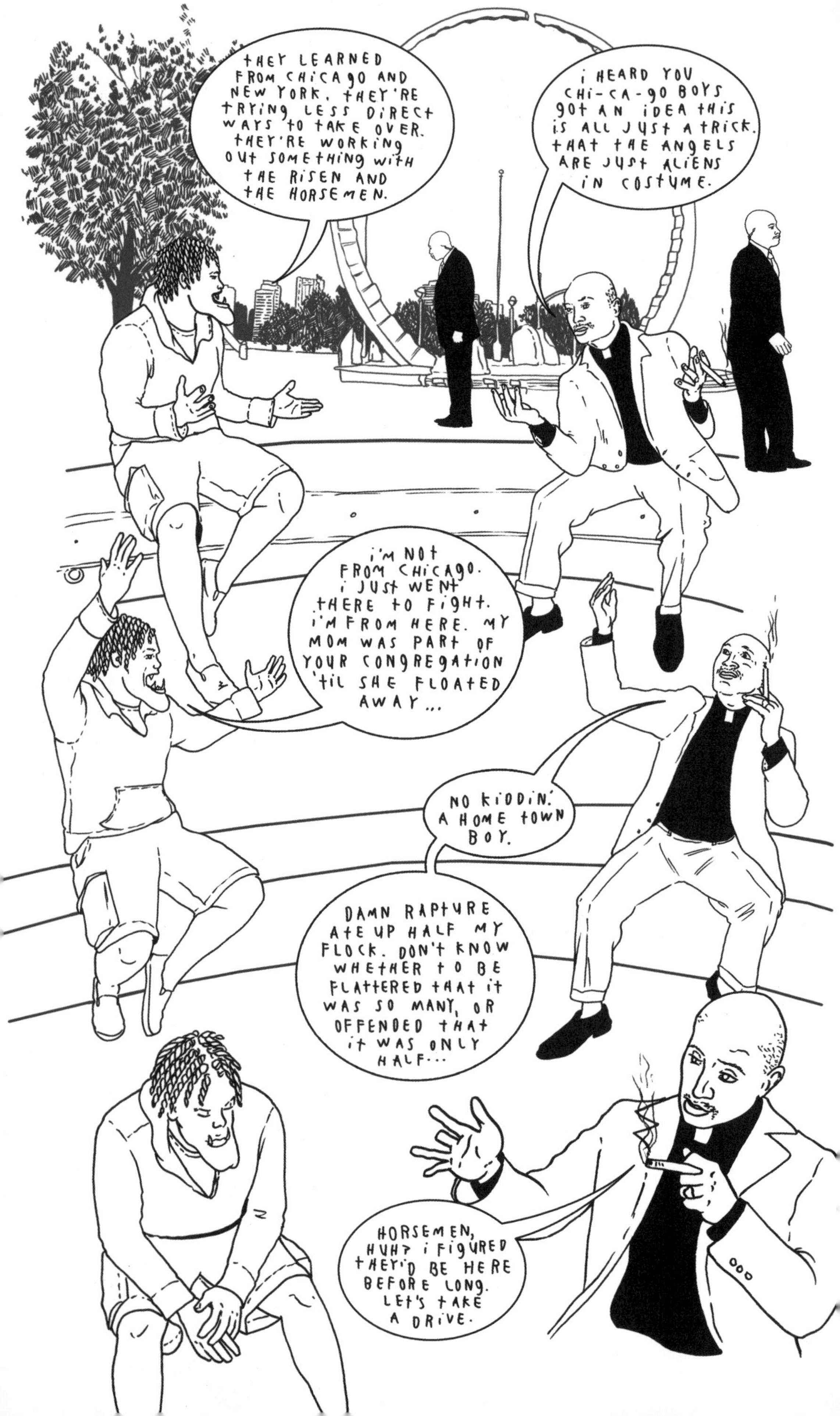
THEY LEARNED FROM CHICAGO AND NEW YORK, THEY'RE TRYING LESS DIRECT WAYS TO TAKE OVER. THEY'RE WORKING OUT SOMETHING WITH THE RISEN AND THE HORSEMEN.
I HEARD YOU CHI-CA-GO BOYS GOT AN IDEA THIS IS ALL JUST A TRICK. THAT THE ANGELS ARE JUST ALIENS IN COSTUME.
I'M NOT FROM CHICAGO. I JUST WENT THERE TO FIGHT. I'M FROM HERE. MY MOM WAS PART OF YOUR CONGREGATION 'TIL SHE FLOATED AWAY...
NO KIDDIN'. A HOME TOWN BOY.
DAMN RAPTURE ATE UP HALF MY FLOCK. DON'T KNOW WHETHER TO BE FLATTERED THAT IT WAS SO MANY, OR OFFENDED THAT IT WAS ONLY HALF...
HORSEMEN, HUH? I FIGURED THEY'D BE HERE BEFORE LONG. LET'S TAKE A DRIVE.

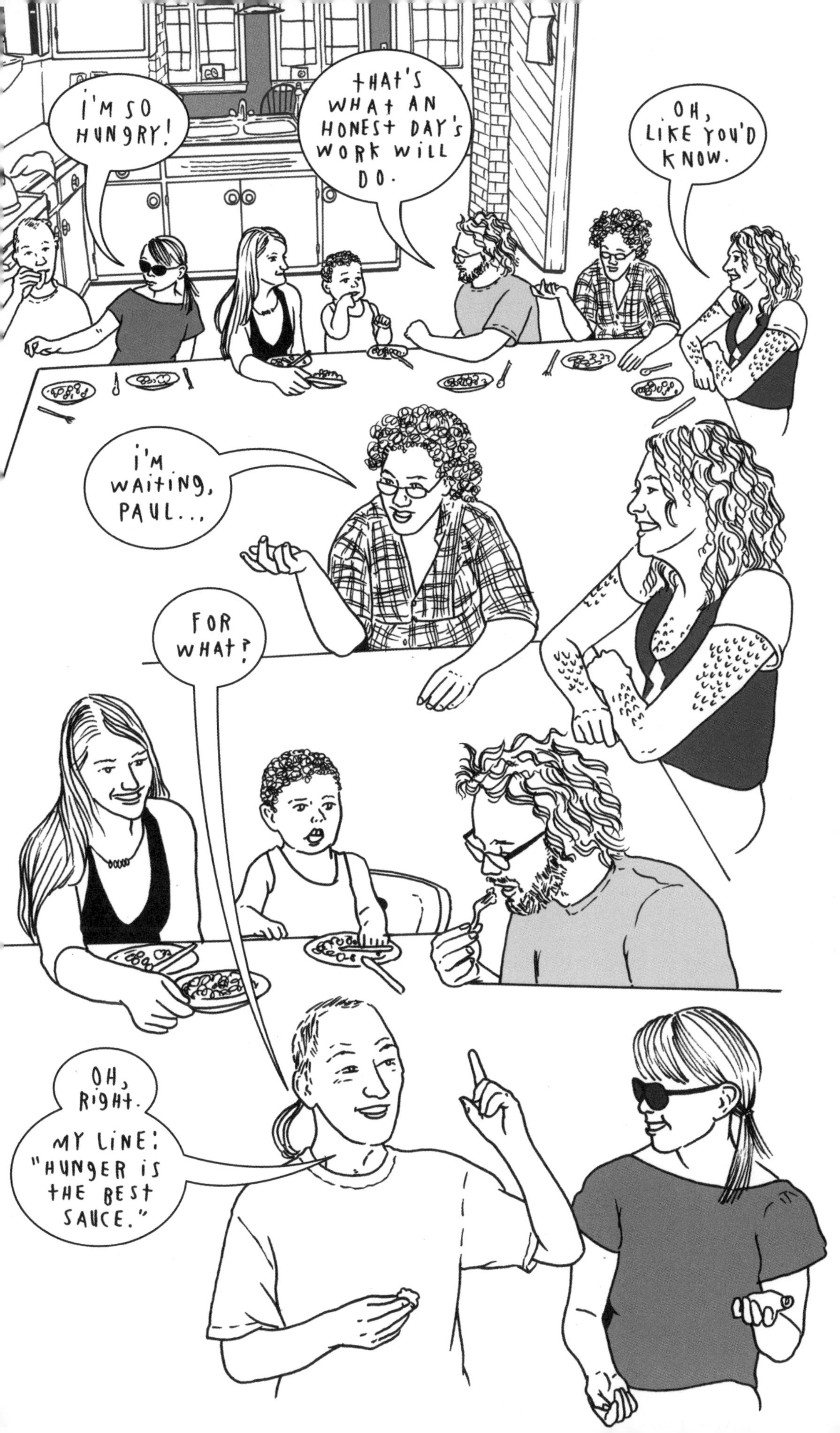
I'M SO HUNGRY!
THAT'S WHAT AN HONEST DAY'S WORK WILL DO.
OH, LIKE YOU'D KNOW.
I'M WAITING, PAUL...
FOR WHAT?
OH, RIGHT.
MY LINE: "HUNGER IS THE BEST SAUCE."

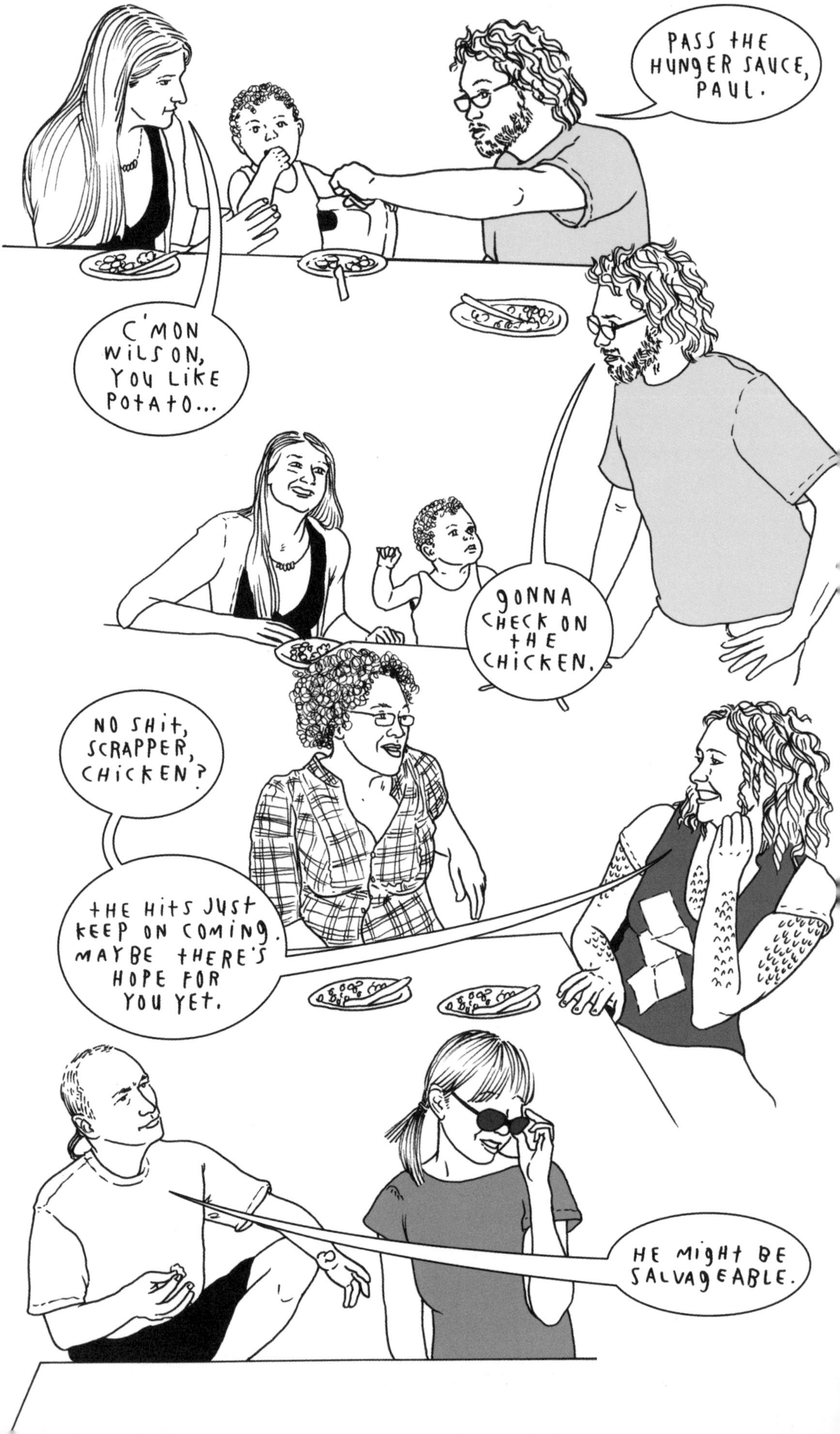
PASS THE HUNGER SAUCE, PAUL.
C'MON WILSON, YOU LIKE POTATO...
GONNA CHECK ON THE CHICKEN.
NO SHIT, SCRAPPER, CHICKEN?
THE HITS JUST KEEP ON COMING. MAYBE THERE'S HOPE FOR YOU YET.
HE MIGHT BE SALVAGEABLE.

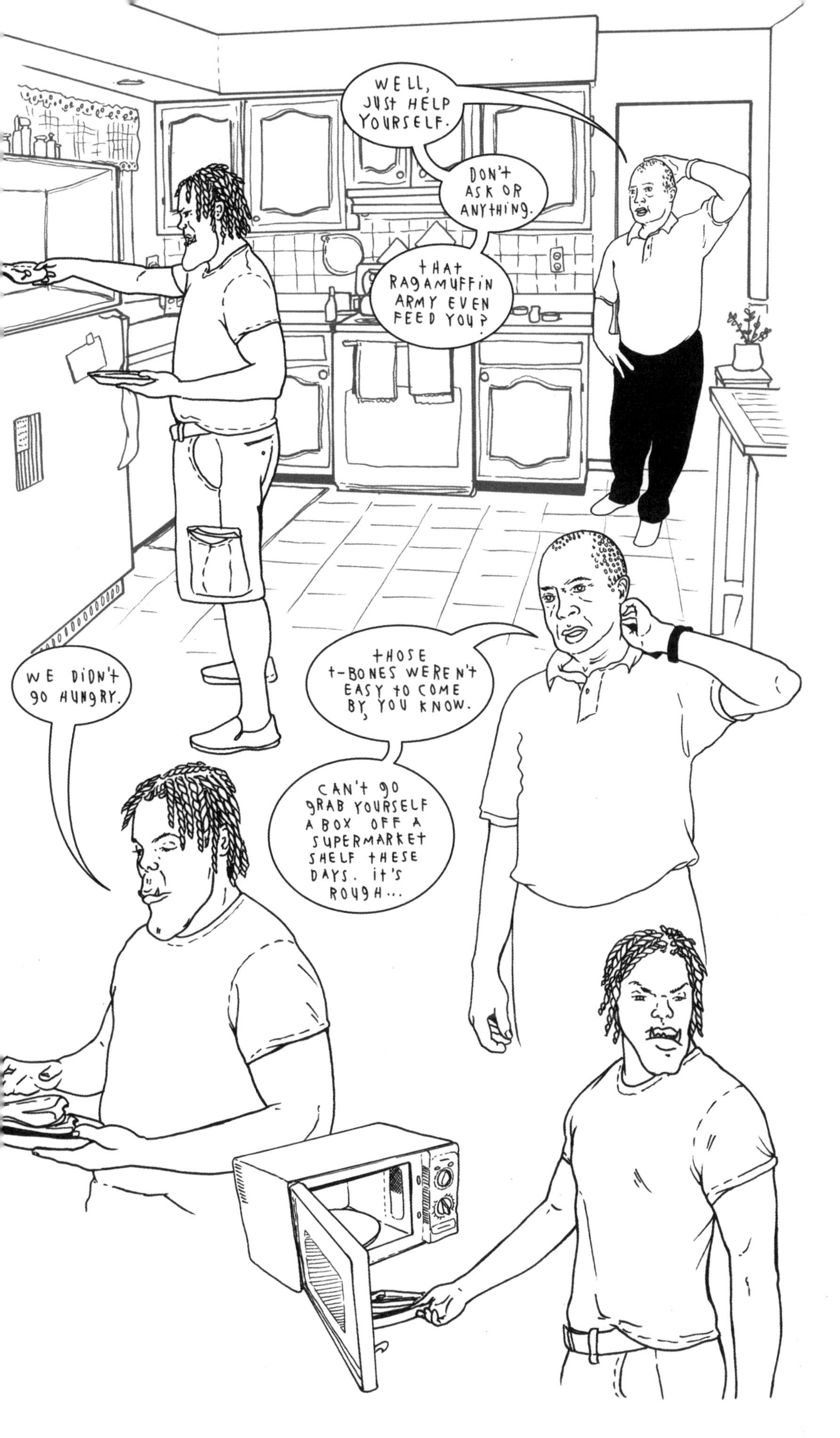
WELL, JUST HELP YOURSELF.
DON'T ASK OR ANYTHING.
THAT RAGAMUFFIN ARMY EVEN FEED YOU?
WE DIDN'T GO HUNGRY.
THOSE T-BONES WEREN'T EASY TO COME BY, YOU KNOW.
CAN'T GO GRAB YOURSELF A BOX OFF A SUPERMARKET SHELF THESE DAYS. IT'S ROUGH...

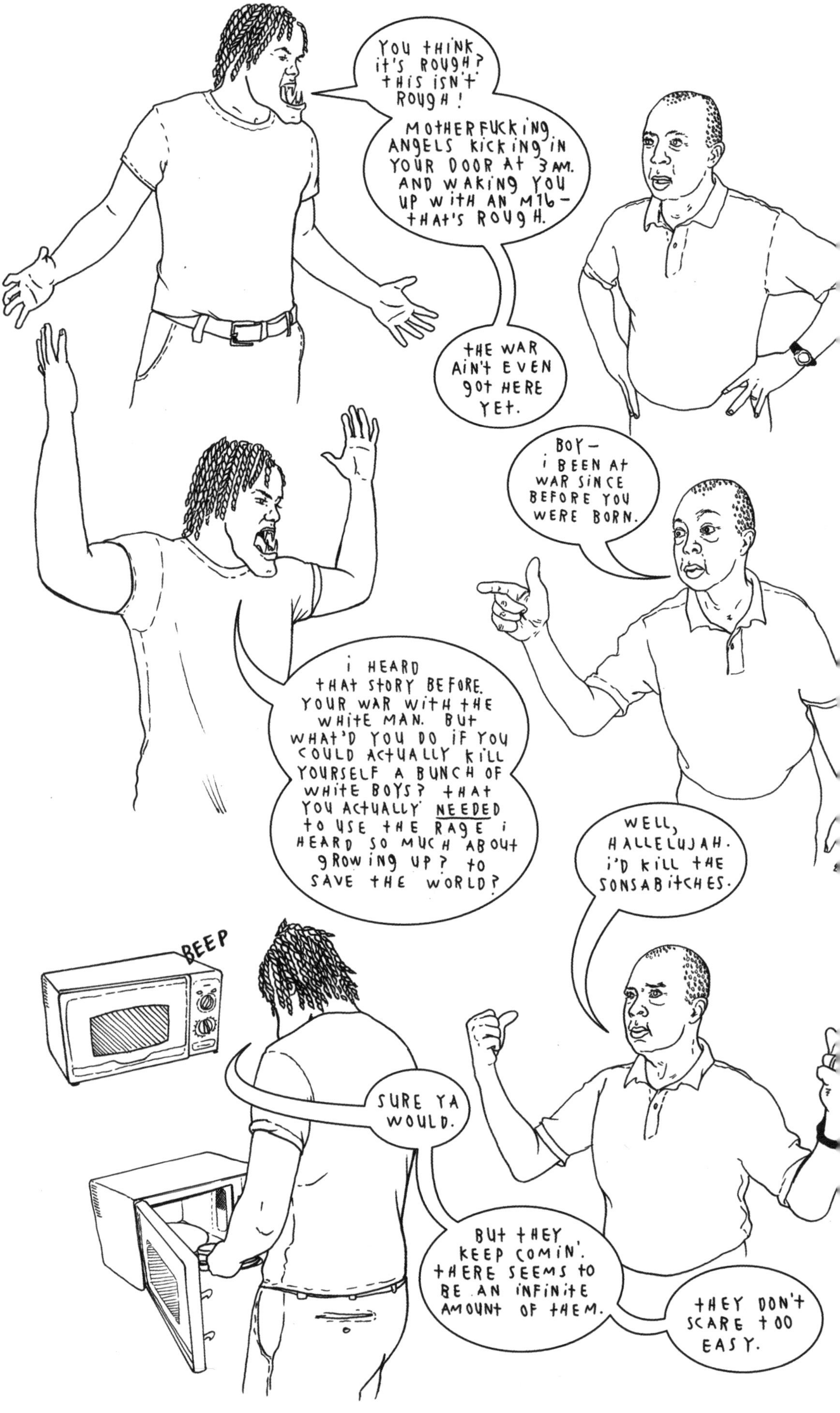
YOU THINK IT'S ROUGH? THIS ISN'T ROUGH!
MOTHERFUCKING ANGELS KICKING IN YOUR DOOR AT 3AM. AND WAKING YOU UP WITH AN M16— THAT'S ROUGH.
THE WAR AIN'T EVEN GOT HERE YET.
BOY— I BEEN AT WAR SINCE BEFORE YOU WERE BORN.
I HEARD THAT STORY BEFORE. YOUR WAR WITH THE WHITE MAN. BUT WHAT'D YOU DO IF YOU COULD ACTUALLY KILL YOURSELF A BUNCH OF WHITE BOYS? THAT YOU ACTUALLY NEEDED TO USE THE RAGE I HEARD SO MUCH ABOUT GROWING UP? TO SAVE THE WORLD?
WELL, HALLELUJAH. I'D KILL THE SONSABITCHES.
BEEP
SURE YA WOULD.
BUT THEY KEEP COMIN'. THERE SEEMS TO BE AN INFINITE AMOUNT OF THEM.
THEY DON'T SCARE TOO EASY.

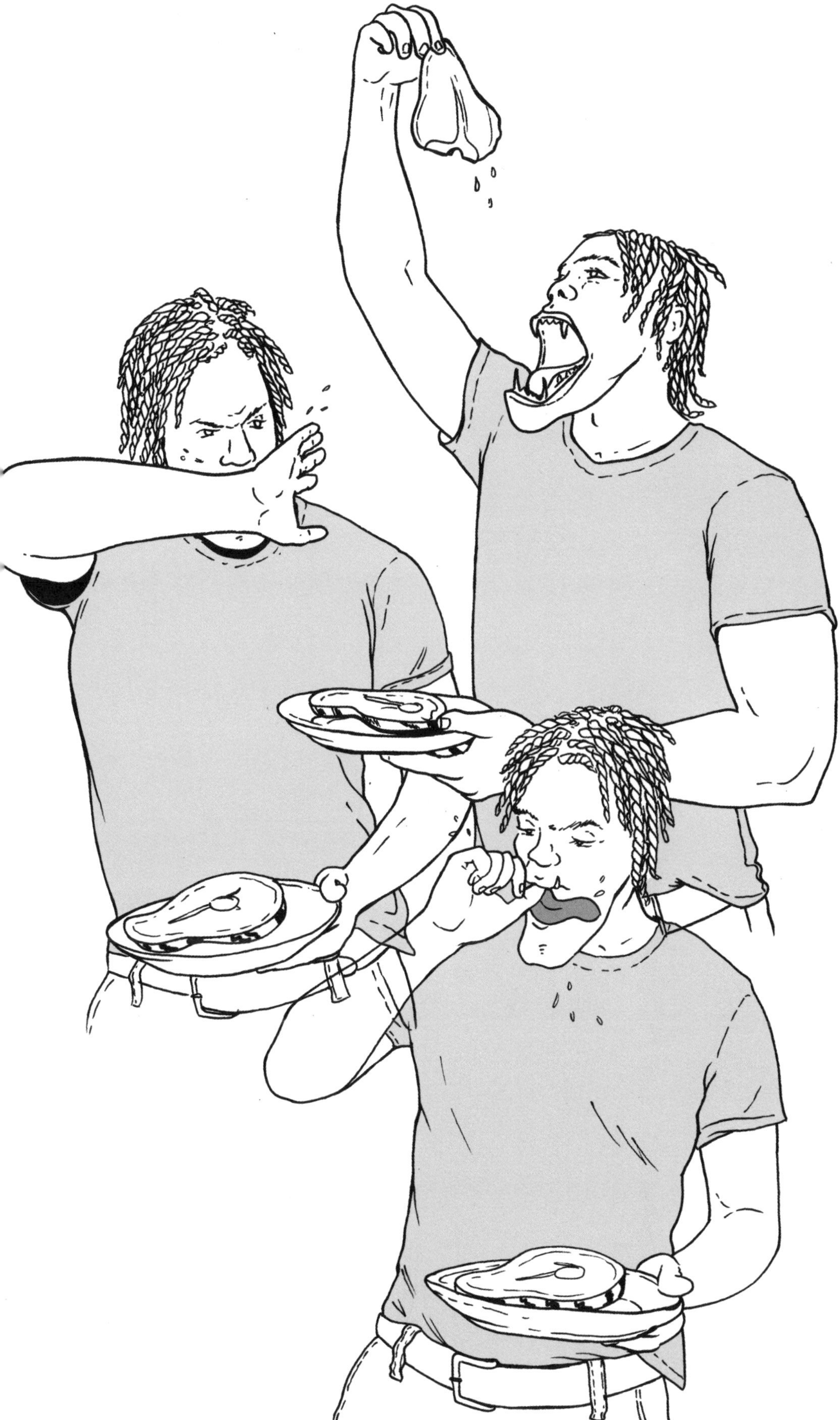

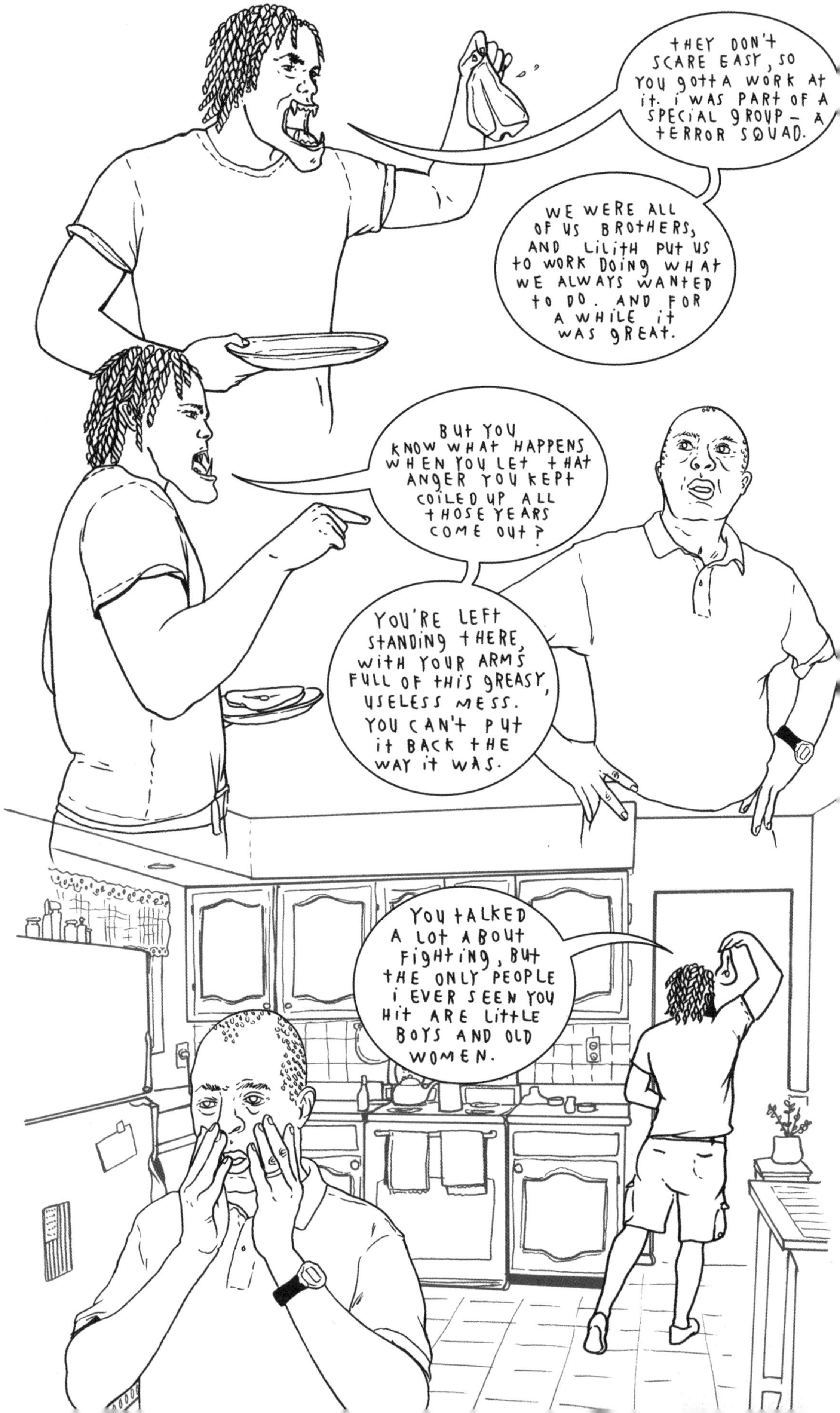
THEY DON'T SCARE EASY, SO YOU GOTTA WORK AT IT. I WAS PART OF A SPECIAL GROUP — A TERROR SQUAD.
WE WERE ALL OF US BROTHERS, AND LILITH PUT US TO WORK DOING WHAT WE ALWAYS WANTED TO DO. AND FOR A WHILE IT WAS GREAT.
BUT YOU KNOW WHAT HAPPENS WHEN YOU LET THAT ANGER YOU KEPT COILED UP ALL THOSE YEARS COME OUT?
YOU'RE LEFT STANDING THERE, WITH YOUR ARMS FULL OF THIS GREASY, USELESS MESS. YOU CAN'T PUT IT BACK THE WAY IT WAS.
YOU TALKED A LOT ABOUT FIGHTING, BUT THE ONLY PEOPLE I EVER SEEN YOU HIT ARE LITTLE BOYS AND OLD WOMEN.

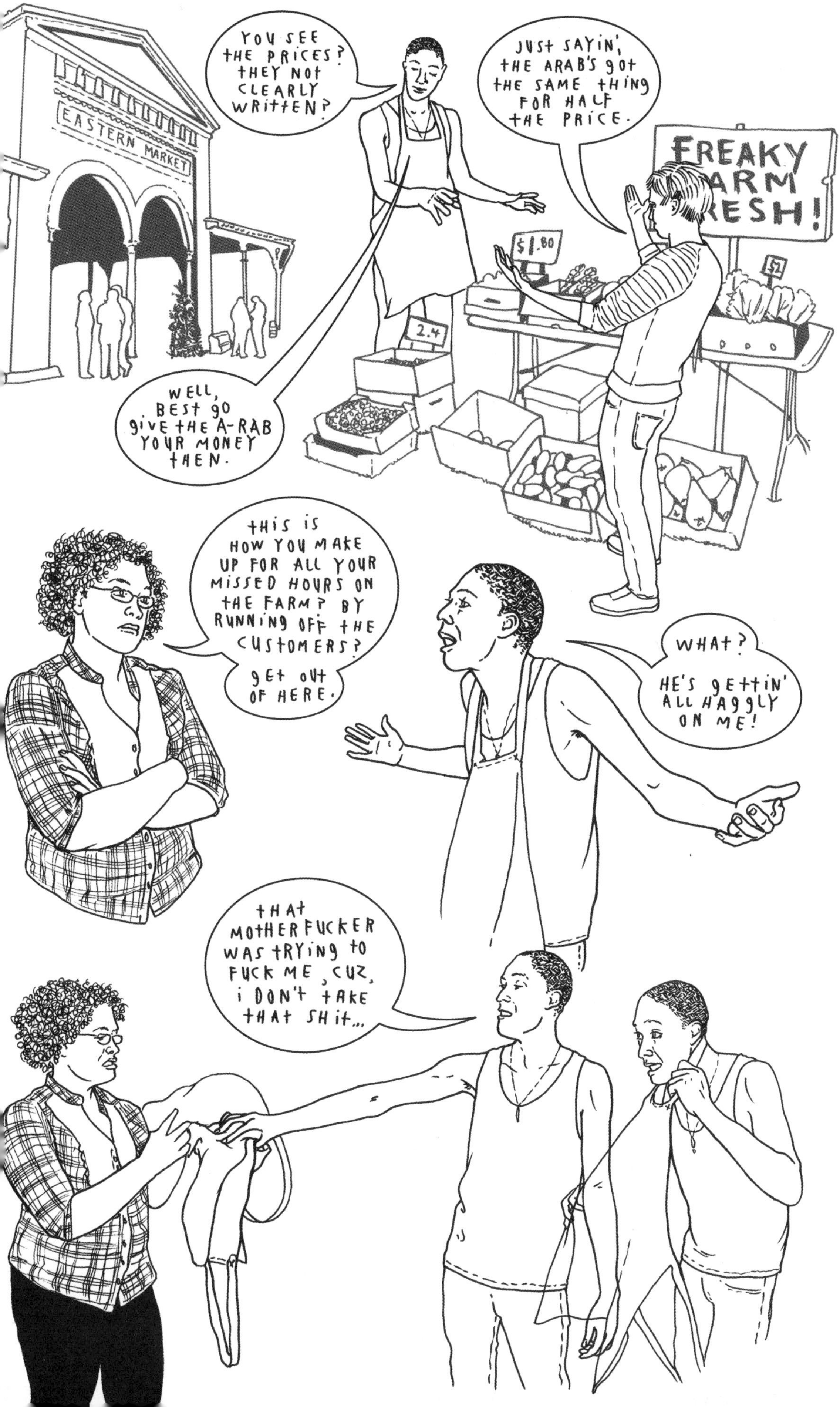
EASTERN MARKET
YOU SEE THE PRICES? THEY NOT CLEARLY WRITTEN?
JUST SAYIN', THE ARAB'S GOT THE SAME THING FOR HALF THE PRICE.
FREAKY ARM RESH!
$1.80
$2
2.4
WELL, BEST GO GIVE THE A-RAB YOUR MONEY THEN.
THIS IS HOW YOU MAKE UP FOR ALL YOUR MISSED HOURS ON THE FARM? BY RUNNING OFF THE CUSTOMERS?
GET OUT OF HERE.
WHAT?
HE'S GETTIN' ALL HAGGLY ON ME!
THAT MOTHERFUCKER WAS TRYING TO FUCK ME, CUZ. I DON'T TAKE THAT SHIT...

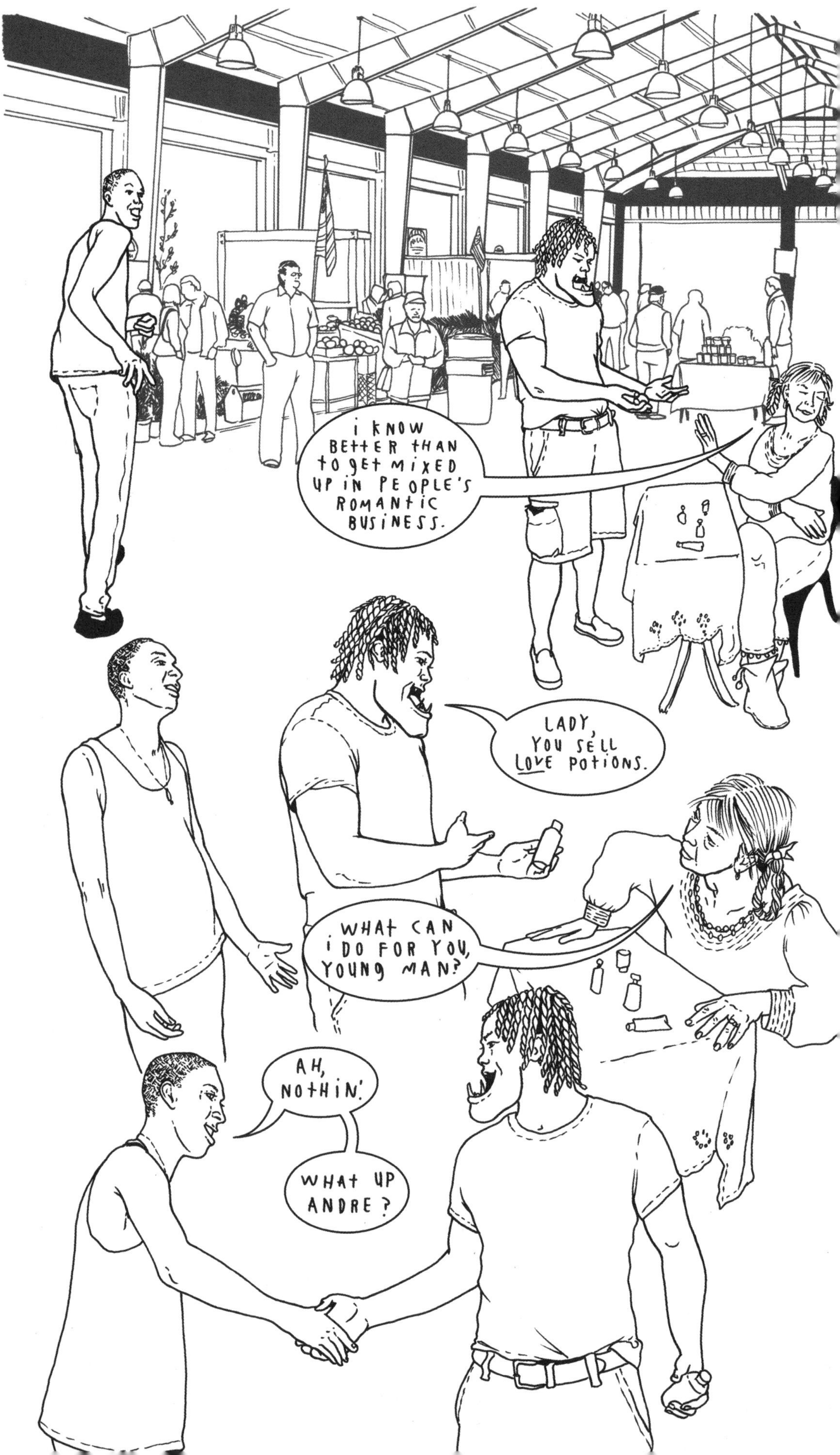
i KNOW BETTER THAN TO GET MIXED UP IN PEOPLE'S ROMANTIC BUSINESS.
LADY, YOU SELL LOVE POTIONS.
WHAT CAN i DO FOR YOU, YOUNG MAN?
AH, NOTHIN'.
WHAT UP ANDRE?

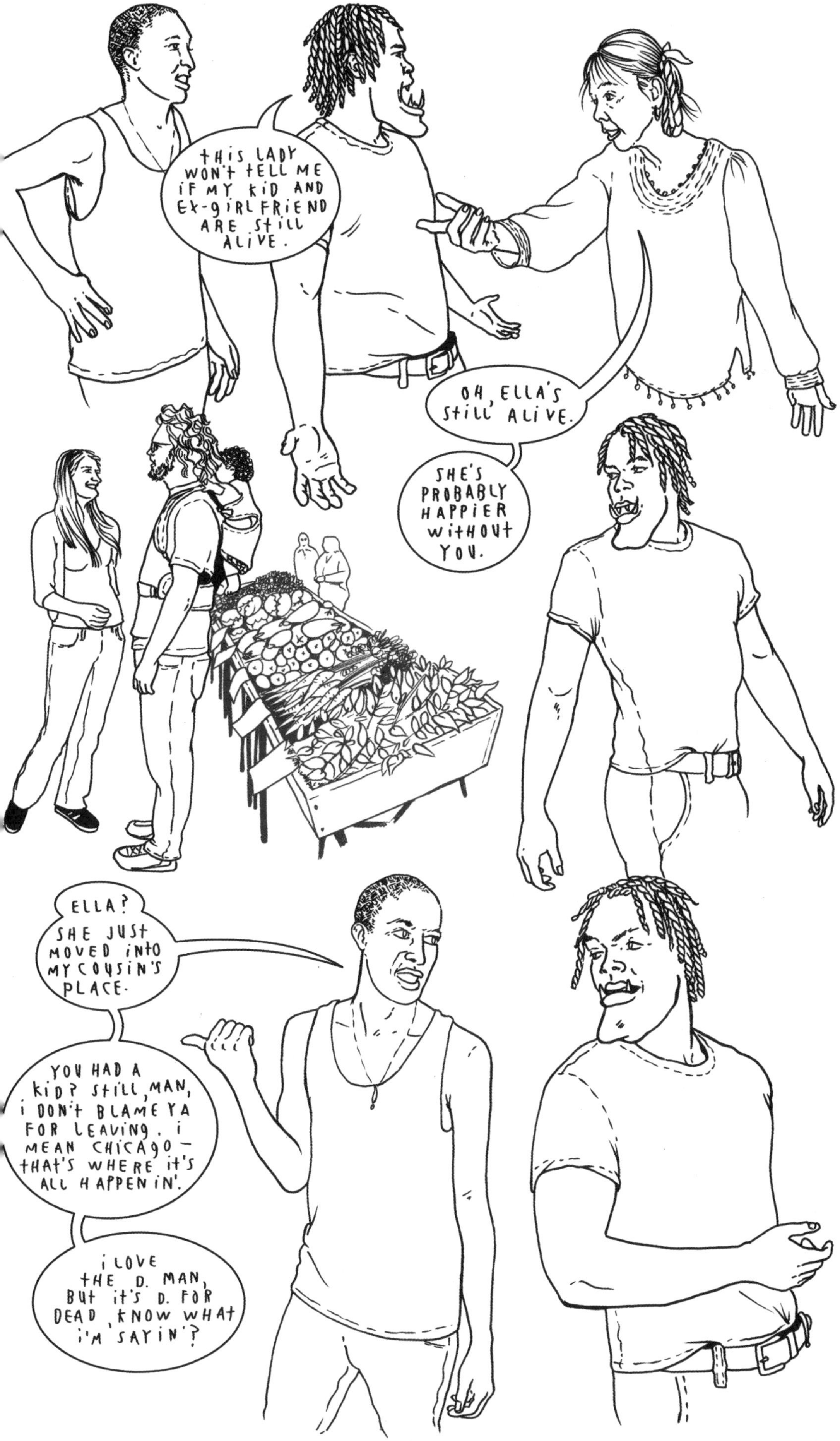
THIS LADY WON'T TELL ME IF MY KID AND EX-GIRLFRIEND ARE STILL ALIVE.
OH, ELLA'S STILL ALIVE.
SHE'S PROBABLY HAPPIER WITHOUT YOU.
ELLA? SHE JUST MOVED INTO MY COUSIN'S PLACE.
YOU HAD A KID? STILL, MAN, I DON'T BLAME YA FOR LEAVING. I MEAN CHICAGO— THAT'S WHERE IT'S ALL HAPPENIN'.
I LOVE THE D. MAN, BUT IT'S D. FOR DEAD, KNOW WHAT I'M SAYIN'?

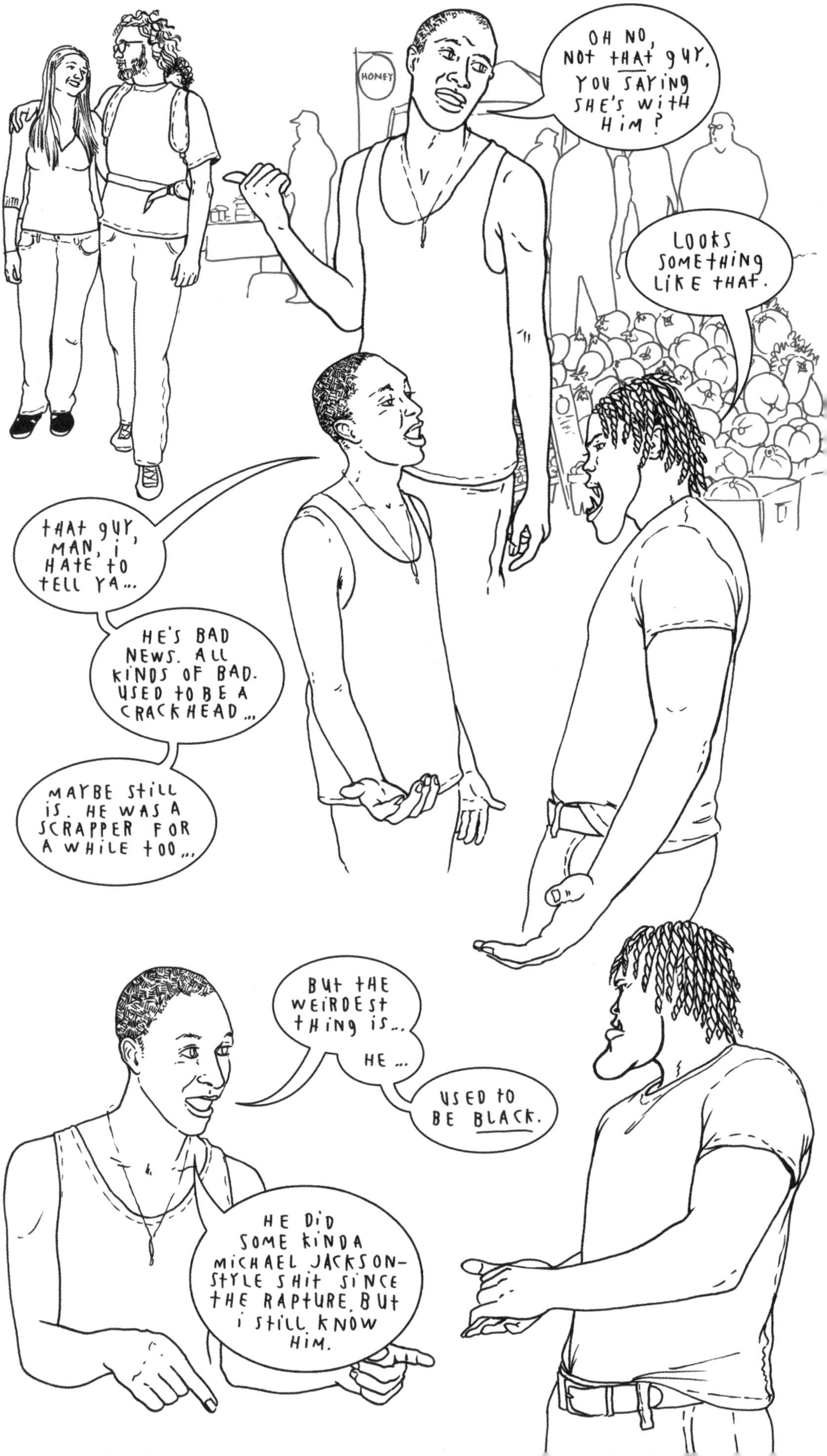
OH NO, NOT THAT GUY. YOU SAYING SHE'S WITH HIM?
LOOKS SOMETHING LIKE THAT.
THAT GUY, MAN, I HATE TO TELL YA...
HE'S BAD NEWS. ALL KINDS OF BAD. USED TO BE A CRACKHEAD...
MAYBE STILL IS. HE WAS A SCRAPPER FOR A WHILE TOO...
BUT THE WEIRDEST THING IS...
HE...
USED TO BE BLACK.
HE DID SOME KINDA MICHAEL JACKSON-STYLE SHIT SINCE THE RAPTURE, BUT I STILL KNOW HIM.
HONEY

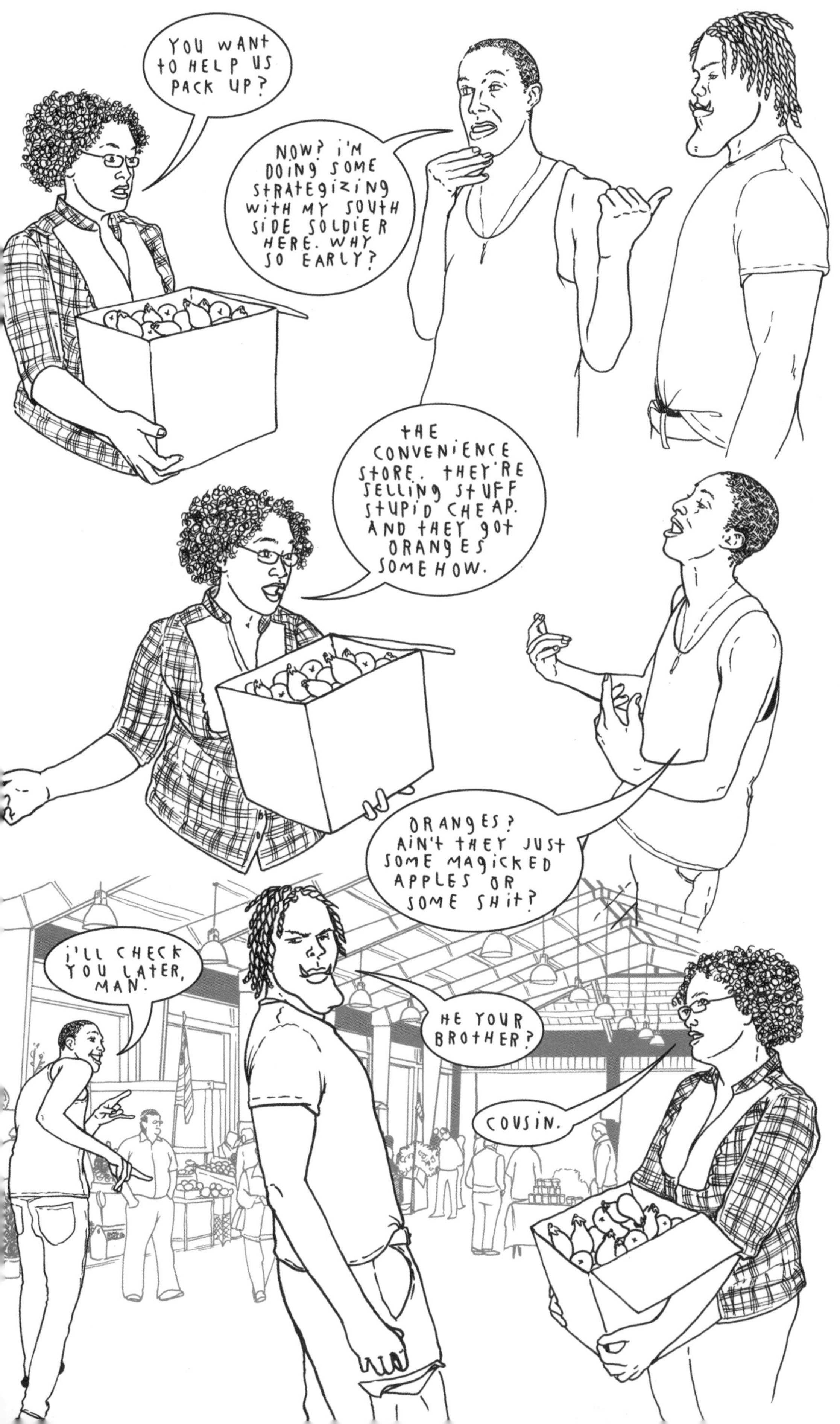
YOU WANT TO HELP US PACK UP?
NOW? I'M DOING SOME STRATEGIZING WITH MY SOUTH SIDE SOLDIER HERE. WHY SO EARLY?
THE CONVENIENCE STORE. THEY'RE SELLING STUFF STUPID CHEAP. AND THEY GOT ORANGES SOMEHOW.
ORANGES? AIN'T THEY JUST SOME MAGICKED APPLES OR SOME SHIT?
I'LL CHECK YOU LATER, MAN.
HE YOUR BROTHER?
COUSIN.

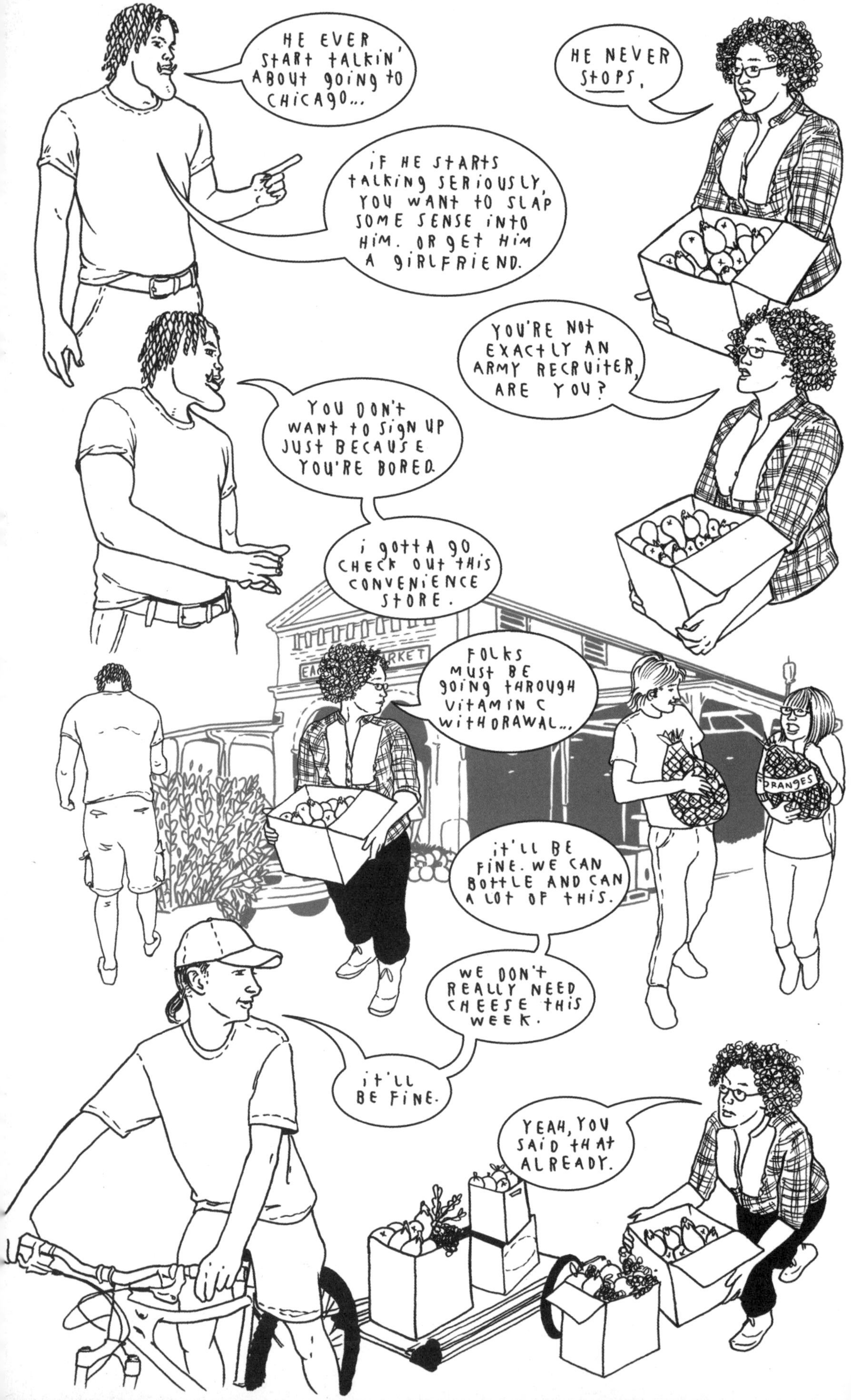
HE EVER START TALKIN' ABOUT GOING TO CHICAGO...
HE NEVER STOPS.
IF HE STARTS TALKING SERIOUSLY, YOU WANT TO SLAP SOME SENSE INTO HIM. OR GET HIM A GIRLFRIEND.
YOU'RE NOT EXACTLY AN ARMY RECRUITER, ARE YOU?
YOU DON'T WANT TO SIGN UP JUST BECAUSE YOU'RE BORED.
I GOTTA GO CHECK OUT THIS CONVENIENCE STORE.
MARKET
FOLKS MUST BE GOING THROUGH VITAMIN C WITHDRAWAL...
ORANGES
IT'LL BE FINE. WE CAN BOTTLE AND CAN A LOT OF THIS.
WE DON'T REALLY NEED CHEESE THIS WEEK.
IT'LL BE FINE.
YEAH, YOU SAID THAT ALREADY.

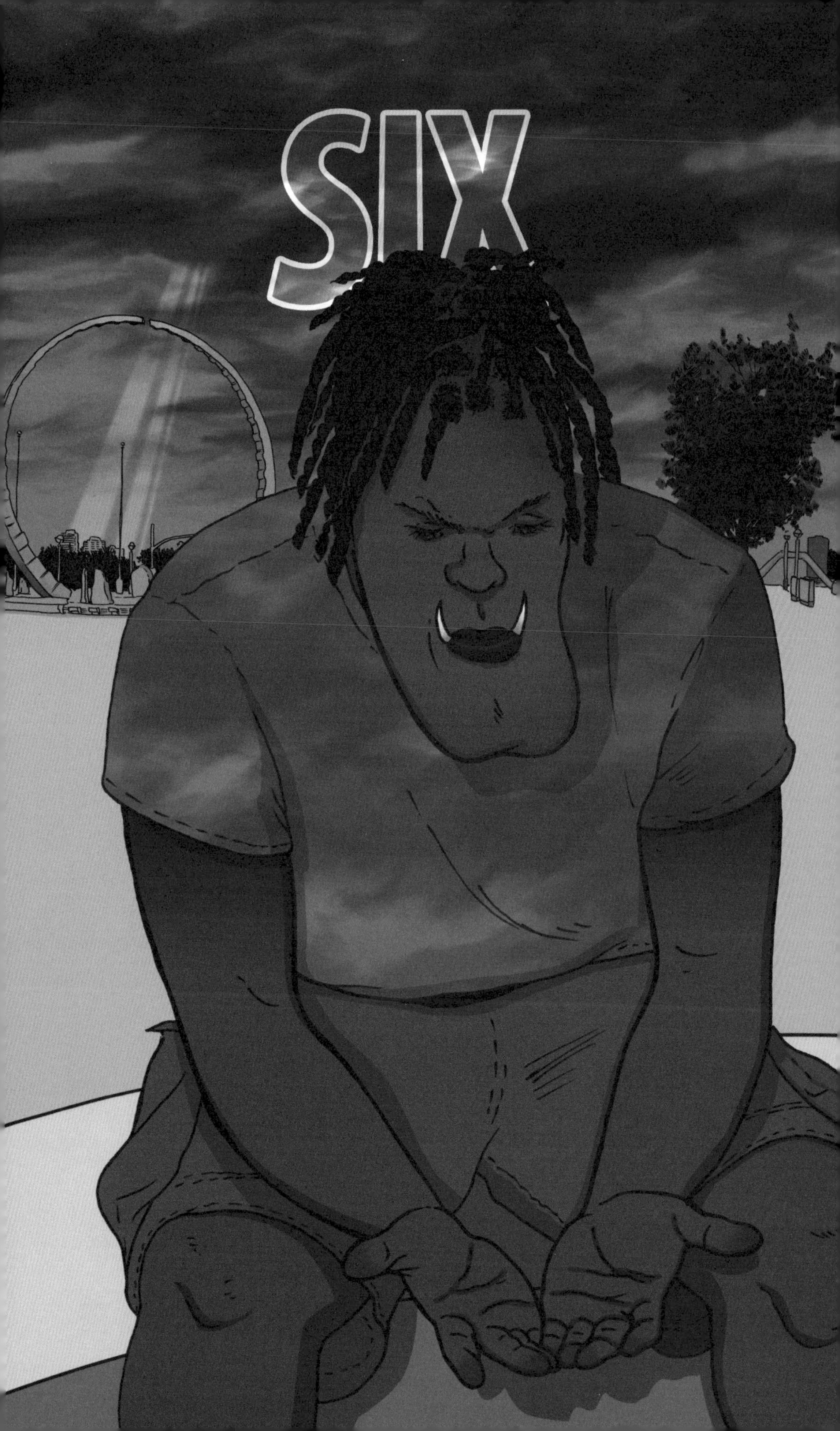
SIX

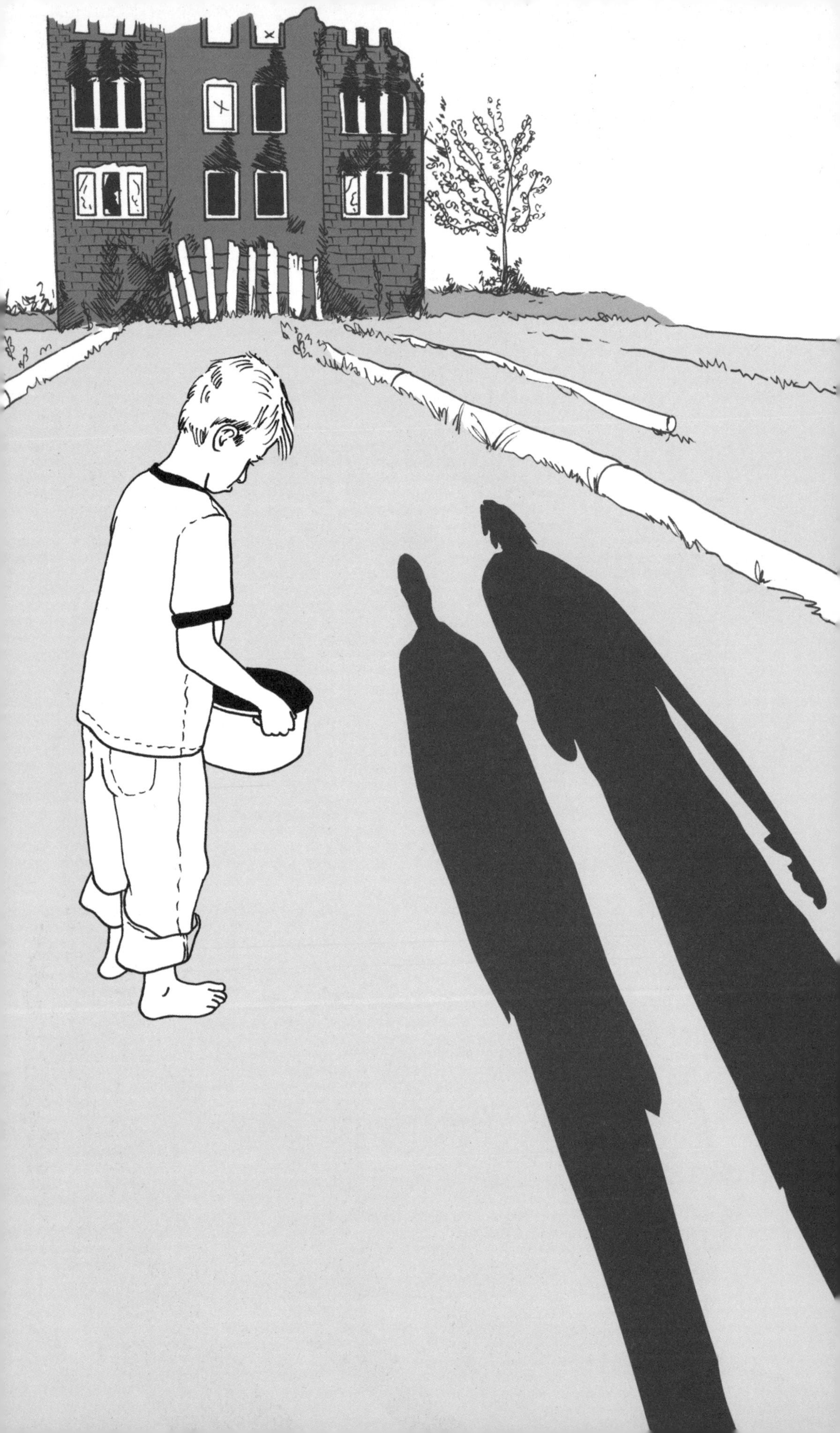

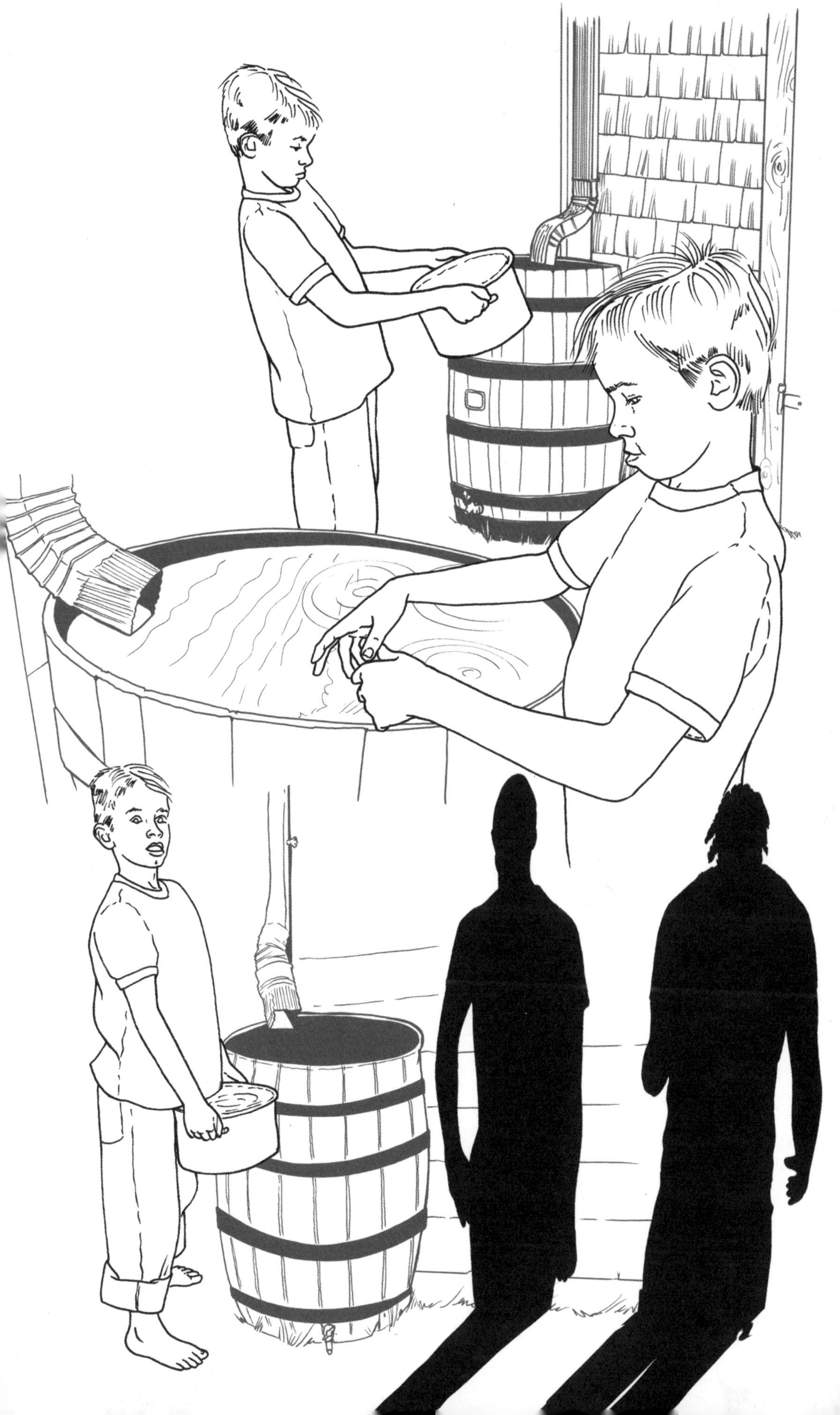

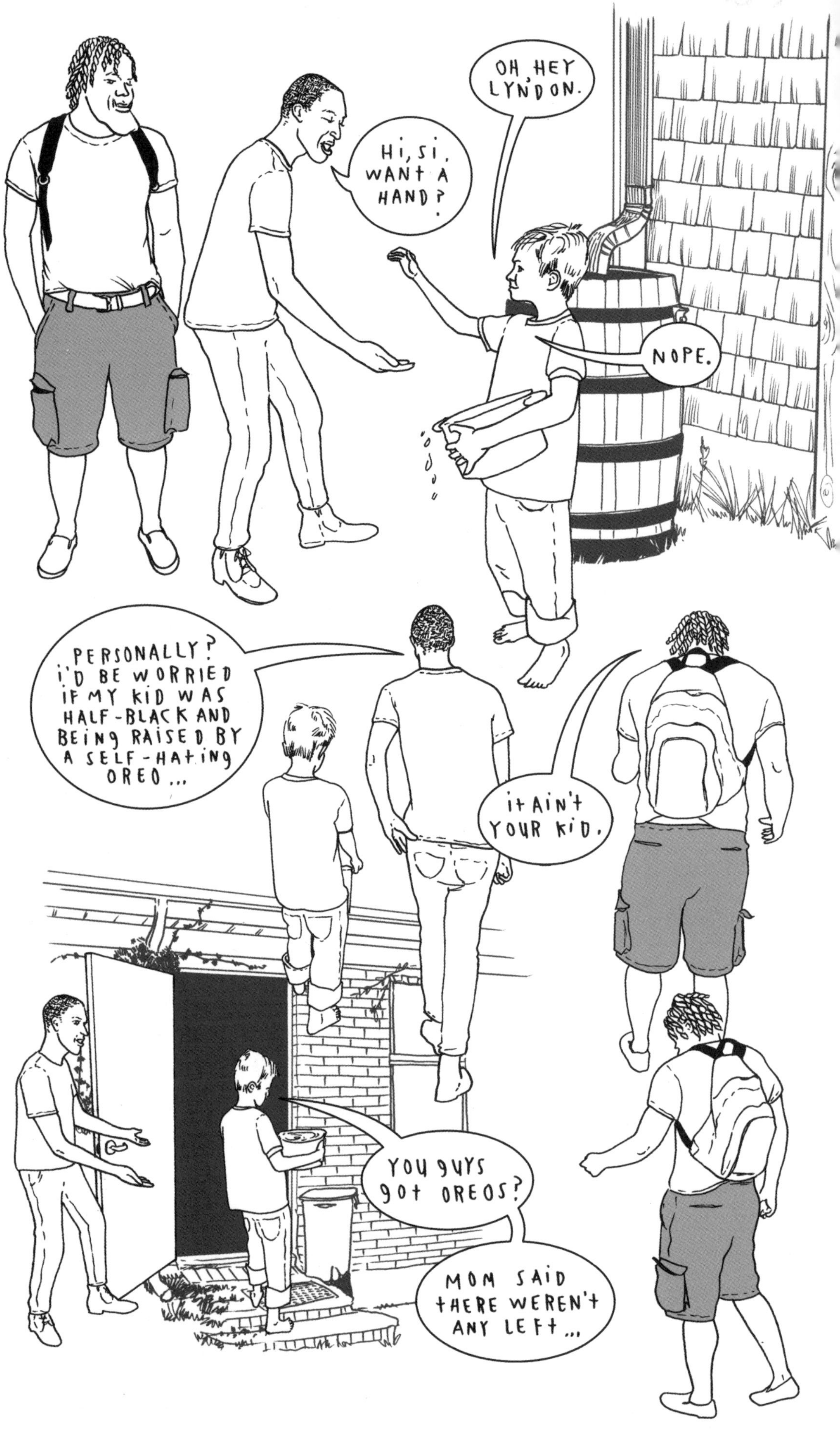
OH, HEY LYNDON.
Hi, Si. WANT A HAND?
NOPE.
PERSONALLY? I'D BE WORRIED IF MY KID WAS HALF-BLACK AND BEING RAISED BY A SELF-HATING OREO...
IT AIN'T YOUR KID.
YOU GUYS GOT OREOS?
MOM SAID THERE WEREN'T ANY LEFT...

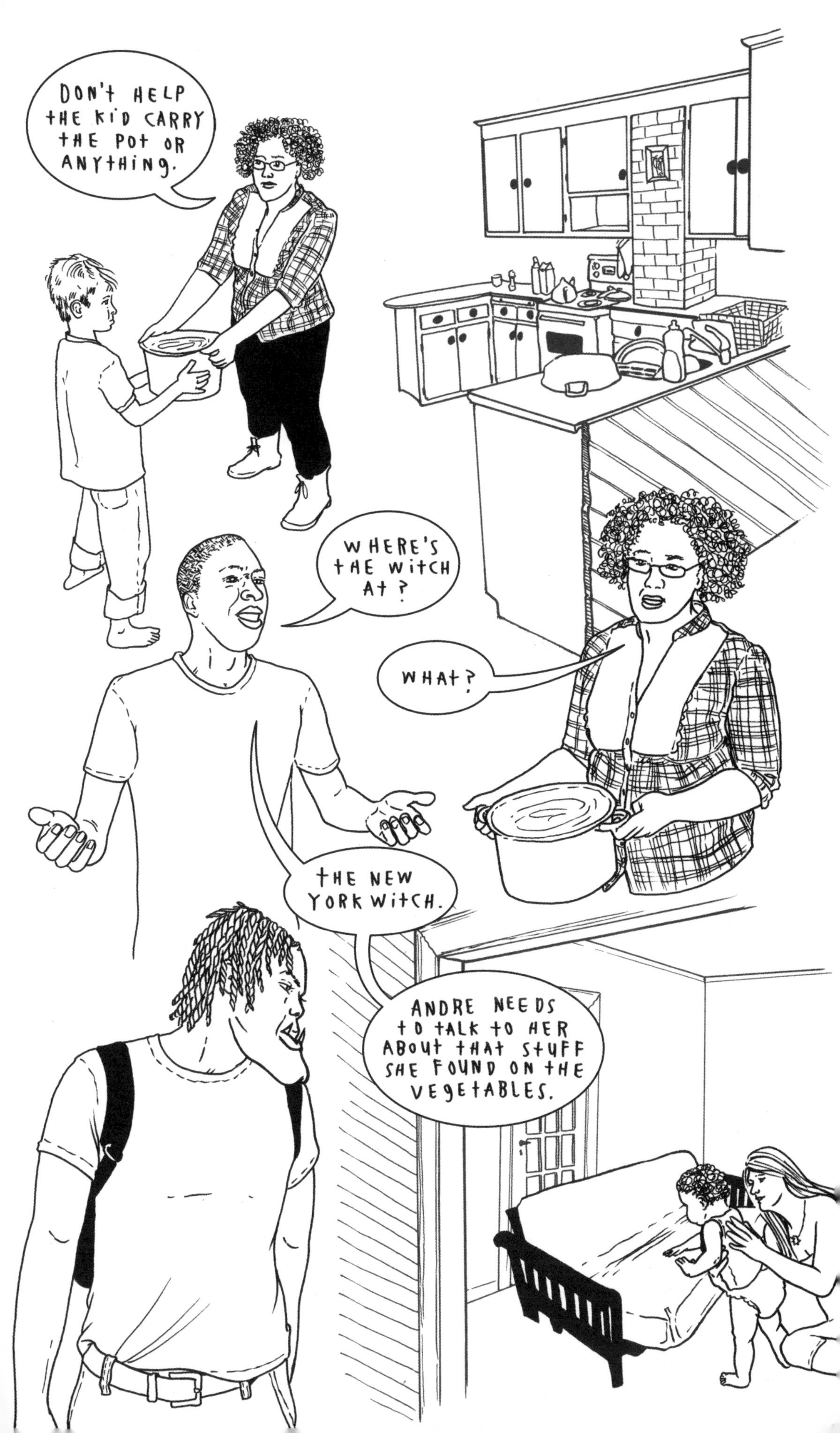
DON'T HELP THE KID CARRY THE POT OR ANYTHING.
WHERE'S THE WITCH AT?
WHAT?
THE NEW YORK WITCH.
ANDRE NEEDS TO TALK TO HER ABOUT THAT STUFF SHE FOUND ON THE VEGETABLES.

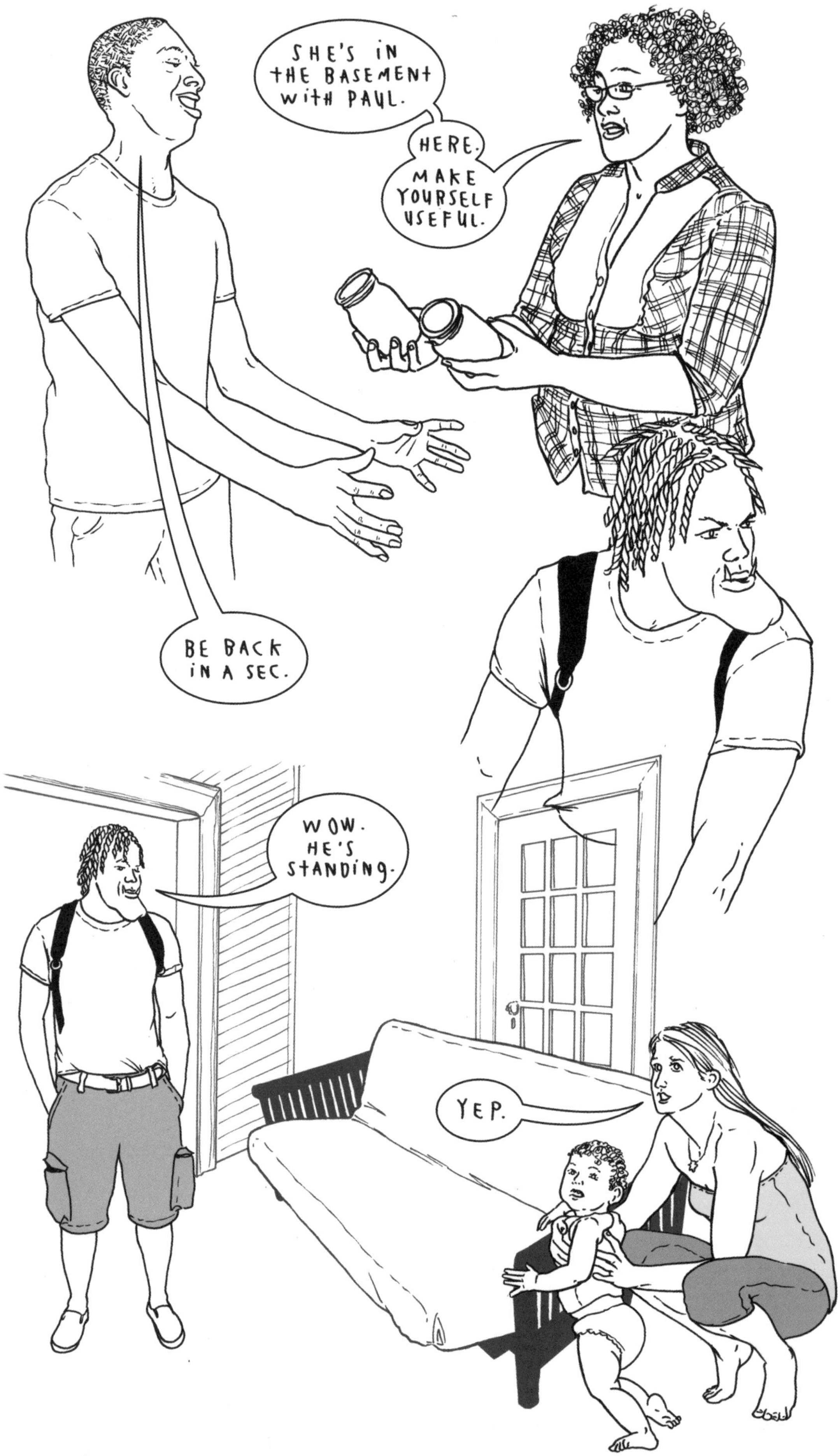
SHE'S IN THE BASEMENT WITH PAUL.
HERE.
MAKE YOURSELF USEFUL.
BE BACK IN A SEC.
WOW. HE'S STANDING.
YEP.

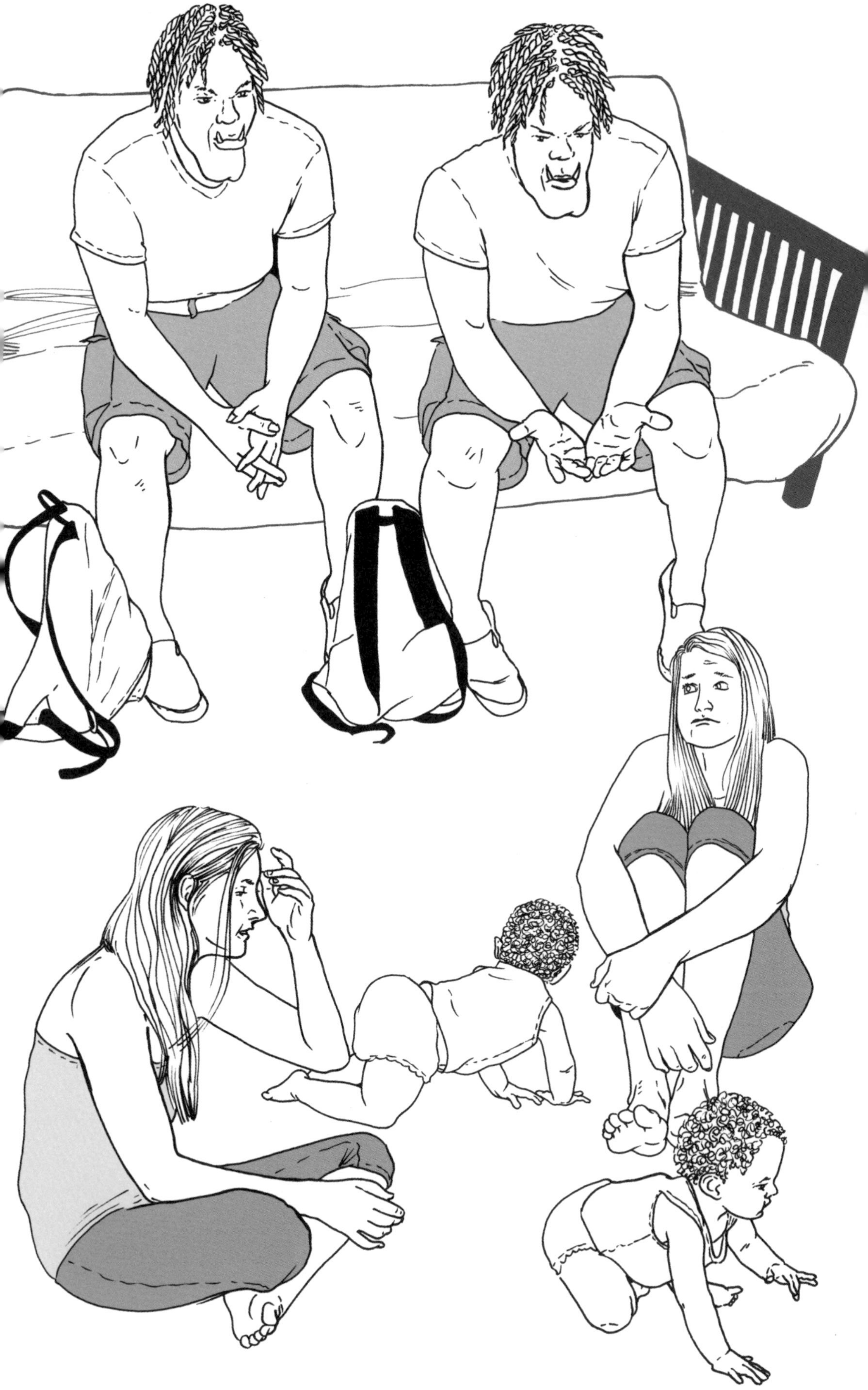

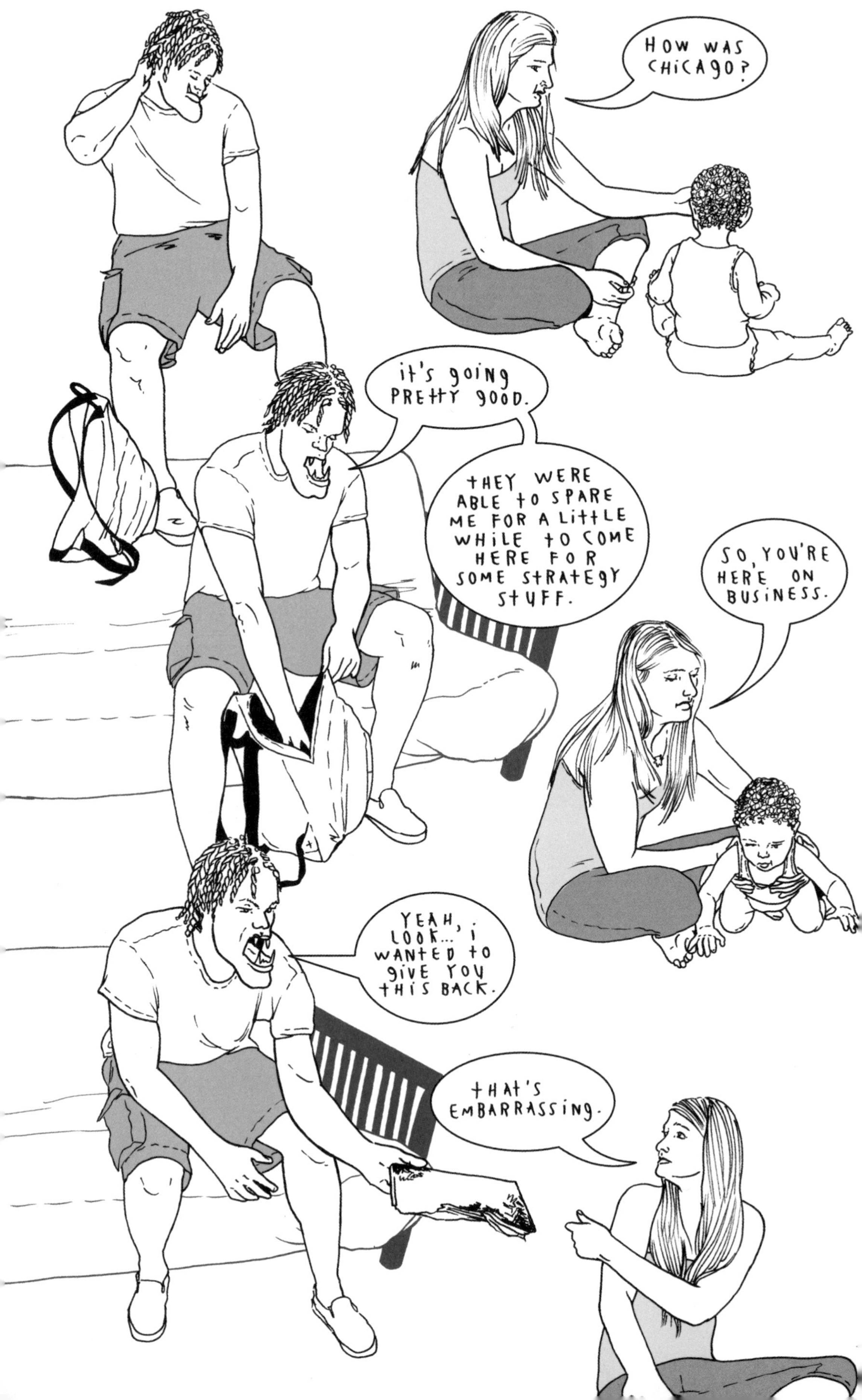
HOW WAS CHICAGO?
it's going PRETTY good.
THEY WERE ABLE to SPARE ME FOR A LITTLE WHILE to COME HERE FOR SOME STRATEGY STUFF.
SO, YOU'RE HERE ON BUSINESS.
YEAH, LOOK... i WANTED to GIVE YOU THIS BACK.
THAT'S EMBARRASSING.

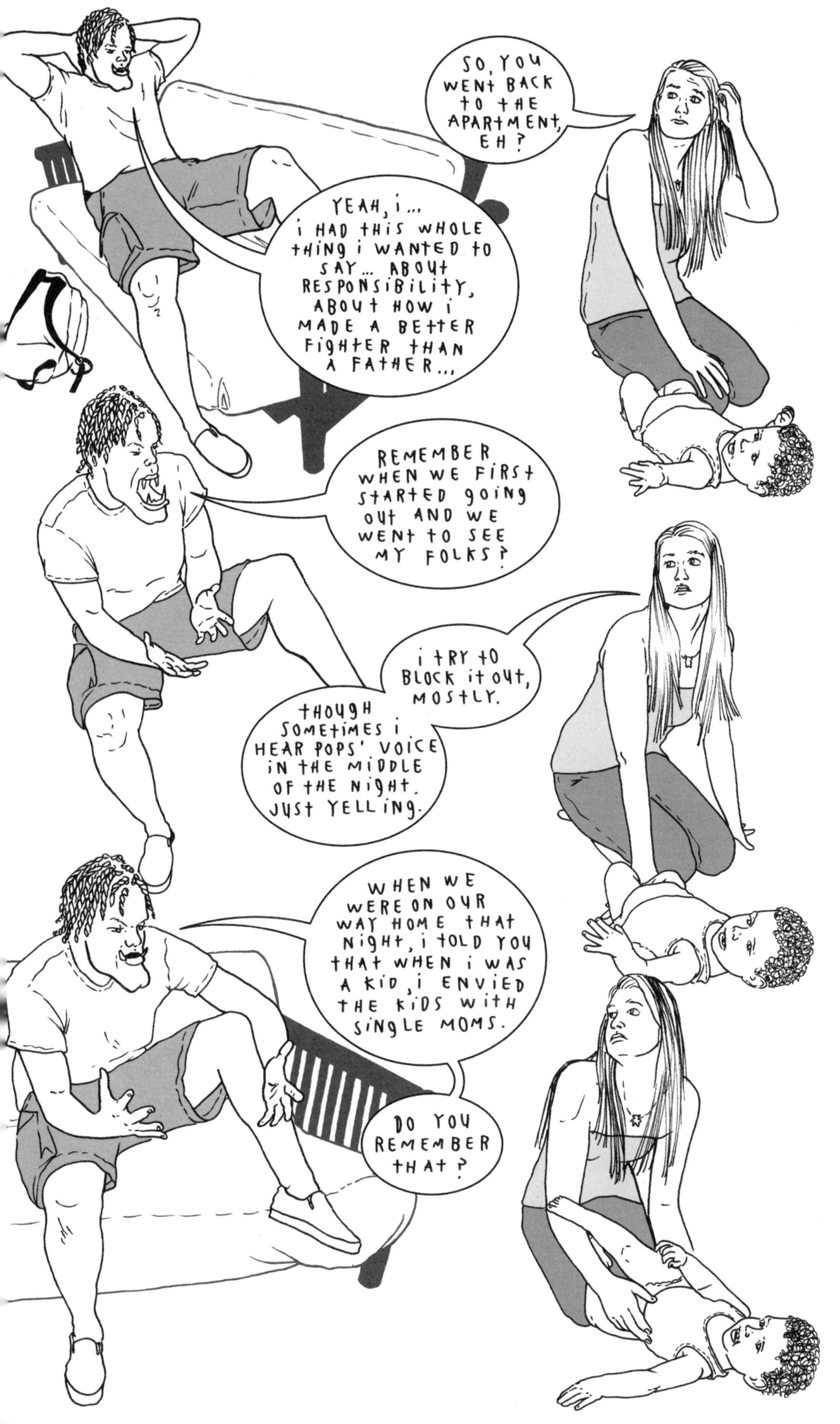
SO, YOU WENT BACK TO THE APARTMENT, EH?
YEAH, I... I HAD THIS WHOLE THING I WANTED TO SAY... ABOUT RESPONSIBILITY, ABOUT HOW I MADE A BETTER FIGHTER THAN A FATHER...
REMEMBER WHEN WE FIRST STARTED GOING OUT AND WE WENT TO SEE MY FOLKS?
I TRY TO BLOCK IT OUT, MOSTLY.
THOUGH SOMETIMES I HEAR POPS' VOICE IN THE MIDDLE OF THE NIGHT. JUST YELLING.
WHEN WE WERE ON OUR WAY HOME THAT NIGHT, I TOLD YOU THAT WHEN I WAS A KID, I ENVIED THE KIDS WITH SINGLE MOMS.
DO YOU REMEMBER THAT?

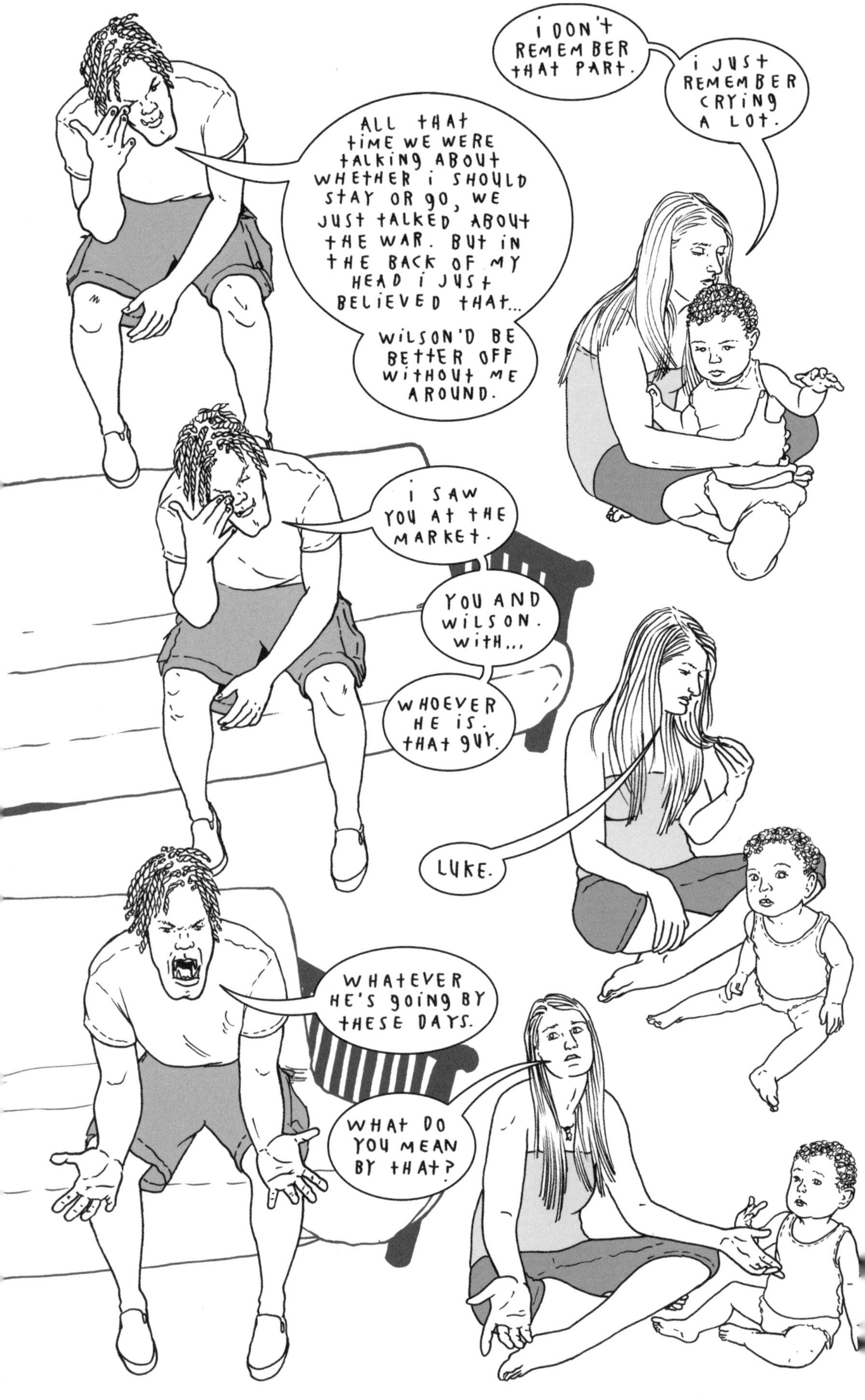
ALL THAT TIME WE WERE TALKING ABOUT WHETHER I SHOULD STAY OR GO, WE JUST TALKED ABOUT THE WAR. BUT IN THE BACK OF MY HEAD I JUST BELIEVED THAT...
WILSON'D BE BETTER OFF WITHOUT ME AROUND.
I DON'T REMEMBER THAT PART.
I JUST REMEMBER CRYING A LOT.
I SAW YOU AT THE MARKET.
YOU AND WILSON. WITH...
WHOEVER HE IS. THAT GUY.
LUKE.
WHATEVER HE'S GOING BY THESE DAYS.
WHAT DO YOU MEAN BY THAT?

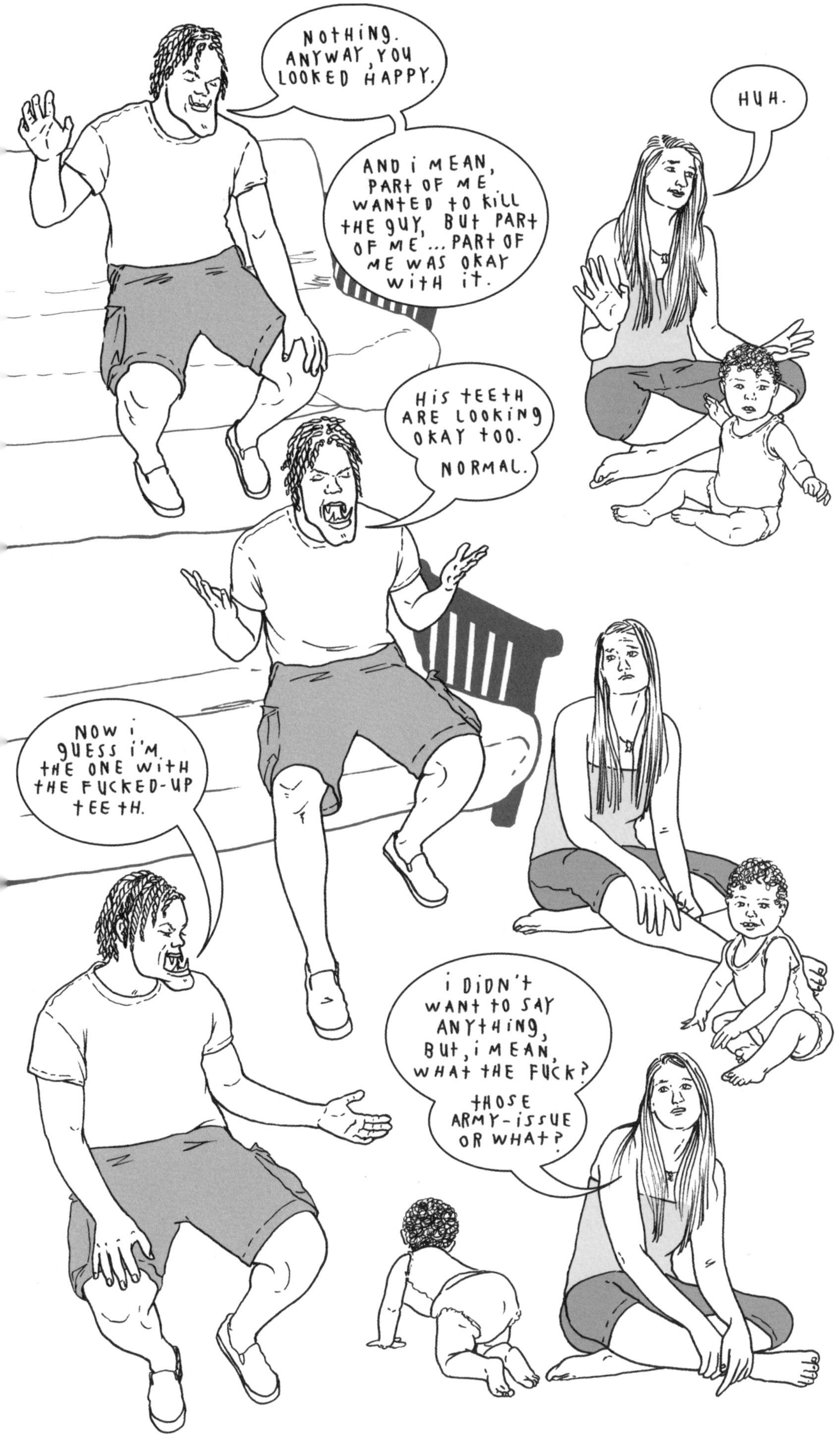
NOTHING. ANYWAY, YOU LOOKED HAPPY.
AND I MEAN, PART OF ME WANTED TO KILL THE GUY, BUT PART OF ME... PART OF ME WAS OKAY WITH IT.
HUH.
HIS TEETH ARE LOOKING OKAY TOO. NORMAL.
NOW I GUESS I'M THE ONE WITH THE FUCKED-UP TEETH.
I DIDN'T WANT TO SAY ANYTHING, BUT, I MEAN, WHAT THE FUCK?
THOSE ARMY-ISSUE OR WHAT?

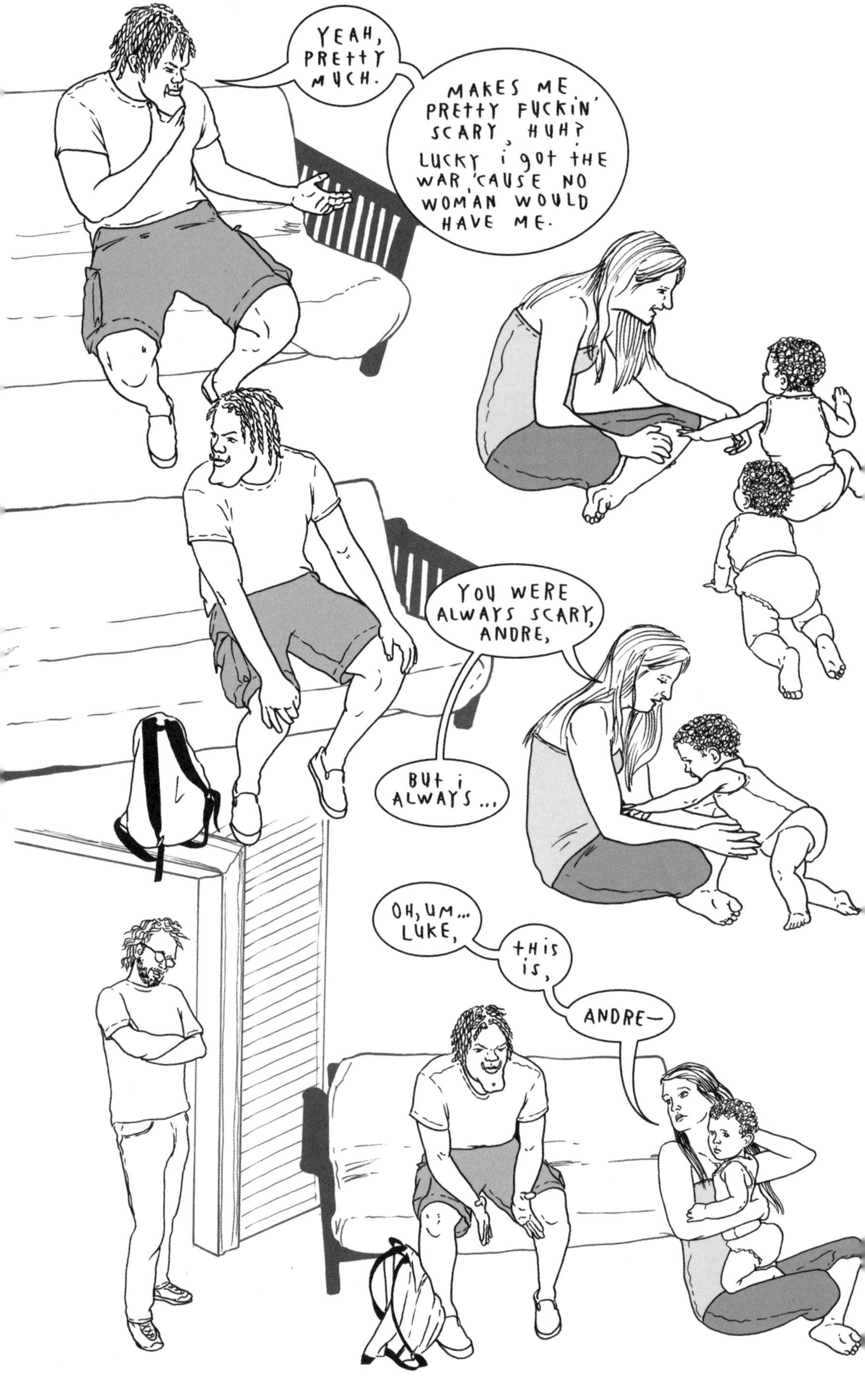
YEAH, PRETTY MUCH.
MAKES ME PRETTY FUCKIN' SCARY, HUH? LUCKY i got THE WAR, 'CAUSE NO WOMAN WOULD HAVE ME.
YOU WERE ALWAYS SCARY, ANDRE,
BUt i ALWAYS...
OH, UM... LUKE,
tHIS IS,
ANDRE—

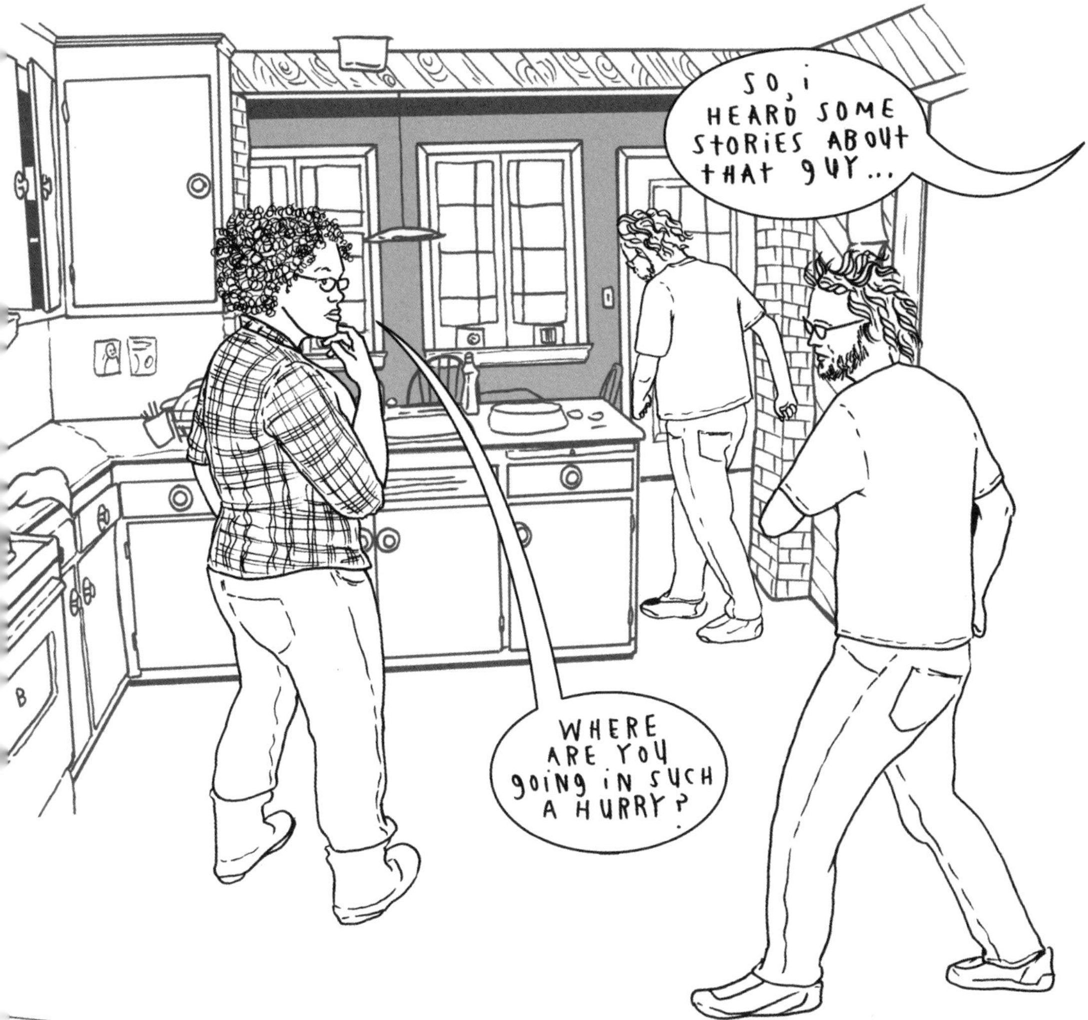
SO, I HEARD SOME STORIES ABOUT THAT GUY...
WHERE ARE YOU GOING IN SUCH A HURRY?

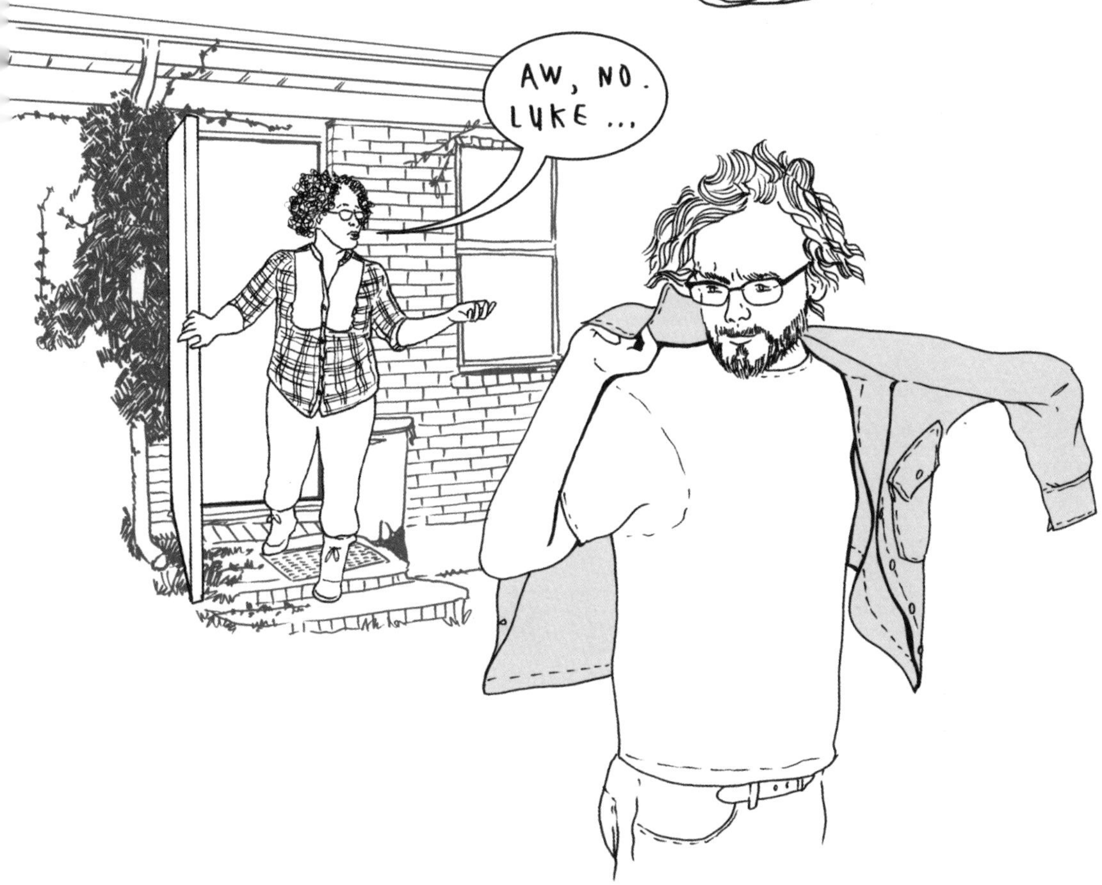
AW, NO. LUKE ...

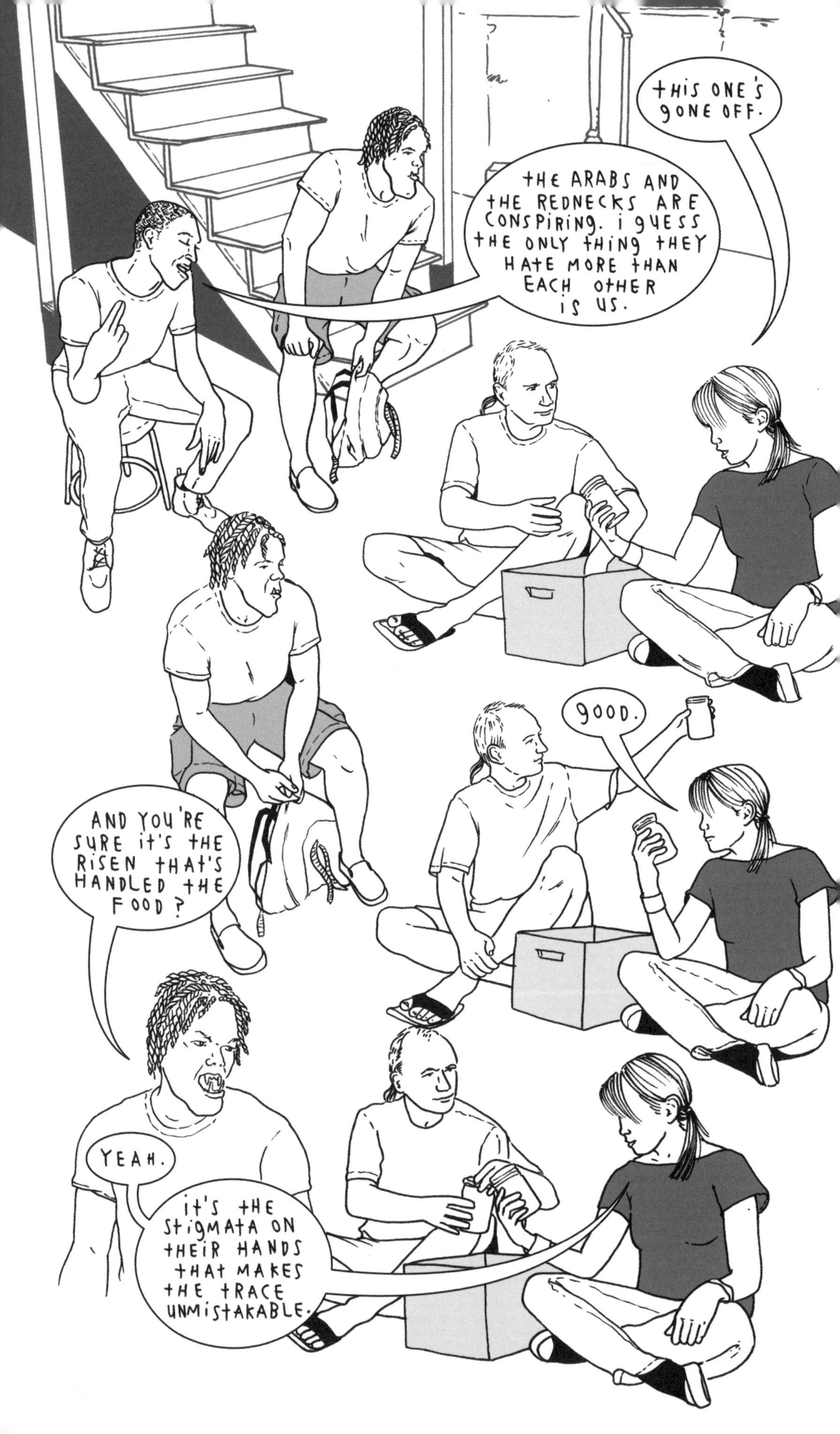
THIS ONE'S GONE OFF.
THE ARABS AND THE REDNECKS ARE CONSPIRING. I GUESS THE ONLY THING THEY HATE MORE THAN EACH OTHER IS US.
GOOD.
AND YOU'RE SURE IT'S THE RISEN THAT'S HANDLED THE FOOD?
YEAH.
IT'S THE STIGMATA ON THEIR HANDS THAT MAKES THE TRACE UNMISTAKABLE.

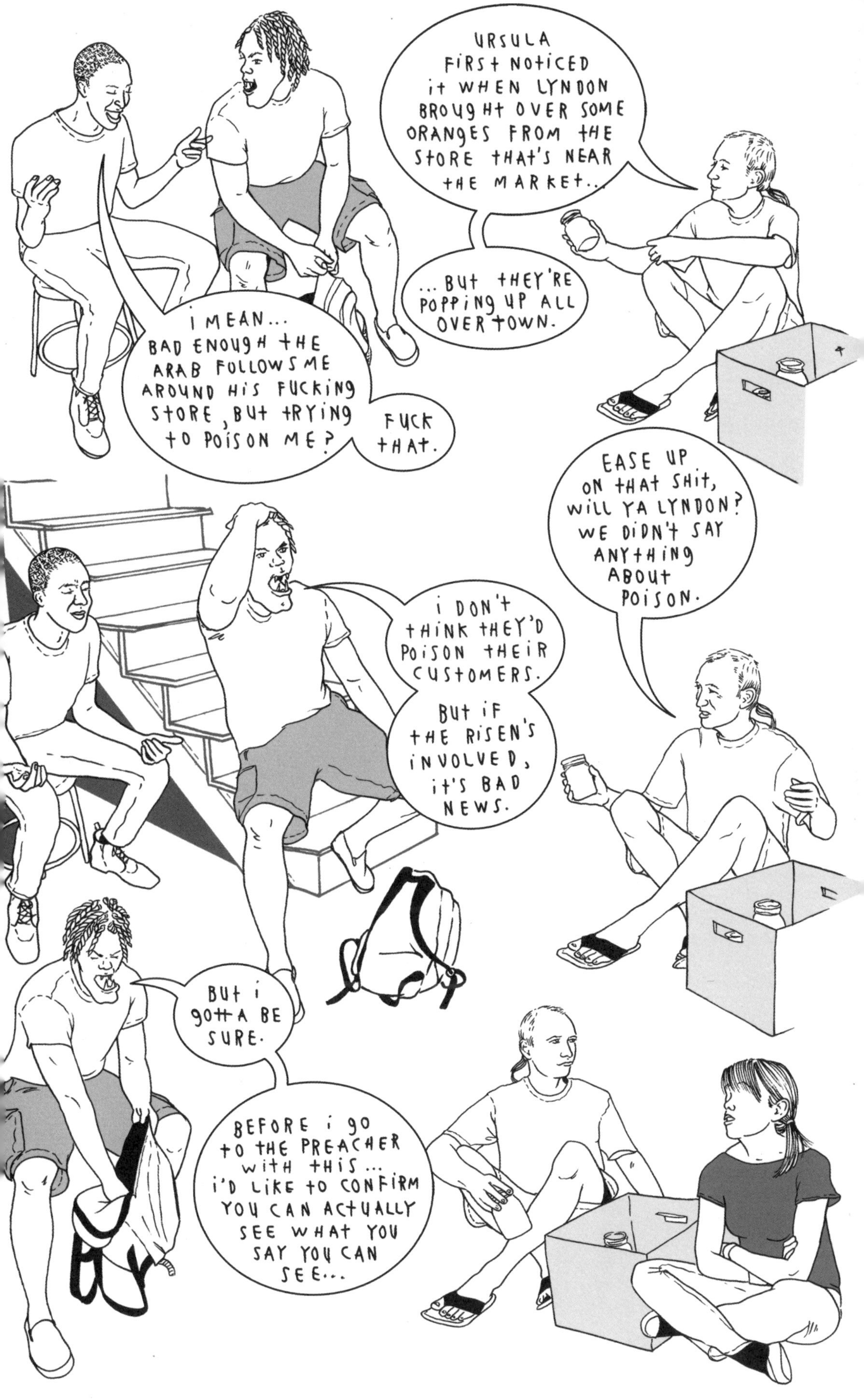
URSULA FIRST NOTICED IT WHEN LYNDON BROUGHT OVER SOME ORANGES FROM THE STORE THAT'S NEAR THE MARKET...
...BUT THEY'RE POPPING UP ALL OVER TOWN.
I MEAN... BAD ENOUGH THE ARAB FOLLOWS ME AROUND HIS FUCKING STORE, BUT TRYING TO POISON ME?
FUCK THAT.
EASE UP ON THAT SHIT, WILL YA LYNDON? WE DIDN'T SAY ANYTHING ABOUT POISON.
I DON'T THINK THEY'D POISON THEIR CUSTOMERS.
BUT IF THE RISEN'S INVOLVED, IT'S BAD NEWS.
BUT I GOTTA BE SURE.
BEFORE I GO TO THE PREACHER WITH THIS... I'D LIKE TO CONFIRM YOU CAN ACTUALLY SEE WHAT YOU SAY YOU CAN SEE...

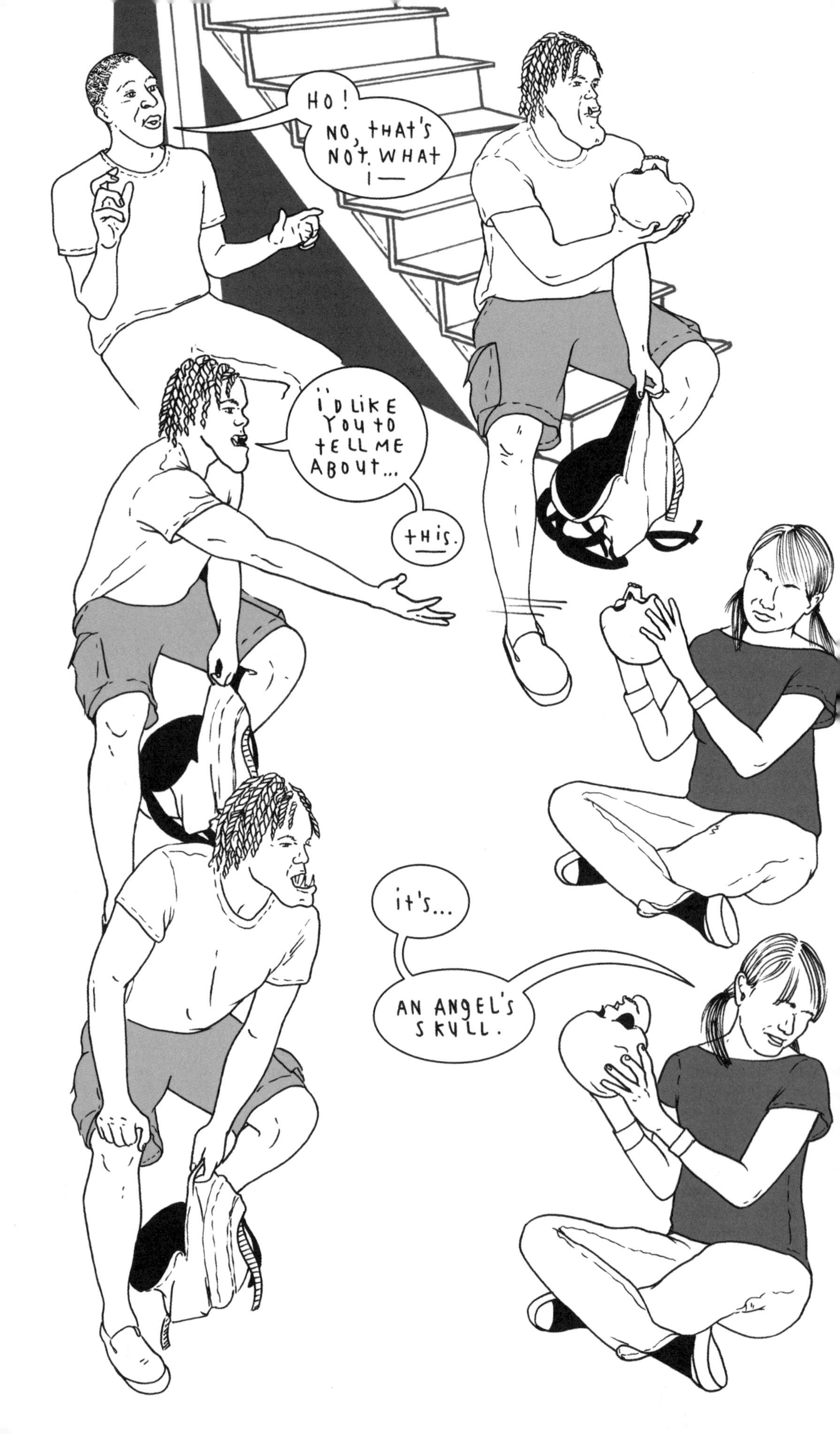
HO!
NO, THAT'S NOT WHAT I—
I'D LIKE YOU TO TELL ME ABOUT...
THIS.
IT'S...
AN ANGEL'S SKULL.

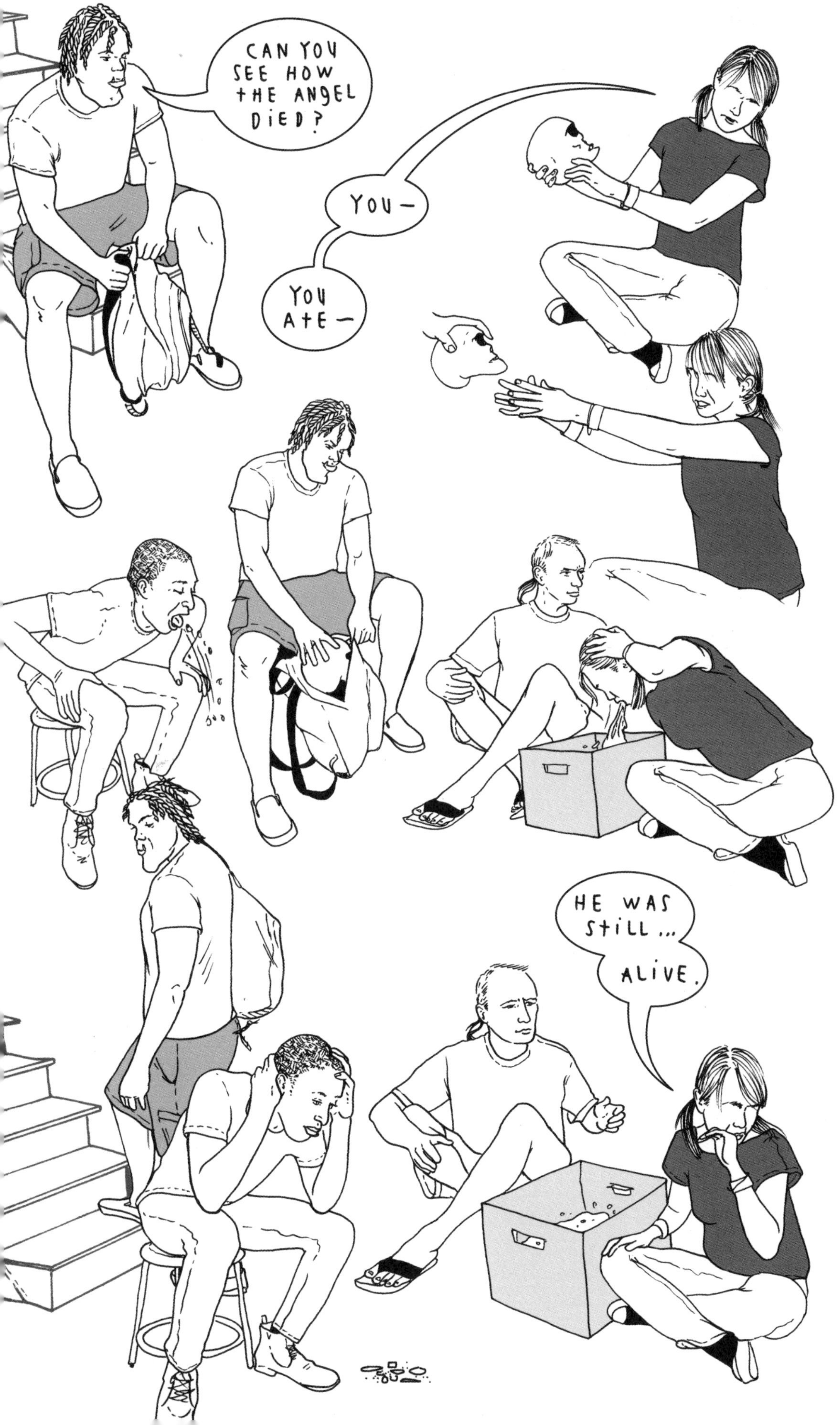

CAN YOU SEE HOW THE ANGEL DIED?
YOU-
YOU ATE-
HE WAS STILL...
ALIVE.

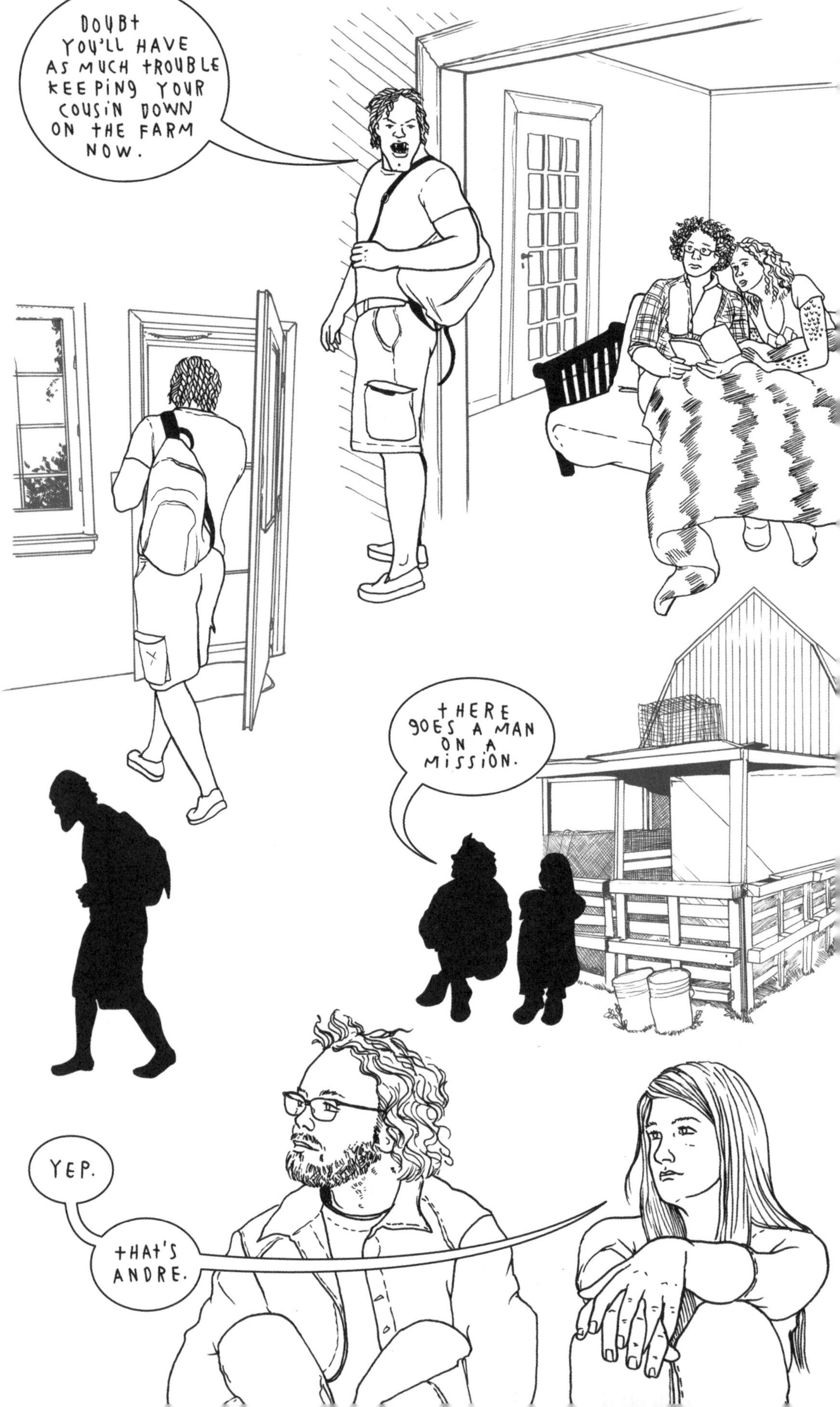
DOUBT YOU'LL HAVE AS MUCH TROUBLE KEEPING YOUR COUSIN DOWN ON THE FARM NOW.
THERE GOES A MAN ON A MISSION.
YEP.
THAT'S ANDRE.

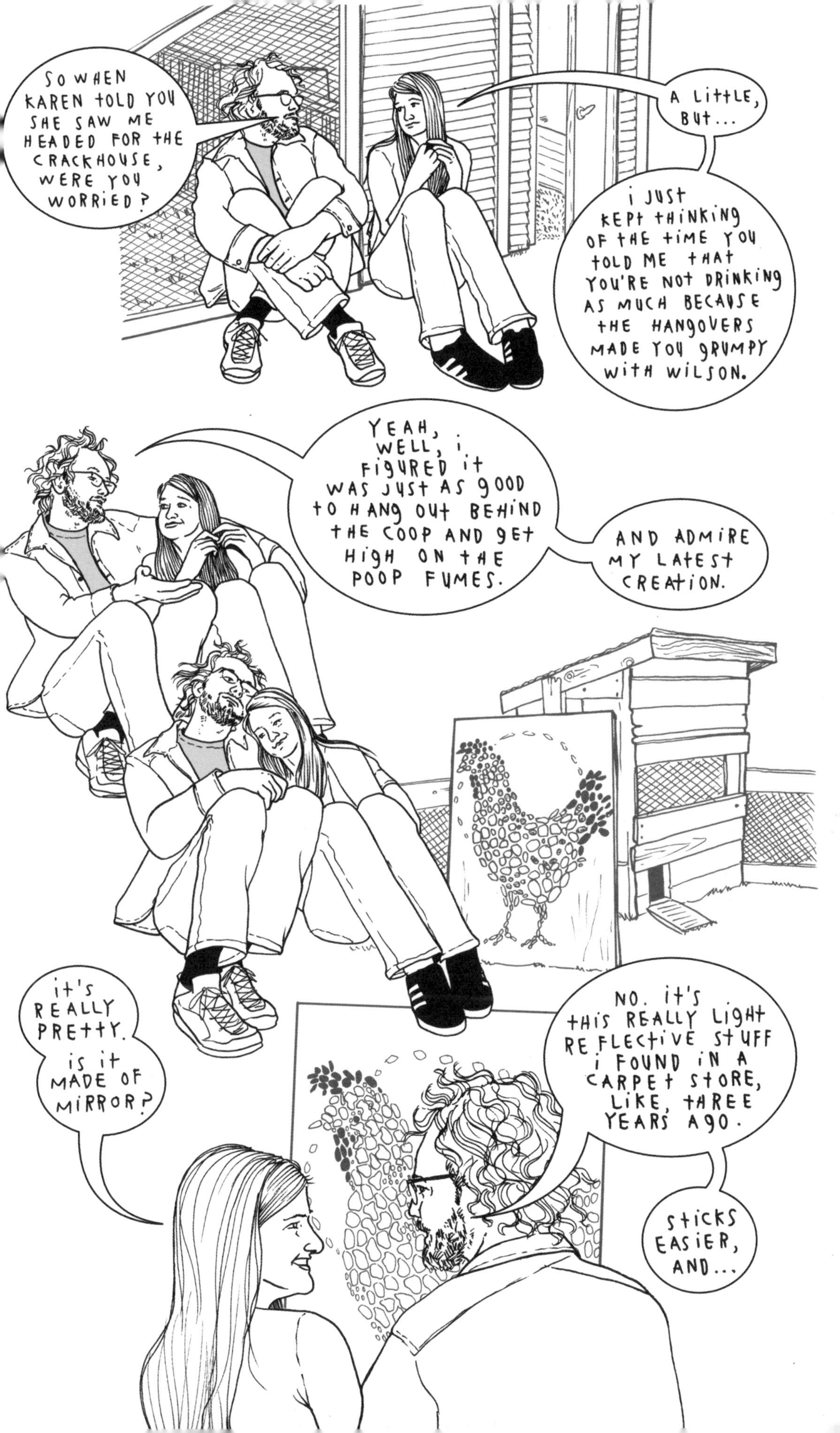
SO WHEN KAREN TOLD YOU SHE SAW ME HEADED FOR THE CRACKHOUSE, WERE YOU WORRIED?
A LITTLE, BUT...
I JUST KEPT THINKING OF THE TIME YOU TOLD ME THAT YOU'RE NOT DRINKING AS MUCH BECAUSE THE HANGOVERS MADE YOU GRUMPY WITH WILSON.
YEAH, WELL, I FIGURED IT WAS JUST AS GOOD TO HANG OUT BEHIND THE COOP AND GET HIGH ON THE POOP FUMES.
AND ADMIRE MY LATEST CREATION.
IT'S REALLY PRETTY. IS IT MADE OF MIRROR?
NO. IT'S THIS REALLY LIGHT REFLECTIVE STUFF I FOUND IN A CARPET STORE, LIKE, THREE YEARS AGO.
STICKS EASIER, AND...

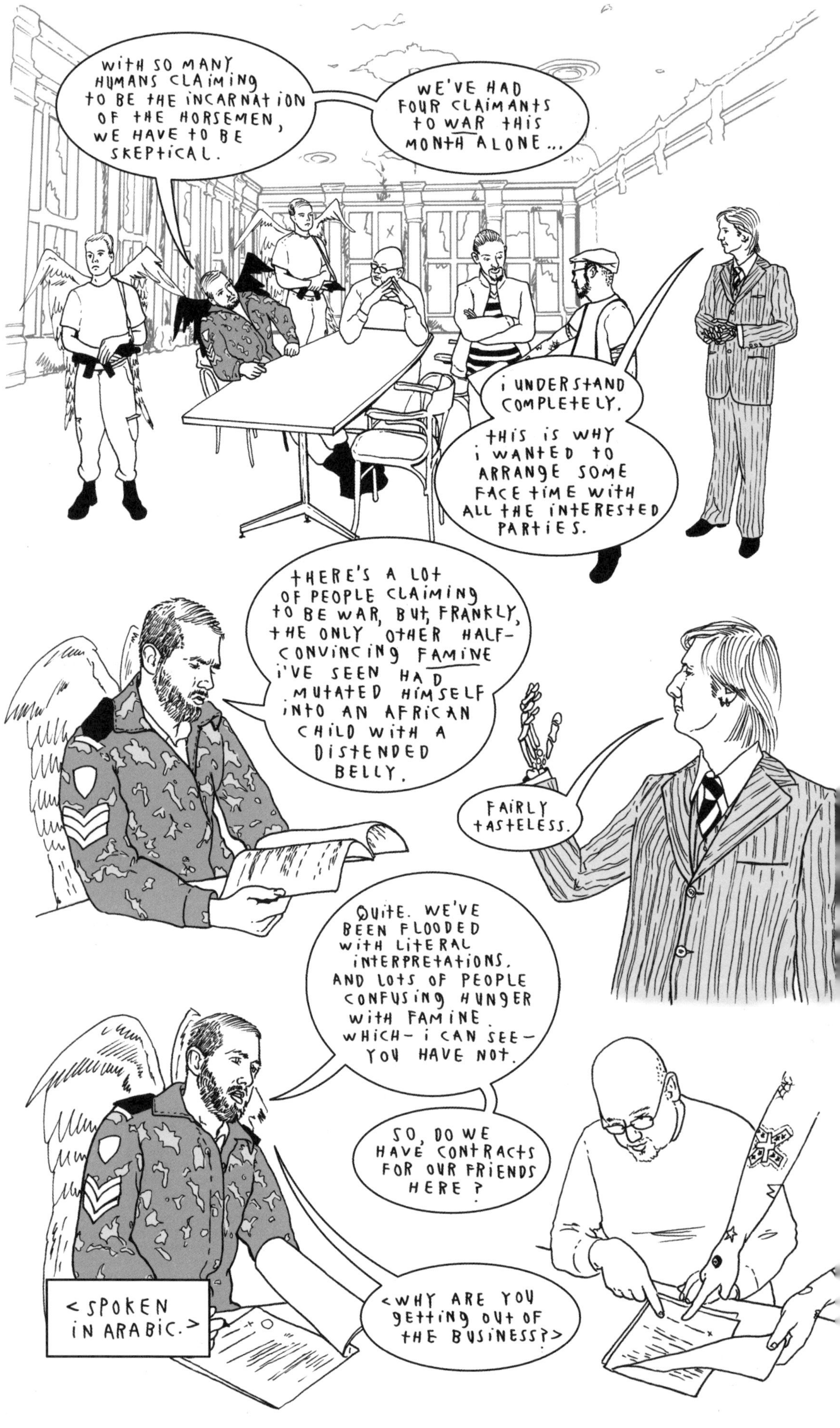
WITH SO MANY HUMANS CLAIMING TO BE THE INCARNATION OF THE HORSEMEN, WE HAVE TO BE SKEPTICAL.
WE'VE HAD FOUR CLAIMANTS TO WAR THIS MONTH ALONE...
I UNDERSTAND COMPLETELY.
THIS IS WHY I WANTED TO ARRANGE SOME FACE TIME WITH ALL THE INTERESTED PARTIES.
THERE'S A LOT OF PEOPLE CLAIMING TO BE WAR, BUT, FRANKLY, THE ONLY OTHER HALF-CONVINCING FAMINE I'VE SEEN HAD MUTATED HIMSELF INTO AN AFRICAN CHILD WITH A DISTENDED BELLY.
FAIRLY TASTELESS.
QUITE. WE'VE BEEN FLOODED WITH LITERAL INTERPRETATIONS. AND LOTS OF PEOPLE CONFUSING HUNGER WITH FAMINE. WHICH- I CAN SEE- YOU HAVE NOT.
SO, DO WE HAVE CONTRACTS FOR OUR FRIENDS HERE?
<SPOKEN IN ARABIC.>
<WHY ARE YOU GETTING OUT OF THE BUSINESS?>

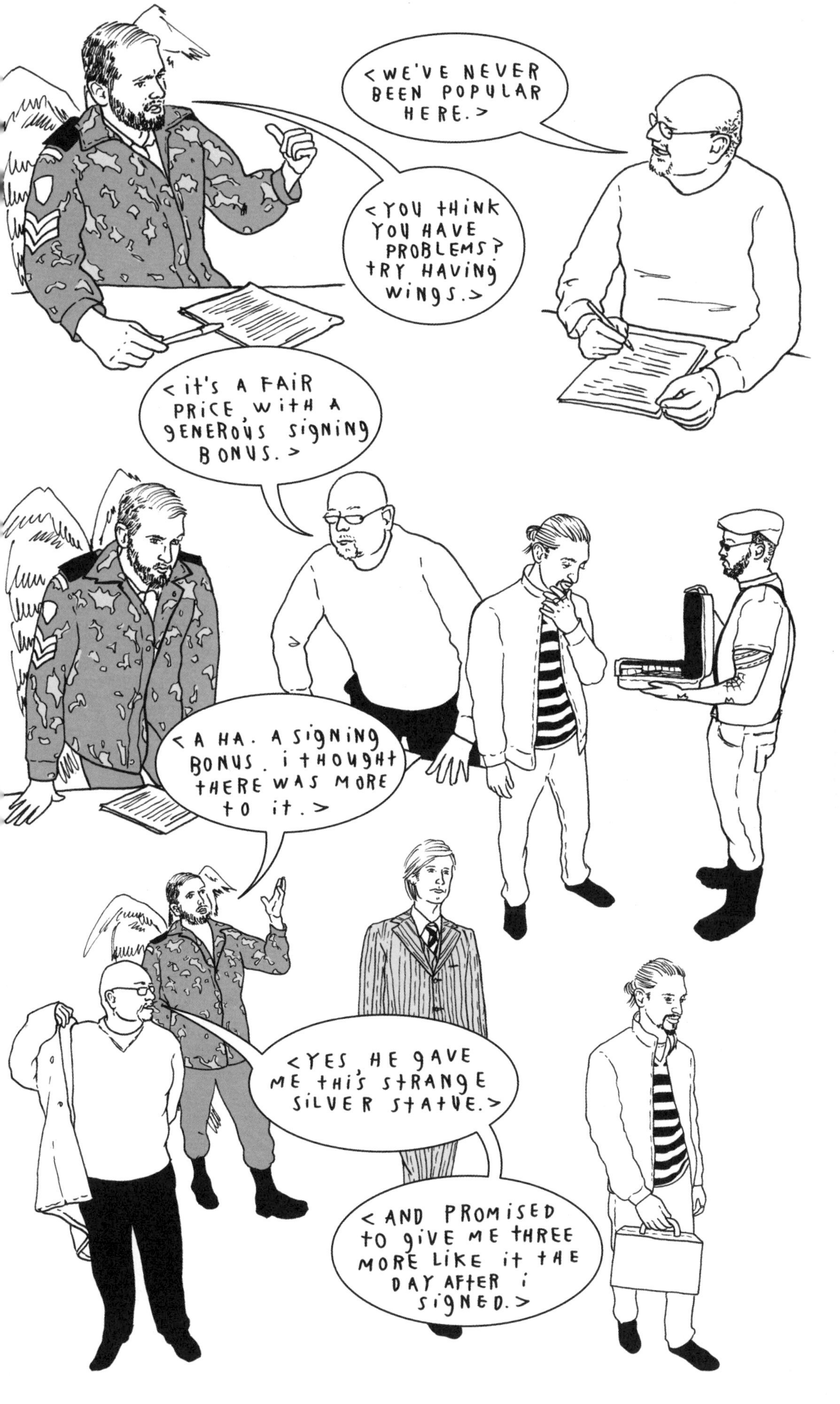
<WE'VE NEVER BEEN POPULAR HERE.>
<YOU THINK YOU HAVE PROBLEMS? TRY HAVING WINGS.>
<IT'S A FAIR PRICE, WITH A GENEROUS SIGNING BONUS.>
<A HA. A SIGNING BONUS. I THOUGHT THERE WAS MORE TO IT.>
<YES, HE GAVE ME THIS STRANGE SILVER STATUE.>
<AND PROMISED TO GIVE ME THREE MORE LIKE IT THE DAY AFTER I SIGNED.>

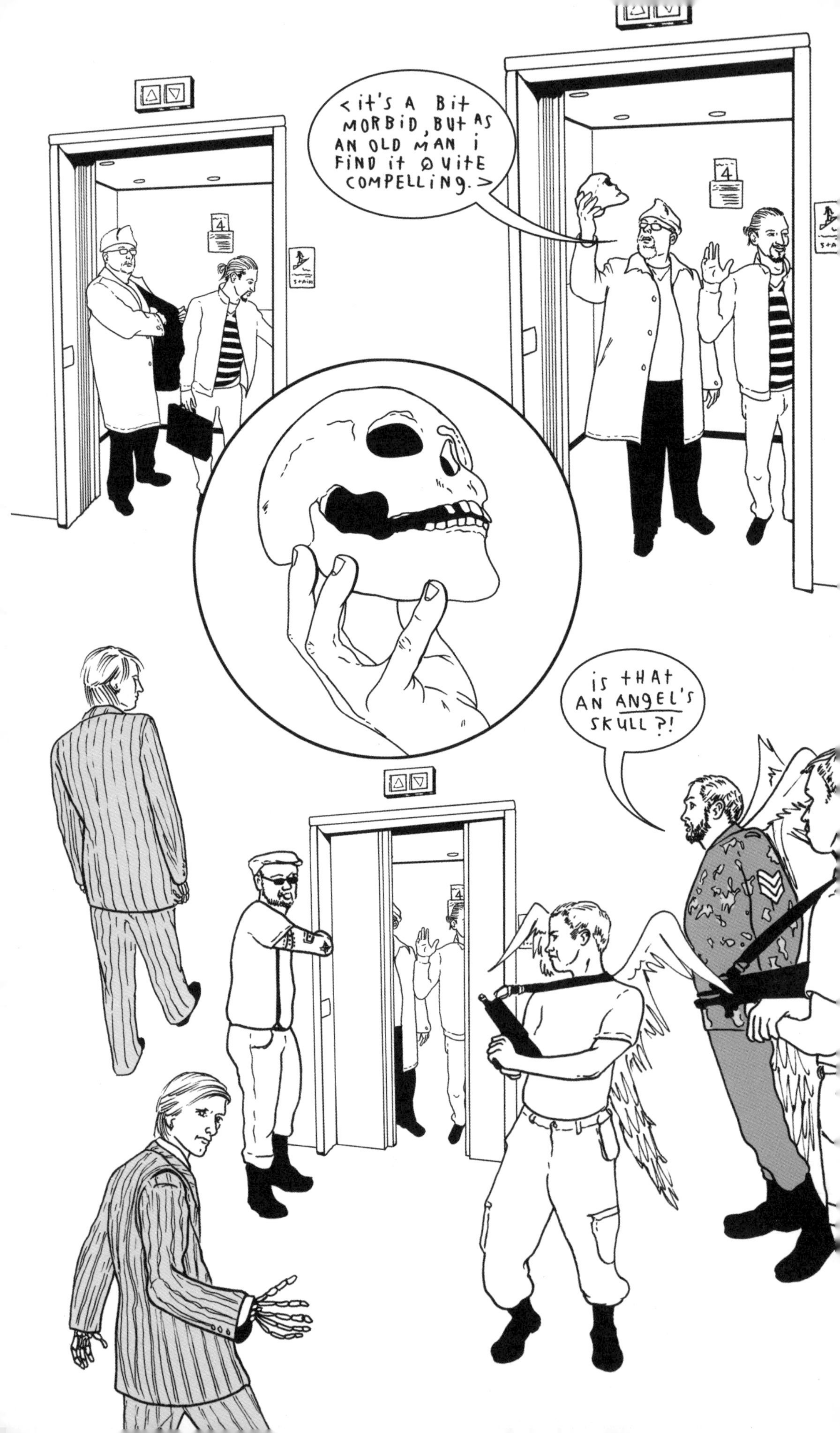
<IT'S A BIT MORBID, BUT AS AN OLD MAN I FIND IT QUITE COMPELLING.>
IS THAT AN ANGEL'S SKULL?!

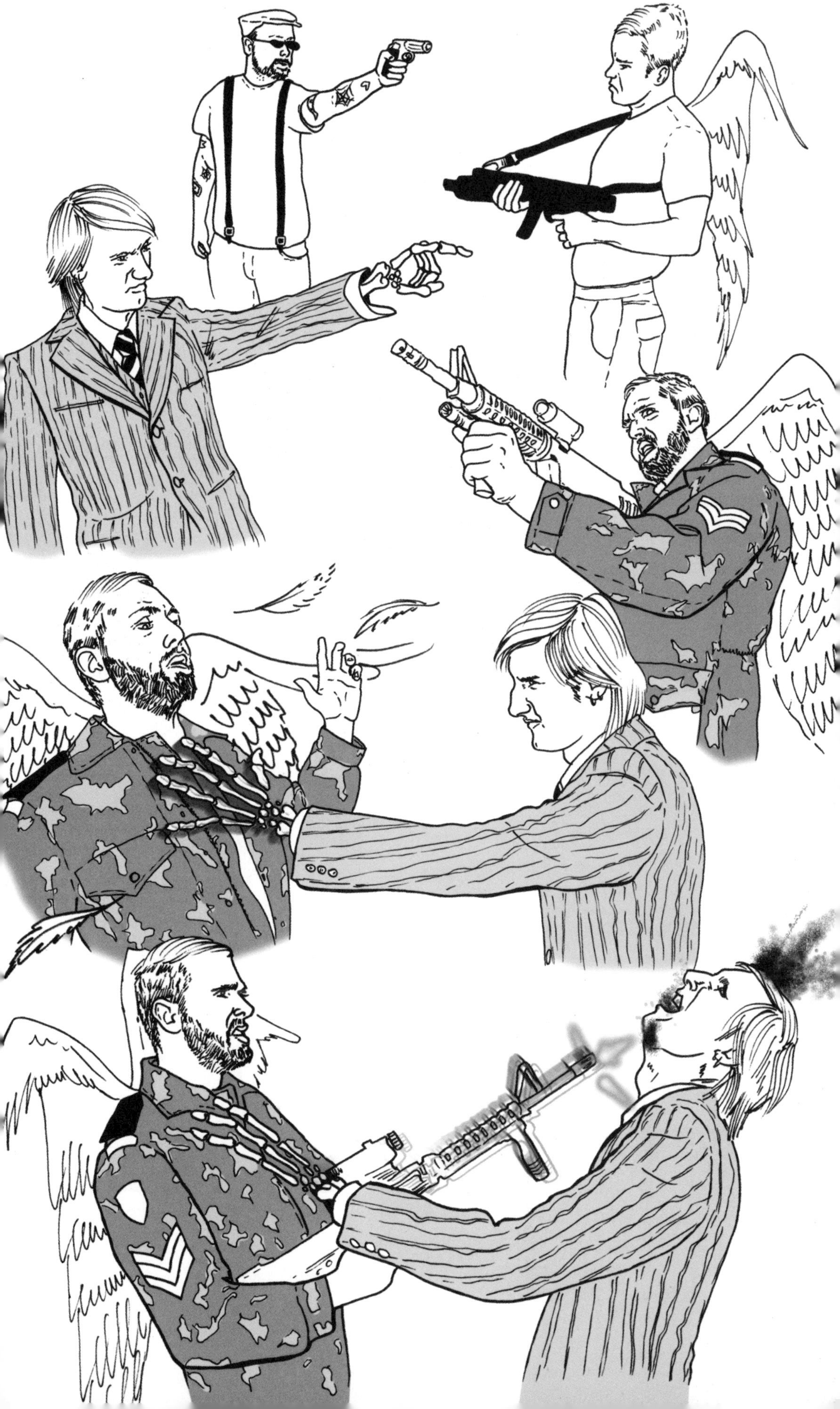

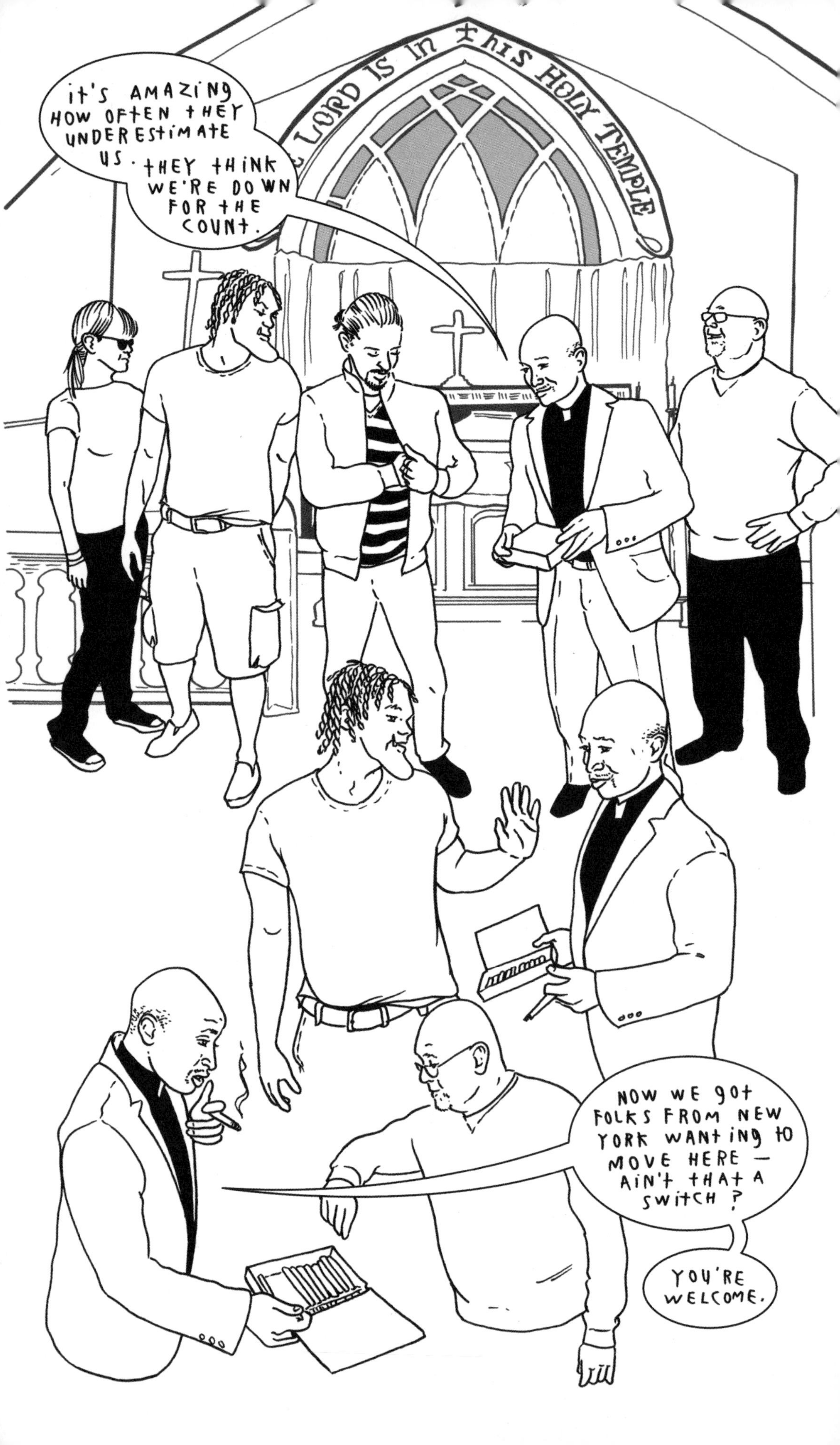
LORD IS IN THIS HOLY TEMPLE
IT'S AMAZING HOW OFTEN THEY UNDERESTIMATE US. THEY THINK WE'RE DOWN FOR THE COUNT.
NOW WE GOT FOLKS FROM NEW YORK WANTING TO MOVE HERE — AIN'T THAT A SWITCH?
YOU'RE WELCOME.

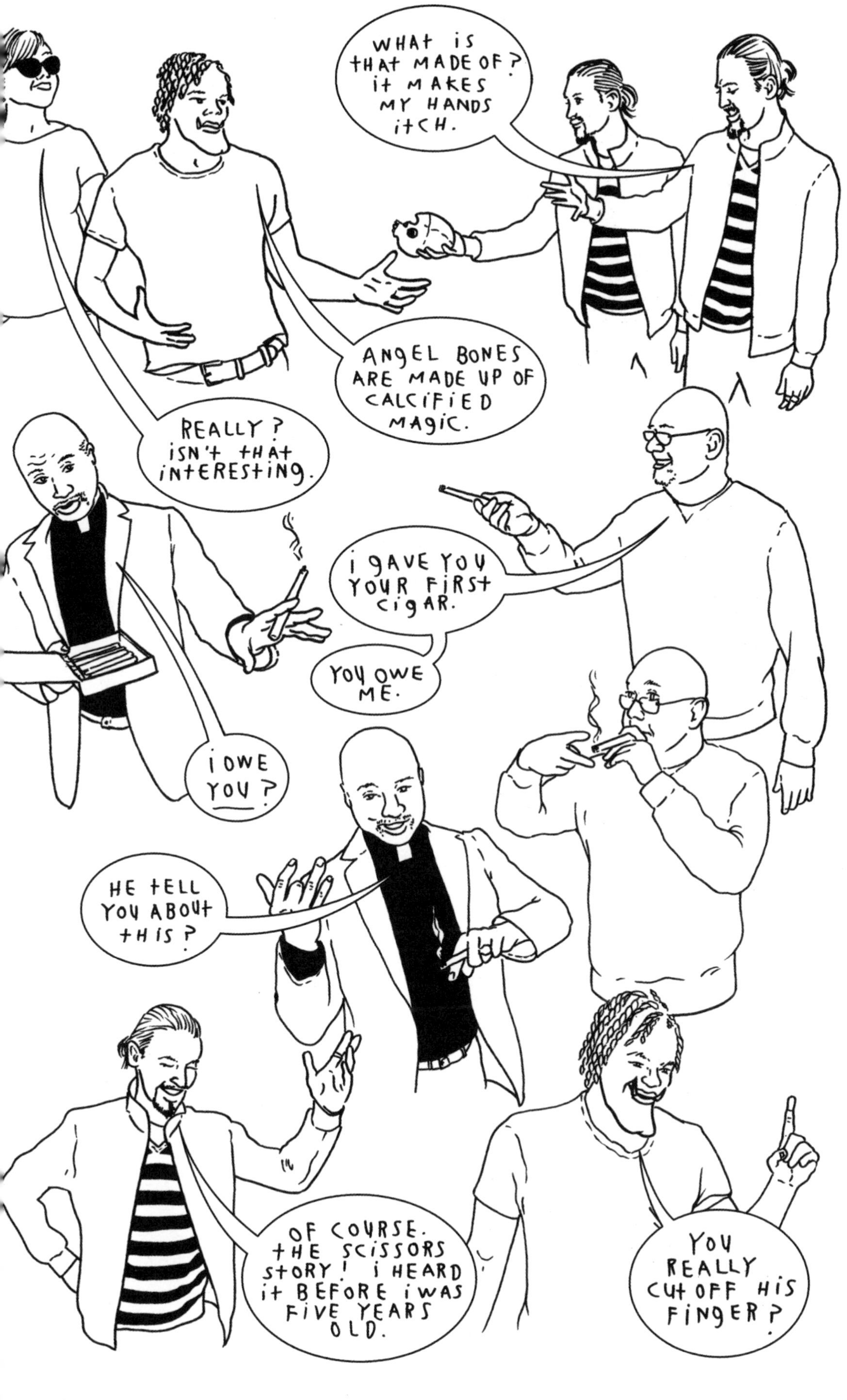
WHAT IS THAT MADE OF? IT MAKES MY HANDS ITCH.
ANGEL BONES ARE MADE UP OF CALCIFIED MAGIC.
REALLY? ISN'T THAT INTERESTING.
I GAVE YOU YOUR FIRST CIGAR.
YOU OWE ME.
I OWE YOU?
HE TELL YOU ABOUT THIS?
OF COURSE. THE SCISSORS STORY! I HEARD IT BEFORE I WAS FIVE YEARS OLD.
YOU REALLY CUT OFF HIS FINGER?

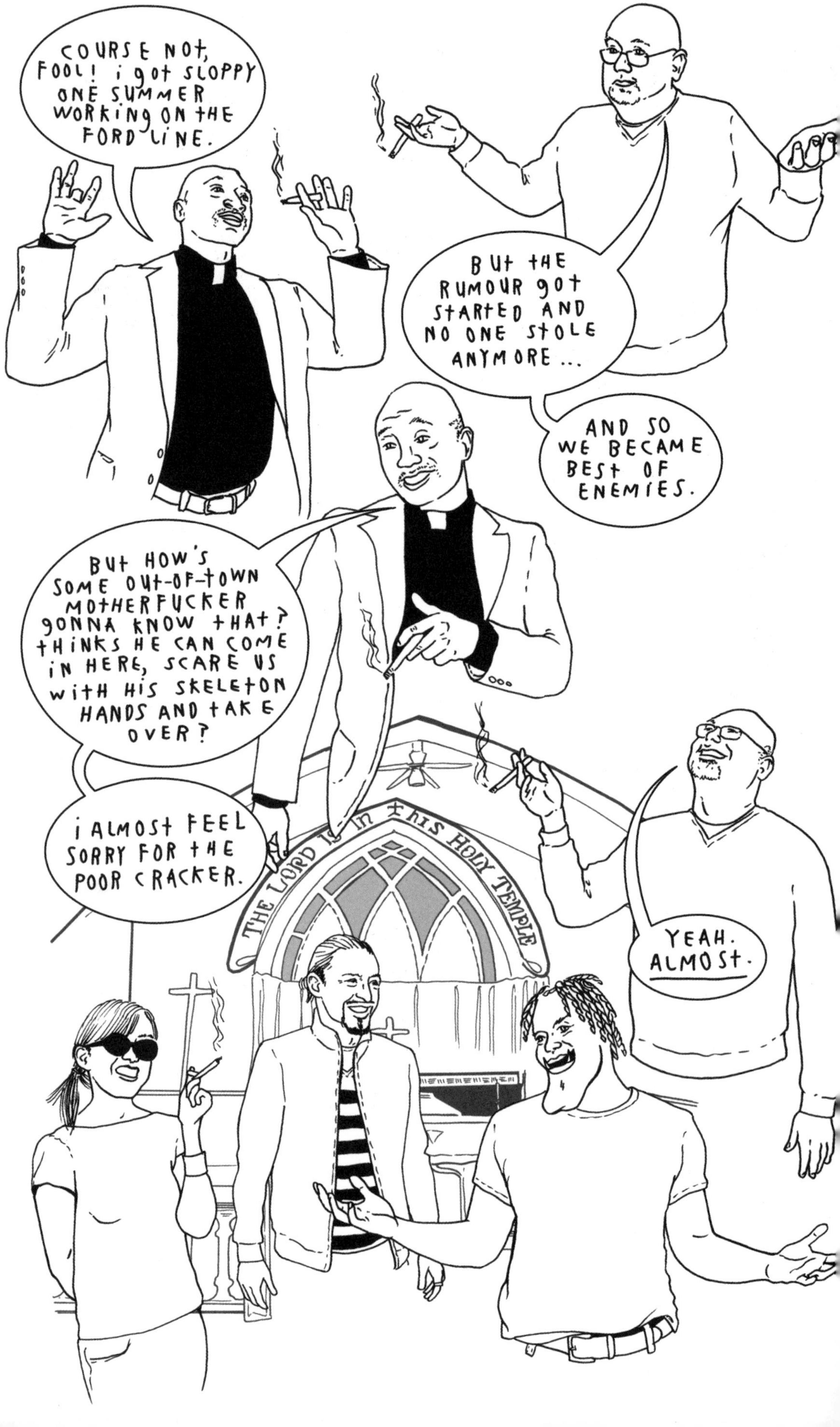
COURSE NOT, FOOL! I GOT SLOPPY ONE SUMMER WORKING ON THE FORD LINE.
BUT THE RUMOUR GOT STARTED AND NO ONE STOLE ANYMORE...
AND SO WE BECAME BEST OF ENEMIES.
BUT HOW'S SOME OUT-OF-TOWN MOTHERFUCKER GONNA KNOW THAT? THINKS HE CAN COME IN HERE, SCARE US WITH HIS SKELETON HANDS AND TAKE OVER?
I ALMOST FEEL SORRY FOR THE POOR CRACKER.
THE LORD IS IN THIS HOLY TEMPLE
YEAH. ALMOST.

Writer/Creator Jim Munroe is an indie culture maker and community organizer. He's spent the last decade making lo-fi sci-fi movies, teenage outcast videogames, and a half-dozen novels. As a byproduct of this medium-hopping he's provided DIY publishing resources, delivered presentations like Time Management for Anarchists, and helped start Toronto's videogame coalition, The Hand Eye Society. Find out more and contact him via his website, nomediakings.org.

Illustrator/Letterer Shannon Gerard works in a variety of media. She writes and draws comics, crochets soft sculptures, binds books, and makes prints. Two current projects are the online illustrated serial *Unspent Love (or Things I Wish I Told You)* for Top Shelf Productions and the conclusion of her autobio series *Hung*. *Sword of My Mouth* is Shannon's first collaborative graphic novel. You can see more of her work online at shannongerard.org.

To view Shannon and Jim's commentary on your complimentary digital version
of this book, register with the invite code "isupportedindiecomics" at
nomediakings.org/sword/register/